Ability Testing:
Uses, Consequences, and Controversies

PART I: Report of the Committee

Alexandra K. Wigdor and Wendell R. Garner, Editors

Committee on Ability Testing
Assembly of Behavioral and Social Sciences
National Research Council

NATIONAL ACADEMY PRESS
Washington, D.C.   1982

NOTICE: The project that is the subject of this report was approved by the Governing Board of the National Research Council, whose members are drawn from the councils of the National Academy of Sciences, the National Academy of Engineering, and the Institute of Medicine. The members of the committee responsible for the report were chosen for their special competences and with regard for appropriate balance.

This report has been reviewed by a group other than the authors according to procedures approved by a Report Review Committee consisting of members of the National Academy of Sciences, the National Academy of Engineering, and the Institute of Medicine.

The National Research Council was established by the National Academy of Sciences in 1916 to associate the broad community of science and technology with the Academy's purposes of furthering knowledge and of advising the federal government. The Council operates in accordance with general policies determined by the Academy under the authority of its congressional charter of 1863, which establishes the Academy as a private, nonprofit, self-governing membership corporation. The Council has become the principal operating agency of both the National Academy of Sciences and the National Academy of Engineering in the conduct of their services to the government, the public, and the scientific and engineering communities. It is administered jointly by both Academies and the Institute of Medicine. The National Academy of Engineering and the Institute of Medicine were established in 1964 and 1970, respectively, under the charter of the National Academy of Sciences.

Library of Congress Cataloging in Publication Data

Main entry under title:

Ability testing.

   Contents: pt. I. Report of the Committee—
pt. II. Documentation section.
   1. Educational tests and measurements—United
States.   2. Ability—Testing. I. Wigdor,
Alexandra K. II. Garner, Wendell R. III. National
Research Council (U.S.). Committee on Ability
Testing.
LB3051.A52   371.2'6'0973   81-18870
ISBN 0-309-03228-8 (pt. I)   AACR2

Available from:
NATIONAL ACADEMY PRESS
2101 Constitution Ave., N.W.
Washington, D.C. 20418

Printed in the United States of America

COMMITTEE ON ABILITY TESTING

WENDELL R. GARNER (*Chair*), Department of Psychology, Yale University

MARCUS ALEXIS, Department of Economics, Northwestern University

WILLIAM BEVAN, Department of Psychology, Duke University

LEE J. CRONBACH, School of Education, Stanford University (psychometrics)

ZVI GRILICHES, Department of Economics, Harvard University

OSCAR HANDLIN, Director of Libraries, Harvard University (history)

DELMOS JONES, Department of Anthropology, City University of New York

LYLE V. JONES, L.L. Thurstone Psychometric Laboratory, University of North Carolina (psychometrics, statistics)

PHILIP B. KURLAND, Law School, University of Chicago

BURKE MARSHALL, Law School, Yale University

MELVIN R. NOVICK, Lindquist Center for Measurement, University of Iowa (statistics, psychometrics)

LAUREN B. RESNICK, Learning Research and Development Center, University of Pittsburgh (psychology, educational psychology)

ALICE ROSSI, Department of Sociology, University of Massachusetts

WILLIAM H. SEWELL, Department of Sociology, University of Wisconsin

JANET T. SPENCE, Department of Psychology, University of Texas

ALAN A. STONE, Law School, Harvard University (psychiatry, law)*

MARY L. TENOPYR, Human Resources Laboratory, American Telephone and Telegraph Company, Morristown, N.J. (industrial psychology)

JOHN W. TUKEY, Bell Telephone Laboratories, Inc., Murray Hill, N.J. (statistics)

E. BELVIN WILLIAMS, Educational Testing Service, Princeton, N.J. (psychology)

ALEXANDRA K. WIGDOR, *Study Director*
SUSAN W. SHERMAN, *Senior Research Associate*
GLADYS R. BOSTICK, *Administrative Secretary*

Member until 1980.

iii

Contents

Preface

The Committee on Ability Testing was established under the auspices of the National Research Council to conduct a broad examination of the role of testing in American life. The project was conceived at a time of widespread public debate about the use of standardized tests in the schools, for college admissions, and in the workplace. That debate has not been stilled by time.

Advocates of testing consider it the best available means of impartial selection based on ability; many are, in addition, enthusiastic about the value of tests in revealing undiscovered talent and extol their contribution to increased efficiency and accountability in a variety of educational and employment settings. Critics of testing have found the negative effects of testing more compelling. They claim that tests measure too little too narrowly. And some spokesmen for minority interests have attacked standardized tests as artificial barriers to social equality and economic opportunity.

Both high expectations and serious complaints have focused public attention on the underlying questions of what tests actually measure and the meaning to be attached to test scores. The increasing interest of courts, legislatures, and governmental agencies in the way tests are used in selection systems has added a significant new dimension to these questions.

The complexity of the issues and the high emotion generated by testing controversies convinced the sponsors of this project of the need for a dispassionate investigation of testing by a multidisciplinary group of people whose breadth of experience and training would provide the requisite technical mastery, balance, and social understanding. The charge to the Committee was, first, to describe as fully as possible the nature, incidence, and impact of testing practices; second, to identify the fundamental policy questions presented by widespread use of standardized tests; and third, to provide guidance on appropriate use and interpretation of test results. This had led us to pay close attention not only to the status of testing technology, but to the legal, political, and social contexts within which testing takes place.

Our report is not primarily an action document, though there are a number of recommendations; nor is it a highly technical study of mental measurement, written by and for psychometricians. It is, rather, a white paper—a document intended to describe accurately the theory and practice of testing; to illuminate competing interests in a balanced fashion; and, ultimately, to help those who make decisions with tests or about testing to reach better-informed judgments than is now the case. It is to those decision makers—judges, lawmakers and their staffs, educators, employers, personnel administrators and the testing industry—that our efforts have been aimed and to whom this report is addressed. Of course, we also hope that the research community will find it useful.

The Committee was chosen with great care. A majority of the members were drawn from areas unconnected with testing: law, history, anthropology, sociology, economics, experimental psychology, mathematics, and education. The variety of their learning and experiences brought to our discussions of testing issues a constant interplay of different points of view, different ways of asking questions. Among the psychometricians and psychologists who completed the group are scholars who have made important contributions to test theory, as well as practitioners with long experience in test development and personnel selection. All of the members gave freely of their time and their knowledge. Each has helped to form the report, and although individual members may not agree with every point in it, this report represents their consensus.

The content and format of this two-part study of ability testing reflect our decisions about scope, purpose, and audience. Part I, the report of the Committee, presents a wide-ranging discussion of testing issues. Because it is addressed to policy makers and test users, the text has been kept largely free of the critical apparatus of scholarly literature. Chapters 1 through 3 provide an overview of the controversies surrounding testing, an introduction to the concepts, methods, and terminology of ability testing, a brief history of testing in the United States, and a discussion of the proliferation of legal requirements that have come to surround the use of tests. Chapters 4 through 6 describe test use for employment selection and educational purposes, point out common types of misuse, and make recommendations about how tests might be better used to preserve the integrity of the technology while at the same time responding to legitimate social, institutional, and individual goals. Chapter 7 takes a close look at the limitations of standardized tests and then attempts to establish a sense of proportion by placing the controversy over testing within the context of the larger social currents that influence the course of national life. The text and recommendations in Part I are the responsibility of the Committee.

Part II is a set of 11 signed papers. Although the Committee has used the papers liberally and major portions of the report reflect the considerable labors of their authors, the Committee does not necessarily subscribe to the views expressed or interpretations offered in them. But it is here that the interested reader will find a rich introduction to the case law, the research literature, and data sources.

ACKNOWLEDGMENTS

This project has been supported with patience and generosity by the Carnegie Corporation of New York, the National Institute of Education, the Office of Personnel Management, the National Institute of Mental Health, and the Ittleson Foundation. In addition to financial support, the Committee is indebted to the Carnegie Corporation, the National Institute of Education, and the Office of Personnel Management for making numerous research reports, data summaries, and other resources available to us.

Our study has been a collaborative venture. In carrying out its work, the Committee met regularly as a whole or in writing groups over a period of 3 years. Individual Committee and staff members produced working papers and position pieces for consideration, two of which appear in Part II. Subcommittees took responsibility for drafting various sections of Part I. The Committee also consulted widely with those who use tests, those who take tests, those who develop tests, and those who regulate testing. In November of 1979, we conducted public hearings in order to give representatives of each group the opportunity to express their point of view and describe their experiences with testing (see Appendix for a list of participants).

We owe a great deal to the various staff members who have worked with the Committee during its life. Our thanks go first to David A. Goslin, Executive Director of the Assembly of Behavioral and Social Sciences, who has been a source of encouragement and support. Barbara Lerner provided staff leadership in the initial phases of the study and was ably followed by Edwin Hollander. Rita Atkinson, Deborah Coates, and Kathleen Kappy assisted with data collection and produced background pieces for discussion. Martha Feldman and Judy Kron served as research assistants. Susan Sherman helped to develop the project and served as senior research associate throughout our work.

Among those who served as consultants to the Committee, we owe a particular debt to Robert Linn, who gave form to our discussions of technical testing matters, and to Matthew Hale, whose digging into the past provided us with a crucial sense of perspective. Our thanks go as well to the other authors of the signed papers in Part II: Melvin Novick, Toby Friedman and E. Belvin Williams, Daniel Resnick, Patricia Hollander, Beverly Anderson, Rodney Skager, Eric Gardner, and Nancy Cole. A number of others contributed working papers that aided discussion: Michael Rothschild, Carol Gargantiel, C. J. Bartlett, Linda Ingram, Henry Acland, David Martin, Rose Giaconia, and James Richards.

Our acknowledgments would not be complete without special thanks to Eugenia Grohman, whose editing skills were surpassed only by her understanding of the workings of the National Research Council; to Chris McShane, who got us to the press on time; to Jean Savage and Elaine McGarraugh, who worked diligently with the authors of the signed papers to locate lost footnotes and dangling participles; and to Gladys Bostick, administrative secretary, who got everyone to meetings, kept track of innumerable drafts of chapters, and accomplished all with efficiency and tact.

WENDELL R. GARNER, *Chair*
ALEXANDRA K. WIGDOR, *Study Director*
Committee on Ability Testing

Overview

The Committee on Ability Testing was convened at a time of widespread controversy about the use of standardized tests to assess individual differences and to evaluate programs. Because its mandate called for a study of testing from a social perspective, the Committee has been especially sensitive to the need to go beyond issues of technical adequacy and to explore the implications of test use for individuals, minority groups, institutions, and the society at large. One of the criteria that influenced the way the investigation was structured, therefore, was topicality—we worked with an eye to the course of public debate and took careful notice of state and federal legislative activities and the emerging case law. At the same time, we tried to understand and present testing issues as expressions of more fundamental social questions about productivity, equity, the rights of individuals, and the allocation of resources.

The Committee was particularly concerned in its study to clarify the issues at controversy; to explain some of the misunderstandings about tests that fuel debate; to provide scientific answers when appropriate; and to delineate with care the issues that are more a matter of policy than science.

In the preface we discussed the nature of the report, the audience addressed, and the relationship between Part I and Part II. The following pages provide a brief account of the organization of Part I and highlight some of the major themes and findings.

Chapter 1   The first chapter presents an introduction to the origins and attractions of quantitative assessment of human performance. It analyzes

1

the functions of testing in modern industrial society and introduces the reader to the kinds of criticisms that have been levelled against tests as assessment instruments. Moving beyond specific points of criticism, the chapter surveys the social and policy questions that the use of tests brings to the fore: questions of adverse impact, regulation of the testing industry, the status of the individual in society, and the use of test results as the basis of policy decisions.

Chapter 2   In order to understand the controversy about testing, one must understand the basic concepts and the essential language of psychometrics; one must, for example, have an idea of what "validity" and "reliability" mean to testers. Chapter 2 provides for the lay reader a discussion of what ability tests are like, how test scores are given meaning, and the common research strategies used to determine how well a test measures the abilities it is said to measure.

Because early testers did not discourage the popular but erroneous belief that ability tests measure innate, unchanging intelligence, the report is careful to emphasize that tests can only measure ability as it exists at the moment of testing. Test results do not say anything about how a test taker reached that level of performance, nor do they portray a fixed or inherent characteristic of an individual. A related and equally important point is that ability tests provide only indirect measures from which abilities must be inferred. For these reasons, the Committee cautions that "intelligence test" can be a misleading label insofar as it encourages misunderstandings about the kind of measurement involved or false notions about intelligence: that it is a tangible and well-defined entity like a heart or even that it is a unitary ability.

The discussion of test validity stresses that validity is not a static characteristic of a test. Rather, validity has to do with scientific judgment, based on empirical data and logical analysis, about the adequacy of a test at a particular time when used for a particular purpose; and it refers to the inferences that can be drawn from a test whose validity is to be examined, not to the test in the abstract. Thus, a single test may have many validities corresponding to the various interpretations and uses made of it and it may exhibit differing degrees of validity over time within the same setting as other factors change. Viewed from this perspective, validation is a continuing process of accumulating evidence to support or refute particular interpretations and uses of test results.

The final sections of Chapter 2 summarize research findings on one of the most debated issues concerning ability tests: differences in average test results between groups in the U.S. population defined by gender, socioeconomic status, and racial or ethnic identity. A sizable body of empirical research supports a finding of rather large differences in average performance for some racial and ethnic groups, although there is also a great overlap in the distributions of scores for all groups. Empirical evidence also indicates that tests predict about as well for one group as for another. That is, the frequently heard contention that ability tests tend to underestimate the actual performance of minority group members on the job or in educational settings has not thus far been borne out by research. Because of the group differences in average test scores, strict reliance on tests for selection can have severe adverse impact on particular minorities. In some situations, the selection of individuals by order of rank on test score would have the effect of excluding minority and majority candidates who could perform well if given the opportunity.

Chapter 3   There are historical antecedents, going back to the early 20th century development of standardized testing and to the application of these techniques to group testing during World War I, that help to illuminate current testing issues. More recently, there have been developments in the law that have had a tremendous influence on the way tests are used. Chapter 3 examines the development and widespread adoption of standardized ability testing in the light of two themes: the search for order and the search for ability. The first impulse was particularly potent early in the century. Businessmen faced with high rates of labor turnover and industrial accidents looked to such new devices as character analysis, application blanks, and tests to make an appropriate match between worker and job. At the same time, school officials, faced with rapidly expanding school populations and the influx of children whose native language was not English, were motivated by a similar desire to increase educational efficiency and found standardized tests, particularly the group-administered tests that became available after World War I, useful for grouping and tracking students. In the period after World War II, standardized ability testing was popularly conceived as a liberating tool. By identifying talent and intellectual ability wherever it may exist in society, tests would, it was felt, act as a democratizing force. It was in this atmosphere that programs like the National Merit Scholarship competition were established. Throughout the entire period, the chapter notes, the federal government exercised an important influence on the development and use of ability tests, particularly in military and civil service testing programs.

Most recently, specifically since the passage of the Civil Rights Act of 1964, the use of tests by employers and school officials has been placed under constraints and frequently challenged because of the federal prohibition against discrimination in employment and educational practices. The second half of Chapter 3 describes the development of federal civil rights law and policy over the last 15 years and explains how tests, often the most visible part of a selection process, have been caught up in the struggle. The Committee's findings indicate that employment tests that are challenged under Title VII of the Civil Rights Act of 1964 rarely survive. There are exceptions to this generalization, particularly where a test has been challenged under the somewhat less demanding constitutional requirements, e.g., *Washington* v. *Davis*.

The extension of federal authority to selection and placement practices in the schools and the workplace has had important effects on test use. For example, any employer who hopes to defend a selection process that screens out larger proportions of minority or female applicants than white male applicants must validate any tests that are part of the process. And the validation strategies used will be judged according to professional standards and the requirements of the *Uniform Guidelines on Employee Selection Procedures*. Although the requirements of federal laws affecting educational testing have not yet received as much explication by the courts, recent decisions suggest that tests used for the placement of children in special classes for the educable mentally retarded also have to be shown valid (in a more or less formal sense of the word) for that use when they effect minority children disproportionately.

The implications of the psychometric facts and the legal developments discussed in the early chapters of the report are spelled out in Chapters 4-6, which are detailed examinations of test use in employment, in the schools, and in college and professional school admissions. Conclusions and recommendations will be found at the end of each chapter.

Chapter 4   This chapter concludes that employment selection is caught up in a disruptive tension between employers' interest in promoting work force efficiency and the governmental effort to ensure equal employment opportunity. Because of the undeniable adverse impact of most employment tests that measure cognitive abilities, they tend to succumb to administrative or legal challenge. Even those tests that are reasonably well developed and researched are vulnerable. The Committee recommends that the validity of a testing process should not be compromised in an effort to shape the distribution of the work force. We call upon federal and state authorities to provide employers with a range of legally defensible decision rules to guide their use of test results so that the effect of differential performance can be mitigated without destroying the utility of testing. In addition, we recommend to the attention of judges and other compliance officers the need to distinguish far more carefully than has yet been done between the technical psychometric standards that can reasonably be imposed on ability tests and the legal and social policy requirements (e.g., proportional selection) that more properly apply to the rules for using test scores and other information in selecting employees. We also suggest that government officials be more open to cooperative validation ventures as an aid to small employers.

Chapter 5   This chapter is organized around the three major functions of testing in elementary and secondary schools: testing for classification of students and instructional planning; testing to certify competence; and the use of tests in policymaking and management. The basic principle underlying the committee's discussion of testing in the schools is that the classification of pupils is warranted only when the decision rules—whether based on tests or not—have instructional validity. No school child should be relegated to a program of instruction that is not expected to enhance his performance.

Chapter 5 makes the general recommendation that tests be used, but rarely if ever used alone. The latter point is particularly important in assessing bilingual children and in deciding about placement of students outside the regular program of instruction. In particular, any local rule or state law that sets a numerical cutoff score on a test or combinations of tests as the basis for decisions about mental retardation or placement in special education programs should be seriously questioned.

The Committee's discussion of minimum competency testing programs notes certain benefits that might result from this movement to revive accountability in education. There are, however, troublesome social implications in competency testing programs that tie high school graduation to passing such a test. Insofar as diplomas are necessary to get jobs, the impact of competency testing will be to reduce the marketability of a group of young people largely characterized by low socioeconomic or minority status. Therefore, equity demands and the Committee strongly recommends that minimum competency testing be introduced early enough in high school for students to have opportunities to retake the test and that the program be accompanied by remedial instruction. In order for the accountability for educational success is shared by all parties, the schools should carry the burden of demonstrating that the remedial instruction offered has a positive effect on test performance.

Chapter 6   Some of the most vociferous debate over testing has concerned admission to college and professional schools. This chapter describes typical admissions practices at various kinds of institutions and explores such issues as test disclosure and coaching. One of the central findings of the chapter is that most undergraduate institutions are not selective enough for test results to be crucial to the selection decision. Most applicants are admitted to the college or university of their choice. Test scores are likely to be a barrier only to the small number of applicants who are marginal and the small number of applicants who want to attend the most selective institutions. As a consequence, the Committee recommends that undergraduate institutions that now require admissions tests reexamine the wisdom of that requirement.

Test results are a far more important factor in admission to graduate and professional schools. Yet the Committee found that few schools perform local validation studies and concluded that greater efforts to justify the use of test scores for admission to the local program are warranted. An important and often misunderstood point is that admissions tests are useful to predict only academic performance, typically first-year grades; the tests are not designed to predict who will be a good doctor or lawyer, and there has been little effort to demonstrate a relationship between test scores and performance in the profession which applicants want to enter. It would, therefore, be foolish to allow test results to completely dominate the decision process. Finally, the Committee counsels against the use of rigid or mechanical decision rules either in the direction of ranking solely on the basis of test scores or in the direction of fixed quotas to increase minority representation. It recommends instead a flexible rule that balances likelihood of success in the program, recognition of academic excellence, and support of demographic diversity.

Chapter 7   The final chapter of the report is a wide-ranging discussion of themes and currents that have emerged from the investigations described in the first six chapters. It begins with an extended discussion of some of the important limitations of standardized ability testing. These limitations range from the compromises required by standardization and by group testing to the traditional emphasis on certain cognitive skills to the exclusion of others and to the exclusion of other characteristics that contribute to excellence. A more fundamental shortcoming lies in the inadequate explanation of abilities that informs current testing. Since a good deal of test misuse stems from the misconceptions of test users and test takers, this discussion is particularly important in light of the popular controversy about ability testing.

The remainder of the chapter represents the Committee's attempt to impart some perspective to the subject of testing by describing the social conditions that have given prominence to testing issues in recent years. The key point is that those conditions exist independent of testing and would continue in the absence of testing. If all tests were eliminated, the issues of fair process, equal opportunity, the right of privacy and other important social concerns would continue to challenge American society.

1
Ability Testing
in Modern Society

INTRODUCTION

Tests and testing are the subject of intense controversy in American society. The signs of the controversy range from polite disagreements among professionals about abstruse technical questions to heated public debates, with strongly political overtones, about the social implications of testing.

When one remembers that only a few years ago tests were widely perceived as impartial instruments of social differentiation, it is striking that there should now be so much controversy. It is also striking that, at a time when tests are subject to vigorous criticism, there has been a continued pressure for additional testing, much of it coming from the federal government. It thus becomes important to examine carefully the functions and consequences of testing, good and bad, in order to recommend sensible policies.

The actions being urged by various parties are not compatible. There are critics who see tests and testing as an example of science and technology run amok, producing discrimination and unequal treatment. These critics prescribe a prompt and radical remedy in the form of a complete moratorium on tests and testing. There are proponents who argue that tests and testing offer the best hope of assuring fairness and objectivity in the treatment of all members of society; that tests are mistakenly criticized as the cause of undesirable conditions that they in fact help to define and could point the way to improving; and that any radical in-

7

terference with further development and application of tests and testing would only exacerbate the conditions about which the critics complain. Between the severest critics and the strongest proponents are many dis-cussants who believe that all is not well in the domain of tests and testing and that some form of corrective action is probably in order.

It has been the purpose of the Committee on Ability Testing over the past three years to examine testing practices and to analyze the contro-versy about tests and testing with a view to suggesting actions appropriate to the resolution of the controversy and consistent with the goals and needs of our increasingly complex society.

Why Testing?

Quantitative assessment of human performance is a relatively recent phe-nomenon. Its rapid development stems from certain intellectual devel-opments of the nineteenth century. One commentator (Goslin 1963) has identified the rise of the notion of individual differences, dissociated from hereditary social status, and the application of that notion to the prediction of an individual's performance as the crucial concept. New-found sta-tistical techniques provided the means of demonstrating difference. Thus, knowledge about the frequency distributions of human performance pro-vided a way of relating the standing of one individual to that of a pop-ulation of individuals, while probability theory enabled scientists to say with a known degree of confidence whether the differences in measured abilities of two individuals reflected real differences or only measurement error. The notion of correlation was used in relating such measurements to expectations of performance. As these intellectual strains coalesced in what was called the science of mental measurement, a variety of methods, which may be subsumed under the technical rubric "validation," were devised to lend evidentiary support to the interpretations given to test scores (see Chapter 2).

These scientific innovations dovetailed with the concurrent social val-ues and needs of Western countries. The growth of industrial economies with diverse job demands, the rapid spread of formal education to new social groups, the concentration of large populations in cities, and the growth of governmental bureaucracies all contributed to a social milieu in which streamlined methods of obtaining knowledge about human performance would be of interest. This interplay of technological capa-bility and social need set the stage for the development of a new tool of measurement, the standardized ability test, as a criterion for making selection decisions.

The ability test as we know it today originated in France with the Binet-Simon scale of intelligence: it was based on the measurement of an ability by testing a sample of the ability. The idea was brought to America through the work of Lewis Terman, who developed the Stanford-Binet test, the first to be standardized, in that it provided definite instructions for administering and scoring and established norms based on a sample of the population. The early tests were individually administered. With the advent of World War I came the transition to testing large numbers of people simultaneously. The resultant Army Alpha test, a group-administered, pencil-and-paper test, was the prototype of virtually all "scientific" testing today.

Every society develops some sort of formalized criteria for making selection decisions. Social characteristics, such as family, class, and the like, in which assessments of ability related to performance play a minor role, traditionally formed the basis of decision. Intuitive opinions based on personal impressions or recommendations concerning assessments of ability have often provided another, more individualized ground of judgment. The claim for testing as a mode of selection was that it was more directly related to performance and more objective. Nowhere did this claim seem more attractive than in this country, for America was perceived as the land of opportunity by the successive waves of immigrants who came here to make a new life. They came from traditionalist societies with the expectation that in America the future could be made—anybody could succeed who tried hard enough and had ability, and nobody could be prevented from trying. Given the great tide of immigrants seeking to find a place in America and the expansiveness of the economy, ability testing offered an ordering device that traditional institutions could no longer provide and that accommodated the aspirations of the ambitious. The convergence of these intellectual, economic, and social forces produced a climate conducive to the acceptance of tests and testing in industrial, educational, and governmental settings during the first half of this century.

In recent decades, however, many have begun to question whether the goals of identifying merit and enhancing productivity are as well served by testing as has been asserted—or whether they are sufficient definitions of the social good. This is the heart of what this committee has been investigating and what is presented in this report, starting in this chapter with an overview of the functions of tests, the criticisms and controversies that have arisen, the policy issues involved, and the implications of these issues in a broader social context.

What is an Ability Test?

This report focuses chiefly on ability testing, defined as systematic observation of performance on a task. There are many kinds of ability tests, including group tests of the paper-and-pencil type, individual tests with oral questions and answers, and tests involving physical activity. While a distinction is often made between tests of aptitude and tests of achievement, this report is not much concerned such this differentiation, because ability is always a combination of aptitude and achievement.

This report focuses more particularly on tests of knowledge, reasoning, and special skills rather than on tests that measure vocational interest, attitude, personality, motivation, or physical activity. It is important to remember, however, that human performance is the product of a more complicated set of factors than those described by tests of cognitive functioning (see Chapter 7:204-240). Motivation, for example, may be an important predictor of job performance.

THE FUNCTIONS OF TESTING

In examining the role and functions of ability testing, it is useful to define the three direct participants in the testing process. They are the test producer or developer; the test user, usually an institution that expects to base decisions at least in part on test results; and the test taker, the individual for whom the test establishes a particular performance score. The roles played by the participants in the testing process are not always distinct, as intended and unintended overlapping of function and benefit occur, but it is helpful to consider the testing process from the viewpoint of each of the participants.

The function of the test producer is relatively clear-cut. The producer develops tests that sample performance, typically with a view either to establishing a standard of a desired level of competence or to predicting later performance in school or on the job. Some 500 testing organizations are included in the survey of standardized test publishers conducted by the Association of American Publishers, and there are many more operating on a less formal scale. These organizations are chiefly commercial, though two of the largest test producers are nonprofit organizations. Other major test producers are government agencies and the armed forces.

The work of the producer is generally oriented to the needs of the test user as the principal decision maker in the testing process. Many tests are bought ready-made; others are developed by the producer for the specific needs of a certain user.

The test user is, typically, an educational institution or an employer. How the tests function may vary with the two types of institution, but in broad outline, both use them as an objective measure of performance to help make various sorting decisions. The most obvious function of ability tests is to facilitate selection decisions. The hope is that sound selection will increase the institution's or the employer's productivity or social efficiency and will give an opportunity to those who are, in some sense, most deserving of it. An employer, faced with 50 applicants for 10 secretarial positions, must select. A college, which has 2,000 applicants for 500 places in the entering class, must select. In all such cases, there are more people available than there are places available, and choices must be made. Drawing people by lot, by order of application, by unstructured reports of past performance, or by family affiliation are possible criteria for selection, but ability tests have gained broad acceptance because they are perceived to be more objective and more predictive of later performance. It is believed that such predictions will help to find the most able or the most suitable candidate for school or work positions and that decisions based on this kind of selection will contribute to the overall performance of the institution or employer.

Selection, as described above, might well be called "positive" selection, since the goal of the process is to identify those who are most capable of a particular activity. Some tests, however, are used for "negative" selection, to exclude individuals from an activity. Driving tests, for example, are designed, not to pick the best performers, but to exclude those who do not meet minimum standards from participating in the activity.

Selection becomes classification when the desire is to match an individual to one of several possible jobs or educational programs. Then it is important to identify specific skills and abilities in order to compare them to job or training requirements. Testing for classification and placement can be found in large institutions, such as the armed forces, as well as in small ones, such as schools.

In educational management, tests are used as a measure of individual achievement in a variety of ways. They are often used to identify excellence or to monitor a student's progress through a course of study. Standardized achievement tests are also used to diagnose a student's particular learning difficulties in order to determine remediation needs and subsequently to monitor progress during remedial training. A more recent, and increasingly prevalent, function is to certify minimum competence of high school students for graduation.

User institutions also frequently use tests to assess the effectiveness of a training or educational program. The focus of such testing programs is an evaluation of programs rather than people.

Although in some instances tests are intended to serve the needs of the test taker (e.g., school testing with a diagnostic purpose) it is important to keep in mind that selection, placement, and achievement measures are primarily intended to serve the decision-making needs of the user institution. But since testing does result in scores for individuals, there are some direct benefits to test takers. Some ability tests, placement tests for example, focus on identifying specific skills—mechanical or scientific, musical or artistic—of the individual test taker. Insofar as the test taker has no accurate knowledge of how skillful he or she is, the function of identifying these skills has potential consequences of value for the test taker. Tests used as a tool in guidance or career counseling, for example, are designed to help the taker make wiser decisions about training opportunities and career choices.

Furthermore, on the basis of his or her score, an individual test taker may receive an educational or employment opportunity. Data in Christopher Jencks' (1979) *Who Gets Ahead* show that a completed college education, for all ethnic groups, is associated with substantial improvement in lifetime income. Although concomitant factors may contribute to higher income, a test score as the first step in access to education is not a trivial consideration. Whether the increase in life chances actually results from further education or from improved employment, it stands as the most likely benefit of the testing process to certain test takers.

While understanding testing from the point of view of the producer, user, and taker is necessary to understand the functions of testing, it is not sufficient for a complete study of the controversy in which testing is now involved. For there is another participant, society as a whole, that stands to benefit or not, albeit less directly, from the various functions of testing. Much of the recent controversy has in fact been initiated in the name of advocacy for the whole society. If, for example, potentially poor pilots are excluded on the basis of tests from becoming commercial airline pilots, then both society in general and potential passengers on airplanes gain. If productivity in the country as a whole is improved by the use of ability tests, then the entire society gains. On the other hand, if some people are improperly excluded from certain educational or work opportunities, it is a loss to society.

Therefore, only by keeping in mind the perspective of producer, user, and taker, as well as the society in which they exist, can we examine the present controversy about tests and testing in America.

THE CONTROVERSY ABOUT TESTING

General Skepticism

The broadest category of criticism contends that tests in general are neither sufficiently reliable nor sufficiently valid to justify their use. The most extreme critics contend that, even at their best, tests do poorly what they are intended to do and are therefore not suitable for use in selection, resource allocation, or guidance. Moreover, critics contend that many tests are inexpertly or thoughtlessly used.

Some critics express dissatisfaction with the limited predictive powers of tests. Even when the validity of a test has been established—that it measures adequately what it purports to measure—it is almost always validity for short-term, not long-term, performance. For example, tests used to determine admission to college predict grade performance reasonably well for the first year, but decreasingly well for successive years. Prediction of what many consider the ultimate performance criterion, in life-after-school, is either weak or unknown. Others argue that most tests measure too limited a range of skills to be useful for meaningful prediction. Illustrative of this view is the comment of consumer advocate Ralph Nader on the passage of the New York State law concerning disclosure of test data for college entrance examinations. He was quoted as saying that tests "do not measure judgment, determination, experience, idealism and creativity, which are rather important attributes" (*The New York Times*, July 15, 1979).[1]

In short, tests are seen by critics as being too limited in scope to measure complex characteristics of the kind required for long-term prediction and oriented only to cognitive skills. More generally, tests are viewed as inadequate for the functions for which they are used.

Test Construction

Another category of criticism focuses specifically on test construction, claiming that tests could be more valuable if only they were constructed properly. These criticisms point out that paper-and-pencil tests, which incorporate a high verbal component, are used in nearly all testing simply because they are comparatively easy to construct and administer. Such use raises questions when the skill being tested does not require much verbal facility or fluency, such as some drafting skills.

There also are criticisms of the multiple-choice format of virtually all standardized tests. It is argued that the "distractor" choices are often deliberately misleading or require overly subtle discrimination. There are also complaints that sometimes more than one answer should be considered correct. Banesh Hoffman (1962) has argued that multiple-choice questions penalize the brighter students, who tend to see more possible associations and are, therefore, attracted to the misleading alternatives. Charlotte Ryan (1979) illustrated this point with the following example:

[1] Nader has recently brought together his organization's criticism of testing in a 550-page report (Nairn et al. 1980).

An orange seed grows into:

(a) an orange tree;
(b) an orange;
(c) another seed;
(d) an orange blossom.

Clearly, all answers are in some way correct.

One of the most fervent criticisms about test construction concerns the way in which test scores are "normed." It is argued that a test normed with members of the majority population will yield test scores that work to the disadvantage of test takers from other populations on whom the test was not normed. To overcome this problem, proponents of tests and their more sympathetic critics have long advocated, as a routine practice, the development of separate norms and the conduct of separate validity studies for majority and nonmajority groups or for males and females. Some critics, moreover, contend that the content of tests is inherently biased in favor of majority groups or males, a bias that cannot necessarily be corrected by the use of separate norms. Tests of mechanical comprehension, for example, may call upon experience that many females have not had. If the purpose of the test is to assess what the test taker will be able to do, after appropriate training, rather than to assess present knowledge, the test will very probably underrate the women. Similarly, tests that are written in standard English or with items (questions) that are embedded in a context familiar only to the majority population may underrate the performance capabilities of people who are more familiar with other linguistic forms or have had different cultural experiences, e.g., American Indians living on a reservation.

Test Use

A third category of criticism has to do with misuses of testing. One charge is that tests are frequently relied upon as the sole criterion for decisions affecting the takers' access to, or exclusion from, a limited resource, such as a professional education. Another is that test scores are used in making irreversible decisions, which should be more tentative and less permanent. Many people, having misjudged the certainty of test scores, are angry to learn that there is bound to be some misclassification of students or job applicants, since test scores predict only the probability of a particular level of performance. That observation must, of course, be made of every selection system, whether or not tests are involved.

In this same vein, critics have articulated considerable concern about the use of tests to track students in school. While such tracking was initiated in the belief that sorting students into groups with similar levels of ability would promote educational efficiency, critics say that a student, once placed in particular track, may never be able to change tracks. Also of concern is the possible use of a test score as the basis for a permanent label. It is all too tempting to use a quantified test score as if there were a perfect relationship between test performance and real-life performance.

Another related issue involves the use of test scores for making decisions far beyond the predictive powers of the test: using an entry-level test score as a basis for promotion or compensation years after it was obtained and years after it may actually have lost its utility, for example; or using LSAT (Law School Admissions Test) scores as the basis of job selection, even though the LSAT's predictive value is primarily for grades in the first year of law school. The test taker, in effect, has career opportunities and compensation influenced by test scores that no longer have any known predictive power.

Test Interpretation

A final category of criticism involves the interpretation of what it is that tests measure. Not without foundation, critics urge that ability tests, and particularly IQ (intelligence quotient) tests, encourage the belief that tests measure fixed genetic characteristics or inherent traits that exist untouched by experience. Although most professional testing specialists have long since rejected any such deterministic assumptions, a number of prominent psychometricians helped to popularize such beliefs early in the century. More recently, the work of Arthur Jensen (1973, 1980), among others, has given new vigor to such ideas. There is understandable concern, therefore, that a person's ranking will be considered fixed, and possibly genetic, despite the fact that professional opinion emphasizes that abilities are affected by experience. This concern becomes distress when the misconception about ability is carried over to a belief that group differences in test performance reflect hereditary differences in ability. The potential for social injustice in such a belief has led some critics to oppose all tests that allow comparisons among individuals; others argue for much more careful public instruction in the meaning of test scores.

What Tests Don't Measure

As noted above, tests are criticized for measuring only certain characteristics, primarily cognitive functioning. The usual test is only tangentially related to determination, motivation, interpersonal awareness and social skills, or leadership ability, yet these qualities contribute to performance in school and work and in some situations are more important than cognitive skills. Who becomes a leader, for instance, has been shown to have only a slight positive relationship with intelligence test scores (Gibb 1969). While a leader must have a sufficient intellect to understand a given task, differences in other attributes are more crucial in determining the most effective leader.

Similarly, not all the characteristics that make for a successful professional career are measured by admissions tests for postgraduate education, or even by performance in professional courses. The compassion and "bedside manner" of a physician or the clever courtroom techniques of a trial lawyer are criteria not predicted by tests oriented primarily to success in first-year, and perhaps second-year, course work in medicine and law. Academic qualities are not irrelevant to professional performance, but they are only part of it.

Although "personality" tests are sometimes used in business and industry, they do not have the professional and public acceptance accorded ability tests. As a result, information about other desired characteristics of applicants is more likely to be sought from personal background data, letters of recommendation, and interviews. Of course, these methods of evaluation have their own limitations. Interviews, for example, have frequently been shown to introduce subjectivity into the decision process, which gives play to conscious and unconscious biases (Webster 1964, Schmitt 1976).

Reaction to the Criticisms of Testing

The response of professional organizations, trade associations, advocacy groups, and government to the criticisms of testing is as varied as the criticism itself. There are ardent proponents of testing and adversaries who would eliminate all testing. Laws have been passed that place constraints on the use of tests or demand more of the tests and their producers. Tests have been increasingly challenged in the courtroom. Actions alleging discriminatory impact have been brought by individuals, interest groups, and government agencies, the net effect of which has been a significant de facto regulation of the use of tests for employment and for certain educational purposes. At the same time, many states have mandated new testing programs to assess students' attainment of minimum levels of competence. And a consequence of employment discrimination litigation has been to rule out all nonobjective selection procedures in situations in which the level of minority employment is at issue, thus increasing the importance of tests in some sectors.

Such contradictory responses are also evident among professional organizations. It is particularly noteworthy that the two largest teachers' organizations, the National Education Association (NEA) and the American Federation of Teachers (AFT), disagree completely on proposed federal legislation regulating educational testing: NEA supports it and AFT opposes it. The two organizations have also generally differed on the use of standardized tests in the schools.[2]

SOCIAL AND POLICY ISSUES

Although the criticisms noted above pose specific problems and questions about testing in their own right, they also emerge as part of larger social and policy issues. Some of the social issues surrounding tests and testing can be discussed mainly from the perspective of test producers, test users, and test takers; others have a broader social context as well. For example, concerns about testing may be a symptom of widespread social development and change. Then, too, the perspective of the larger society may lead to perceptions concerning such developments that differ from those of the more direct participants in the testing process. This section first discusses the narrower policy and social issues, then the broader ones.

Adverse Impact

The social issue of greatest significance regarding the use of tests and testing is adverse impact. The term was popularized by the Equal Employment Opportunity Commission and has been incorporated into law by judicial construction of Title VII of the Civil Rights Act of 1964 (P.L. 88-352). In general, adverse impact means a substantially different (lower) rate of selection in hiring or other employment decisions for members of racial, ethnic, or gender groups protected by the Act. The concept of adverse impact is an extrapolation from the specific wording of Title VII of the Act, which prohibits "discrimination because of race, color, religion, sex, or national origin." In practice, tests and other selection procedures have been judged unlawful if they result in adverse impact and cannot be shown to be valid.

In recent years, American society has devoted a great deal of attention

---

[2] As part of the background for this report, the Committee conducted public hearings in November 1978 at which 25 individuals and organizations (see Appendix) presented statements on the issues involved in the controversy about testing. Many other organizations contributed written statements for the record. Together they provided an abundant record of the current controversy about testing in America.

to eliminating discrimination against women and minority groups such as blacks, Spanish-speaking people, and American Indians. Government action has taken the form of prohibiting discrimination and, more recently, encouraging affirmative action programs to improve the economic position of these groups.

Testing has frequently been challenged because certain social groups tend, as groups, to score consistently lower on the average than more advantaged groups, and this holds true on both achievement tests and more abstract reasoning tests (those with items requiring the manipulation of symbols independent of subject mastery). Females, for example, tend to score lower as a group than males on items that measure certain spatial abilities and some forms of mathematical reasoning and higher on certain verbal items. Blacks and Hispanics tend to score lower on both verbal and quantitative items. As a consequence, the use of tests for selection in education or employment often produces a higher selection rate among white male applicants than among other categories of applicants.

The reasons for differential performance of particular groups on tests are extremely complex, but the consequence of that difference, insofar as tests are predictive of everyday performance, is to place in conflict the desire to encourage maximum productivity and the desire to distribute the benefits of society as broadly as possible. Translated into political terms, the issue involves balancing the principle of equal opportunity for every individual in society with the reality of unequal background and preparation.

Alternatives to Testing

Defining a useful role for tests amidst conflicting claims of equity and notions of right has so far eluded practitioner and policy maker alike. Many people have placed their hopes on alternative modes of selection that might produce equal outcomes without sacrificing the efficiencies of selecting on the basis of ability, but alternatives have so far been accompanied by equally confounding problems.

Many such "alternatives" are already in use, although typically as supplements to, rather than substitutes for, tests. These alternatives include letters of recommendation, interviews, previous performance in similar or related activities, and work samples. In the case of college or graduate school admissions, grade-point averages serve as a basis for selection along with standardized admissions tests. In the employment setting, promotion can be based on objective records of work performance and absenteeism, as well as the more subjective ratings by supervisors.

Most of these means of making judgments about an individual's probable performance predate the use of ability tests. In fact, the introduction of standardized testing was seen as a forward step in compensating for the unreliability of these other assessments. College admissions tests, such as the SAT (Scholastic Aptitude Test) and ACT (American College Test), were designed to provide a "third view" of candidates, in addition to grade-point average and personal information from applications, interviews, and letters of reference. It was seen to be in the candidate's interest to have this view available to offset potential inequalities of the traditional system. Critics worry, however, that in actual use test scores dominate rather than supplement and caution against "reliance on any single system, process, or instrument," as it was put in a recent NEA report (Quinto and McKenna 1977) on the topic of alternatives.

Teacher-made tests, which are the main basis for students' grades, have largely escaped the criticisms aimed at standardized tests. They are seen as somehow more benign. For example, the NEA report just cited says that they "can be tailored to specific situations . . . and individual needs." Critics, however, point out that teacher-made tests can be poorly constructed and can be biased. In a similar vein, Morton Deutsch (1979) has recently criticized grading for being a contest in which "merit" is assigned by the teacher on the variable basis of "ability, drive, and social character." Supervisory ratings are also subject to some of the same variability, including an element of personal affinity, which can differentially shape the evaluations a subordinate receives.

If more reliance is placed on alternative indicators of future performance, it must be recognized that these alternatives may have their own sources of adverse impact, including the possibility of bias, and many of the controversial issues about testing will simply shift from tests to the alternatives. Concerns about the reliability and validity of tests will become concerns about the reliability and validity of grade-point averages, letters of recommendation, and supervisory ratings. Indeed, in the absence of testing, the problem of predicting performance would increase. Prediction of school and job performance from presently available alternatives to tests—with the exception of records of past performances in similar situations—has generally not been as accurate as prediction from tests (Reilly and Chao 1980).

There is, of course, always the possibility of discovering new predictive devices as minorities and females move into higher education and the work force in greater numbers. This would demand a major research effort, but could be of considerable value. One possible advantage of new alternatives to testing might be that adverse impact would be more easily prevented or rectified (although it is also possible that more accurate predictive devices would increase adverse impact). If that were so, it would be a strong argument for increasing the use of such alternatives. If not entirely so, it might even be reasonable to consider a trade-off between validity and the ease in compensating for adverse impact. Therefore, evaluating the desirability of an alternative to testing may not be answered simply by asking whether the alternative can predict well, but by asking whether the particular problems that may exist with certain tests can be eliminated or corrected with the alternative.

Regulation of Test Use

Tests can be useful instruments, but they are clearly open to abuse—by producers as well as by the decision-making users, and even by the individual test takers. One of the most difficult policy questions to emerge from the controversy about testing concerns regulation: If tests continue to be used (and some use seems inevitable), what can society do to prevent their misuse?

In almost any profession or industry, some form of control of practices exists to maintain standards, to control competition, and to prevent abuse. Some observers have suggested that the testing industry itself should take a far more active role in combatting test abuse. For the test producers, self-policing might include giving users more information about the statistical properties and theoretical assumptions of the test, providing instruction in test administration and interpretation, and allowing independent researchers greater access to test data, particularly validation data.

Professional organizations whose members develop, produce, and use tests—such as organizations of psychologists, of employers and managers, and various educational organizations—provide a second possible source of regulation. The American Psychological Association, the American Educational Research Association, and the National Council for Measurement in Education have been the most active in setting standards for testing. A major weakness of this source of quality control is that most test users are not members of the organizations that have taken the lead in setting professional standards and are thus not subject even to their mild forms of quality control.

Of late, increasing numbers of people have supported a third form of regulation by state and federal governments. Because government agencies are expected to protect individual rights and guard against discrimination, many feel that governmental regulation would represent the interests of the test taker, while other modes of regulation are more likely to focus more on the interests of producer and user.

Regulation of tests already exists of course. The questions are whether any further activity is required and, if so, what might best be done and by whom. In other words, which mode of regulation is best suited to balance the various interests of the participants in the testing process? For example, one alleged misuse is the continued use of test scores in a person's record long after their purpose has been served. Who, if anyone, is to monitor records in widely scattered files? At what point does the cost of surveillance outweigh the benefits of up-to-date records?

As noted earlier, legal actions that affect the testing process and its participants have introduced a layer of governmental regulation to the self-regulation by professional organizations and testing companies. Ideally, governmental intervention should occur only in response to some manifest need: there is always the chance that a regulation or accumulation of regulations will generate second-order effects that are worse than the ills they were designed to cure. Also, regulations may create obligations for participants that go beyond what they are capable of providing. In sum, granting that regulation is needed, the questions of how and how much remain problematic.

Test Scores as a Basis for Policy Decisions

Another set of issues arises when government agencies use test results in determining policy. For example, it has been proposed that subsidies for school districts, designated to help improve student performance, be scaled according to test scores. Following this formula, districts having lower test scores would get a higher subsidy on the grounds that a greater need had been demonstrated. Another example would be the use of competency test scores for evaluating the effectiveness of the educational unit. In at least one state, school certification is tied to such scores.

An important aspect of the current status of testing in the United States is the dichotomous influence of government. While some laws and court decisions discourage the use of tests in making decisions about individuals, others require or encourage such use. When conflicting policies affect a single program—such as the selection of employees under civil service merit systems—the user institution is often left frustrated and confused. In employment selection, the weight of governmental policies that affect the use of tests seems at the moment to be leaning in the direction of discouraging test use; in education, given the popularity of program evaluation, the pressure for added testing may be stronger than the pressure against test use.

Decisions About Individuals

There is nothing new about the need to make decisions about people and their educational and employment opportunities. Tests represent only one of the many sources of information used in making such decisions, and the concerns about tests are, therefore, quite legitimately also concerns about alternative instruments used in making the decisions.

There has been increased rejection of the right of institutions to have complete discretion when their policies affect people's life chances. In an earlier generation, labor unions sought and secured participation in many aspects of decision making formerly the province of management alone. In 1964, the Civil Rights Act removed race, color, ethnic origin, sex, and religion from the selection criteria within the discretion of the employer.

This democratization of power has also reached educational institutions, for example, in the so-called sunshine laws. These statutes establish the right of students to have access to their academic files, including letters of recommendation, teacher evaluations, and test scores. Not too many years ago, it was considered inappropriate to tell a student his or her test score on a college entrance examination. The scores were sent to the local guidance counselor, if there was one, or to the administrative offices: the student was considered likely to misunderstand the test score unless a professional acted as intermediary. A recent New York State law requires that not only the test score, but also the entire test and scoring key, be disclosed so that the test taker can evaluate the test and his or her performance on it. This law represents a considerable change in social attitudes regarding the rights of individuals in the decision process.

Insofar as the criticisms of testing are actually criticisms of the nature of the decision process itself, some of the policy issues discussed above take on a different aspect. For example, if tests are inadequate, we can search for alternatives to testing. But if the real concern is how and by whom selection decisions are made, alternatives to testing may be of no help unless the ground rules for decision making are changed. In fact, it is possible that some critics should be asking for alternative decision-making processes rather than for alternatives to testing. And if there are alternatives to testing that are socially more acceptable, it may well be that their acceptability derives chiefly from the ease with which the decision process can be changed. As an illustration, an interview is notoriously lower in validity than most tests. Yet many people perceive it as more acceptable because it involves a direct interchange between the decision maker and the applicant, even to the point that the decision is truly a joint one. Thus, the interview might well be perceived as more acceptable by a person about whom the decision is made despite its lower validity.

In sum, it must be recognized that, although tests are of concern in their own right, they also are important because they are a major means for institutionalizing the decision process about individuals. If the true issue is the nature of the decision process, then concerns about the construction, reliability, validity, and other formal aspects of testing are not the major consideration, and those concerns should be seen as the means to an end. Taken in this light, it is the end to which tests are put, not their characteristics as a means to that end, that motivates the controversy about testing.

Costs and Benefits to Society

Each of the two proximate actors in the testing process, the user and the taker, incurs costs, and presumably benefits, from the enterprise. For test users, the costs might include procuring and administering the tests, interpreting the results, and conducting validation studies. The benefits would derive from the increased likelihood of successful performance by those who are selected or placed by the tests. Admissions tests, for example, were initially attractive to law schools because of very high attrition rates that wasted the resources of the institution as well as the time and resources of the unsuccessful students.

For test takers, the consequences of testing are the opportunities gained or lost. Unsatisfactory performance will cost the test taker access to one sort of future. The benefits of testing accrue to the taker who gains access to a limited opportunity, is assigned to a potentially more rewarding position, is barred from an opportunity that would have led to failure, or can gain self-knowledge that will help in choosing among educational or vocational options.

But the question of costs and benefits of testing goes beyond the immediate interests of users and test takers; indeed, it goes to the very nature of the society one wishes America to be. Tests are, by and large, elitist. The aim of testing is to identify those who are best prepared by nature and training to perform well in a given role. Is there a place in a democratic society for excellence? Can the selection of the "best" one of ten people into a superior job, college, or occupation balance the "loss" to the others, those who are not selected? Should society nurture some outstanding institutions—the Metropolitan Opera, the Green Bay Packers, Harvard University—which exist because of stiff selection criteria? Would society be better off with ten mediocre colleges, or a combination of one excellent school, six mediocre, and three poor ones?

The answers to these questions used to seem fairly clear. Western nations, at least since the Renaissance, have held a world view that reveres excellence. America, with its open spaces and expanding wealth and constant infusions of new hands and energy from abroad, has had the luxury of combining respect for excellence with widespread upward mobility. During much of this century there was a broad consensus that if access to the most desirable things (good schools, good jobs, wealth) is "fair," i.e., based on ability and achievement, then the resulting inequality is acceptable.

This consensus has dwindled along with optimism about an ever-expanding economy. The recognition of excellence, Americans have come to realize, also creates invidious comparisons and more visible inequality. In good part, the attack on tests is an attack on the outcomes of the overall social and economic system in America, which are no longer perceived as "fair." In this light, tests validate the existing social structure rather than opening it up. In the present state of ambivalence about testing, one question assumes central importance: Who would get the good jobs if tests were not used?

REFERENCES

Deutsch, M. (1979) Education and distributive justice: some reflections on grading systems. *American Psychologist* 34:391-401.

Gibb, C. A. (1969) Leadership. In G. Lindzey and E. Aronson., eds., *Handbook of Social Psychology*, 2nd ed. Reading, Mass.: Addison-Wesley.

Goslin, D. A. (1963) *The Search for Ability*. New York: Russell Sage Foundation.

Hoffman, B. (1964) *The Tyranny of Testing*. New York: Collier Books.

Jencks, C. (1979) *Who Gets Ahead?* New York: Basic Books.

Jensen, A. (1973) *Educability and Group Differences*. New York: Harper and Row.

Jensen, A. (1980) *Bias in Mental Testing*. New York: The Free Press.

Nairn, A., and Associates (1980) The Reign of ETS. The Corporation That Makes Up Minds. The Ralph Nader Report on the Educational Testing Service.

Quinto, F., and McKenna, B. (1977) *Alternatives to Standardized Testing*. Washington, D.C.: National Education Association.

Reilly, R., and Chao, G. (1980) Validity and Fairness of Alternative Employee Selection Procedures. Unpublished manuscript. Research Division, American Telephone and Telegraph Co., Morristown, N.J.

Ryan, C. (1979) *The Testing Maze*. Chicago: National Parent Teachers Association.

Schmitt, N. (1976) Social and situational determinants of interview decisions: implications for the employment interview. *Personnel Psychology* 29:79-101.

Webster, E. C. (1964) *Decision Making in the Employment Interview*. Montreal: Eagle.

2
Measuring Ability: Concepts, Methods, and Results

INTRODUCTION

There are many different kinds of ability tests designed to assess a variety of abilities for a variety of uses. Some are intended to measure highly specific skills (e.g., the ability to take shorthand) while others are intended as measures of general intellectual ability. Some require the use of special apparatus and must be administered by a highly trained examiner. More often they are paper-and-pencil tests with multiple-choice questions, administered by nonspecialists; this form is encountered regularly by almost all school children in this country.

Despite the great variety of kinds and uses of ability tests, they all share some fundamental characteristics. They are intended to assess how well a person can perform a task when trying to do his or her best. Thus, the tests are meant to measure the upper limit of what a person can do, which may be quite different than typical performance. In addition, an ability test can measure a person's best performance only if the person is motivated to do well and understands what is expected. As we shall see, many variables can influence a test taker's motivation and expectations.

Another characteristic that is common to all ability tests is that they assess only a person's current status. An ability test "yields a sample of what the individual knows and has learned to do at the time he or she is tested; it measures the level of development attained by the individual in one or more abilities. No test, whatever it is called, reveals how or why the individual has reached that level" (Anastasi 1980:4).

Ability, the upper limit of what a person can do now, should not be confused with "potential" or "capacity." Many of the controversies considered in this report have grown out of the mistaken idea that test scores directly measure an inborn, predetermined capacity. This idea is mistaken in two crucial ways. First, as just quoted from Anastasi, the assessment is only of the ability at the time of testing; it cannot reveal how the person developed the level of ability suggested by the score. Second, tests provide only indirect measures of ability: the ability is inferred from performance on the test; it is not observed directly.

Because ability is not observed directly, as it would be, say, in a piano competition, the explanation of test performance depends on careful test design and a continuing process of validation research. To illustrate, a test that is intended to measure one ability can also reflect other abilities—ones that the test is not intended to measure. For example, a test designed to measure mathematical ability may place substantial reading demands on some takers. If so, the measure of mathematics ability becomes confounded with reading ability. Consequently, low math test scores could erroneously suggest limited ability in mathematics for some people or groups of people for whom the real difficulty was in reading. Thus, it is important that tests be designed to minimize the influence of abilities other than the one(s) they are intended to measure.

The concepts discussed in this chapter could apply to all kinds of abilities—social, athletic, artistic—but we focus primarily on tests, usually paper-and-pencil tests, of knowledge, reasoning, and special skills. The following section provides a description of what ability tests are like and presents examples of questions from a few of the widely used ones. The description of tests is followed by a discussion of the analyses that are applied to judge how well a test serves particular purposes. Finally, the results of research on some of the crucial, and sometimes controversial, issues in testing are discussed. In particular, we discuss the results and interpretations of the use of tests with different groups and some of the variables that influence test scores.

WHAT ABILITY TESTS ARE LIKE

The tests considered in this chapter are commonly referred to as "standardized tests." Although we also use this term, it unfortunately has several meanings, and so it is important to distinguish among them. "Standardized" sometimes refers to tests that are accompanied by a table of norms, sometimes to tests whose content reflects "standard" school curricula, and sometimes to tests in which a uniform testing procedure is applied. We refer in this report only to the latter property: a standardized test may or may not be accompanied by a table of norms and may or may not contain content that is considered part of "standard" school curricula, but it must be uniform in administration and scoring for all who take it.

For standardized tests, as with any scientific observation, there is a need for controlled conditions to minimize the effects of extraneous variables. Uniformity of procedure in standardized tests is intended to minimize the differential effects of examiners, instructions, time, scorer, and various other factors. In reality, standardization is obviously a matter of degree; not every conceivable extraneous factor can be controlled. Standardization is designed to reduce the influence of such factors. When they are discovered, it is incumbent upon the developer of a standardized test to try to devise procedures to remove such influences; or failing that, to estimate and report the magnitude of the error caused by such uncontrolled variations.

Attempts are often made to distinguish between two categories of ability tests: aptitude tests, intended to predict what a person can accomplish with training; and achievement tests, intended to measure accomplished skills and indicate what one can do at present. Actually, however, achievement and aptitude tests are not fundamentally different. They both measure developed ability, they often use similar questions, and they have often been found to yield highly related results. Rather than two sharply different categories of tests, it is more useful to think of "aptitude" and "achievement" tests as falling along a continuum.

Tests at one end of the aptitude-achievement continuum can be distinguished from those at the other end primarily in terms of purpose. For example, a test for mechanical aptitude would be included in a battery of tests for selecting among applicants for pilot training since knowledge of mechanical principles has been found to be related to success in flying. A similar test would be given at the end of a course in mechanics as an achievement test intended to measure what was learned in the course. Of course, it would not be surprising to find that many people who did well on one of the tests would also do well on the other, nor that the achievement test could also be used to predict flying success.

Tests at the two ends of the aptitude-achievement continuum can also be distinguished in terms of the specificity of the definition of relevant prior experience (Anastasi 1980). The questions on the achievement test for the course in mechanics would be determined by the content covered in the course. By mastering the course material, a person should have the knowledge needed to answer the questions on the achievement test.

For the mechanical aptitude test, the knowledge needed for the questions would not be so clearly specified. A wide variety of experiences, including but not limited to a course in mechanics, would be relevant for developing the knowledge measured by the mechanical aptitude test. Thus, an aptitude test should be less dependent than an achievement test on particular experiences, such as whether or not a person has had a specific course or studied a particular topic.

In addition to the aptitude-achievement distinction, ability tests may also be considered on a general-to-specific continuum. At the general end of the continuum are tests that sample a fairly broad array of verbal and quantitative tasks and summarize performance with a single general score. At the other end of the continuum are highly specific tests that provide separate scores for many different abilities. J. P. Guilford (1967), for example, has distinguished 120 separate, albeit interrelated, abilities. The question of how many abilities there are is intriguing, but it cannot be answered from results with tests. The fineness of the distinctions depends upon one's purpose and on the investigator's judgment of what is useful or significant. Very fine distinctions also depend on the technological capability of developing sufficiently sensitive tests.

The general-versus-specific distinction applies to both achievement and aptitude tests. A competency test of high school graduation is an across-the-board, general measure. Closer to the specific end of the continuum, there are separate tests for most school subjects, and tests can be made for particular skills within a subject. For example, there is a test that measures reading as a whole and also the decoding of syllables.

For tests of general ability, most of the tasks require a complex mixture of the abilities to analyze, to understand abstract concepts, and to apply prior knowledge to the solution of new problems. Few of the items can be answered by simple recall or the rote application of practiced skills.

Tests of general ability are often called intelligence tests, but this is an unfortunate label. It is too easily misunderstood to mean that intelligence is a unitary ability, fixed in amount, unchanged over time, and for which individuals can be ranked on a single scale. It is legitimate, however, to speak of general ability and to say that some people have more of it than others. Older, more experienced people, on the average, perform better than people half their age on a wide variety of tasks; this is true from childhood to at least middle age. Within a grade, students who have superior competence in arithmetic are likely to have better-than-average records in other academic subjects. Adults who can follow a complex legal argument would be expected to comprehend, more easily than the average person, the diagram of a complex football play or an account of research on protein synthesis. In summary, then, and as used in this report, general ability or "intelligence" refers to a repertoire of information-processing skills and habits, such as the ability to subdivide a problem, the ability to encode stimuli for efficient memory storage, persistence, and flexibility. These skills and habits must be developed. Furthermore, in any application, these skills and habits have to be integrated (Resnick 1976), although any given task places greater demands on certain processes than on others.

Although a summary index of general ability is often useful, abilities are by no means so consistent that a person who is average at one task is average at all tasks. A graphic profile of a person's scores on tests of several different abilities side by side will have a characteristic elevation, referred to as a generally high or generally low profile. But profiles are irregular, and some are so jagged that a statement about general level would be a poor description. For purposes of guidance and counseling, it is often useful to have information on several abilities rather than only one or two. Batteries of tests that provide scores on mechanical reasoning, clerical speed and accuracy, spatial ability, and possibly others as well as verbal and quantitative abilities provide such information.

Emphasis on multiscore batteries has increased over the years. Scores to describe patterns of ability are used in vocational guidance, in assigning military recruits to specialized training, in diagnosing aphasics, and in similar applications. In selection and classification for employment, combining scores in several ways permits the tester to make separate predictions for diverse jobs. Speed of list-checking is highly relevant to some clerical jobs, while quantitative skills are more relevant for a cashier's job.

Because standardized ability tests are so diverse that few statements hold true for all of them, it is useful to consider a few specific examples. Tasks, materials, item formats, responses required, mode of administration, and kind of score reported are among the important variations in tests. The tests that are briefly described below illustrate, but do not exhaust, the range of ability tests; they are all well-known, widely used tests.

An Individual Test of General Ability

The Wechsler Adult Intelligence Scale (WAIS) is an individually administered test used to measure cognitive abilities in adults. (There are comparable tests for preschoolers, the Wechsler Preschool and Primary Scale of Intelligence, and for children aged 6 to 16, the Wechsler Intelligence Scale for Children—Revised.) The WAIS consists of 11 subtests organized into separate verbal and performance scales (see Figure 1).

Verbal Subscale

1. *General Information.*
What day of the year is Independence Day?

2. *Similarities.*
In what way are *wool* and *cotton* alike?

3. *Arithmetic Reasoning.*
If eggs cost 60 cents a dozen, what does 1 egg cost?

4. *Vocabulary.*
Tell me the meaning of corrupt.

5. *Comprehension.*
Why do people buy fire insurance?

6. *Digit Span.*
Listen carefully, and when I am through, say the numbers
right after me.

7   3   4   1   8   6

Now I am going to say some more numbers, but I want
you to say them backward.

3   8   4   1   6

Performance Subscale

7. *Picture Completion.*
I am going to show you a picture with an important part
missing. Tell me what is missing.

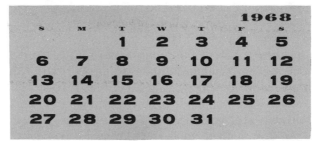

8. *Picture Arrangement.*
The pictures below tell a story. Put them in the right
order to tell the story.

FIGURE 1 Subscales and illustrative items on the Wechsler Adult Intelligence Scale (not
actual test items).
SOURCE: Thorndike and Hagen (1977: 307–309).

9. *Block Design.*

Using the four blocks, make one just like this.

10. *Object Assembly.*

If these pieces are put together correctly, they will make something. Go ahead and put them together as quickly as you can.

11. *Digit-Symbol Substitution.*

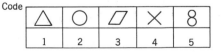

The verbal scale measures a person's understanding of verbal concepts and ability to respond orally. As can be seen from the illustrative items in Figure 1, performance on the verbal scale depends on familiarity with general information and vocabulary. It also depends on the ability to understand verbal arithmetic problems and perform the necessary arithmetic operations. The performance scale measures the ability to solve problems involving the manipulation of objects and other materials.

In addition to an IQ for the entire test, the WAIS yields a verbal IQ and a performance (nonverbal) IQ. Scaled scores are also obtained for each of the subtests. These subtest scores are used to get some idea of a person's strengths and weaknesses. For example, they may tell how well the test taker does under pressure—some subtests are timed, others are not—or how verbal skills compare with the ability to solve nonverbal problems. A large discrepancy between verbal and performance scores prompts the tester to look for specific learning problems—e.g., reading disabilities or a language handicap.

The WAIS must be given individually by a trained tester, and the process is time-consuming. Its advantage over a group test, however, is that the tester can determine whether the test taker understands the questions, can evaluate motivation, and by carefully observing how the test taker approaches different tasks can gain additional clues as to strengths and weaknesses.

A Group Test of General Ability

Group tests, required whenever large numbers of people are to be tested, are available for employment and military use and for all the school grades. Such tests usually offer a verbal score and one for spatial or quantitative tasks. The Scholastic Aptitude Test (SAT) is a well-known group test given to high school students who wish to attend college.

The SAT is a multiple-choice test that yields separate verbal (SAT-V) and mathematics (SAT-M) scores. The SAT-V contains a total of 85 questions spread over four item types: antonyms, analogies, sentence completion, and reading passages. Examples of each item type are provided in Figure 2, along with a brief description of what the items are thought to measure. The SAT-V provides a general measure of developed verbal ability, i.e., the ability to understand what is read and the extent of a student's vocabulary. The SAT-M is a measure of a student's ability to solve arithmetic reasoning and algebraic and geometric problems. A third of the 60 items are presented in the form of quantitative comparisons while the remainder are "regular" multiple-choice questions. The number of questions by content area is as follows: arithmetic reasoning, 18 or

1. Antonyms ("test extent of vocabulary")

   "Choose the word or phrase that is most nearly the *opposite* in meaning to the word in capital letters."

   "PARTISAN: (A) commoner (B) neutral (C) unifier (D) ascetic
                   (E) pacifist"

2. Analogies ("test ability to see a relationship in a pair of words, to understand the ideas expressed in the relationship, and to recognize a similar or parallel relationship")

   "Select the lettered pair that *best* expresses a relationship similar to that expressed in the original pair."

   "FLURRY: BLIZZARD: (A) trickle:deluge   (B) rapids:rock
                          (C) lightning:cloudburst   (D) spray:foam
                          (E) mountain:summit"

3. Sentence Completion ("test . . . ability to recognize the relationships among parts of a sentence")

   "Choose the word or set of words that *best* fits the meaning of the sentence as a whole."

   "Prominent psychologists believe that people act violently because they have been _____ to do so, not because they were born _____ :

       (A) forced--gregarious   (B) forbidden--complacent
       (C) expected--innocent   (D) taught--aggressive
       (E) inclined--belligerent"

4. Reading Passages (test ability to comprehend a written passage)

   Blocks of questions are presented following passages of roughly 400 to 500 words. Some questions ask about information that is directly stated in the passage, others require applications of the author's principles or opinions, still others ask for judgments (e.g., how well the author supports claims).

FIGURE 2   Item types and illustrative items on the verbal section of the Scholastic Aptitude Test.
SOURCE: Test items and directions are taken from the sample SAT in *Taking the SAT* (College Entrance Examination Board 1978). Reprinted by permission of the Educational Testing Service.

NOTE: The illustrative items are of middle difficulty, i.e., are answered correctly by 50 to 65 percent of the test takers. Answers: B, A, D.

19 questions; algebra, 17 questions; geometry, 16 or 17 questions; and miscellaneous, 7 to 9 questions. Questions in the last category "often involve newly defined concepts or novel settings" (Braswell 1978:170). Examples of the two formats and the three main content areas are shown in Figure 3.

The SAT measures both aptitude and achievement. It samples the skills a person has acquired during 12 years of education; however, the developers of the test try to avoid items that require knowledge of specific topics (e.g., American history, biology), focusing instead on the ability to use acquired skills to solve new problems.

Tests of Special Abilities

The Differential Aptitude Test (DAT) is a widely used battery of ability tests that are intended primarily for educational and vocational counseling for students in grades 8 to 12. The battery consists of eight tests: verbal reasoning, numerical ability, abstract reasoning, clerical speed and accuracy, mechanical reasoning, space relations, spelling, and language usage. Illustrative items from each test are shown in Figure 4.

A profile of the eight scores on the DAT yields information about areas of particular strength or weakness in addition to information about general level. The information from the various scores is not unique, however. People with high scores on verbal reasoning tend to have high scores on language usage and to a slightly lesser extent high scores on numerical reasoning and abstract reasoning. Indeed, the best prediction is that someone who has a score on verbal reasoning that is well above average will have a score that is somewhat above average on any of the other seven tests.

Some indication of the degree of relationship among the tests on the DAT can be obtained by considering students who rank in the top quarter on the verbal reasoning test. On an unrelated test, only a random 25 percent of them would be expected to rank in the top quarter on the second test. But on the numerical reasoning test, 62 percent of them would be expected to rank in the top quarter, and on the space relations test (assuming a bivariate normal distribution), 56 percent would be expected to rank in the top quarter. The agreement is not perfect, but it is substantial.[1] While there is evidence that the tests have sizable inter-

[1] In fact some disagreement would be expected if an alternate form of the verbal reasoning test were administered since the test scores are subject to errors of measurement (see section below on reliability). Specifically, 73 percent of those in the top quarter on the first verbal reasoning test would also be expected to be in the top quarter on an alternate form of the verbal reasoning test.

1. Regular Items

   Algebra:

   "If $x^3 = (2x)^2$ and $x \neq 0$, then $x =$

   　　(A) 1　(B) 2　(C) 4　(D) 6　(E) 8"

   Geometry:　$\ell \dfrac{\quad x^{\circ} \diagup y^{\circ} \quad}{P}$

   Note: Figure not drawn to scale.

   "If P is a point on line ℓ in the figure above and $x - y = 0$, then $y =$

   　　(A) 0　　(B) 45　　(C) 90　　(D) 135　　(E) 180"

2. Quantitative Comparison

   "Questions—each consists of two quantities, one in Column A and one in Column B. You are to compare the two quantities and on the answer sheet blacken space:

   　　(A)　if the quantity in Column A is greater;
   　　(B)　if the quantity in Column B is greater;
   　　(C)　if the two quantities are equal;
   　　(D)　if the relationship cannot be determined from the information given."

	Column A	Column B
Arithmetic:	"Number of minutes in 1 week"	"Number of seconds in 7 hours"

   Algebra:

   $\dfrac{5}{x} = \dfrac{1}{3}$

Column A	Column B
$\dfrac{3}{x}$	$\dfrac{1}{5}$

FIGURE 3　Item formats and illustrative items on the mathematical section of the Scholastic Aptitude Test.
SOURCE: Test items and directions are taken from the sample SAT in *Taking the SAT* (College Entrance Examination Board 1978). Reprinted by permission of the Educational Testing Service.

NOTE: Items are of middle difficulty, i.e., are answered correctly by between 48 and 63 percent of the test takers. Answers: C, C, B, C.

VERBAL REASONING

Choose the correct pair of words to fill the blanks. The first word of the pair goes in the blank space at the beginning of the sentence; the second word of the pair goes in the blank at the end of the sentence.

. . . . . . is to night as breakfast is to . . . . . .

A. supper —— corner
B. gentle —— morning
C. door —— corner
D. flow —— enjoy
E. supper —— morning

The correct answer is E.

NUMERICAL ABILITY

Choose the correct answer for each problem.

Add	13	A	14		Subtract	30	A	15
	12	B	25			20	B	26
		C	16				C	16
		D	59				D	8
		N	none of these				N	none of these

The correct answer for the first problem is B; for the second, N.

ABSTRACT REASONING

The four "problem figures" in each row make a series. Find the one among the "answer figures" that would be next in the series.

The correct answer is D

CLERICAL SPEED AND ACCURACY

In each test item, one of the five combinations is underlined. Find the same combination on the answer sheet and mark it.

FIGURE 4 Sample items from the Differential Aptitude Tests.
SOURCE: Anastasi (1976:380-381).

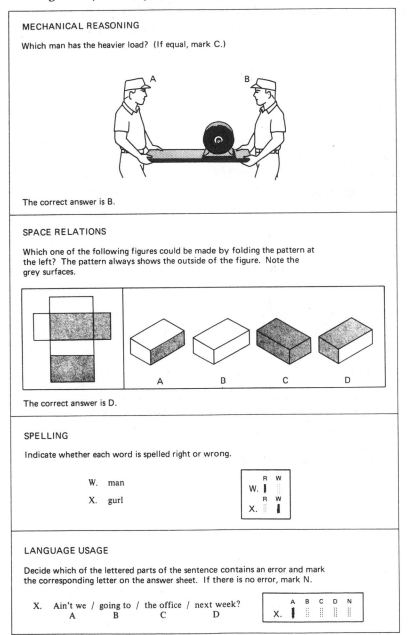

MECHANICAL REASONING

Which man has the heavier load? (If equal, mark C.)

The correct answer is B.

SPACE RELATIONS

Which one of the following figures could be made by folding the pattern at the left? The pattern always shows the outside of the figure. Note the grey surfaces.

A   B   C   D

The correct answer is D.

SPELLING

Indicate whether each word is spelled right or wrong.

W.   man

X.   gurl

       R   W
W. ▌   ⋮
       R   W
X. ⋮   ▌

LANGUAGE USAGE

Decide which of the lettered parts of the sentence contains an error and mark the corresponding letter on the answer sheet. If there is no error, mark N.

X.   Ain't we / going to / the office / next week?
     A   B   C   D

     A   B   C   D   N
X. ▌   ⋮   ⋮   ⋮   ⋮

FIGURE 4   (*Continued*)

relationships, there is also an indication that the individual tests provide some unique information. Thus, it may be concluded that the separate tests contain both general and specific information about ability.

An Employment Test

The Professional and Administrative Career Examination (PACE) was developed by the U.S. Civil Service Commission for use in the selection of employees for over 100 different government occupations. It is the means by which several thousand college graduates get government jobs each year. In addition to a written examination (called Test 500), the PACE includes an evaluation of an applicant's education and experience, which includes the assignment of credits for outstanding scholarship in college and for veterans preference; we consider here only Test 500.

Test 500 is intended to measure five abilities, labeled verbal comprehension, judgment, induction, deduction, and number. A description of the five abilities and of the type of questions used to measure each ability is provided in Figure 5. Each of the subtests consists of 30 items; test takers are allowed 35 minutes to complete each subtest. As can be seen in Figure 5, each ability subtest has two different types of items except judgment, which has only one type of item.

CONVERTING SCORES INTO MEANINGFUL FORM

The fact that a person has 10 correct answers on a test is, by itself, meaningless. It begins to have some meaning when one knows that the test consisted of 30 multiplication problems. Still more information is needed for sensible interpretation, however, because the difficulty of the task can vary substantially depending on such factors as the amount of time provided, the format of presentation (e.g., multiple choice vs. free response), the numbers involved (e.g., 5×5 vs. $876 \times 9,453$). Knowing that the average score on the test for students in the same grade is 20 correct answers and that 5 percent of the students in that grade get less than 10 correct answers also helps in interpreting a raw score of 10 correct answers.

Because raw scores generally lack meaning and those from one form of a test are not comparable to those from another, raw scores on standardized tests are usually converted to some scale. The converted form of the score usually provides some information about how one individual's score compares to the scores of others. The group of people used to provide the comparison is called the norm group and the results for that group are commonly referred to as norms.

Norms obviously depend on the group on which they are based. For example, norms for 6th-grade students would presumably be quite different from norms for 4th-grade students. Similarly, the proportion of people with test scores below some specified value in a local norm group (e.g., 6th-grade students in Chicago public schools) might differ substantially from that in a national norm group (e.g., a sample of 6th-grade students from throughout the United States). Thus, in considering scores that are based on norms, the norm group should be clearly specified. A few of the more common scales that depend on norms are briefly described below.

Percentile Ranks

One of the more common and easily understood scales for reporting test scores is the percentile rank scale. The percentile rank is equal to the percentage of persons in the norm group who fall below a given raw score. In the above example the student's percentile rank on the multiplication test would be 5, since he or she scored higher than 5 percent of the students. The dependence of the scores on the norm group is quite apparent in the case of percentile ranks. The time of the school year as well as the definition of the norm group is important. A score on the multiplication test that yielded a percentile rank of 20 using 4th-grade norms in the fall might result in a percentile rank of only 5 using 4th-grade norms in the spring.

The main advantage of percentile ranks is their simplicity: they are easily understood. The main disadvantage is that they tend to exaggerate small differences in raw scores near the average relative to the same differences near the extremes. The tendency to exaggerate differences near the average is a consequence of the shape of the distribution of raw scores that is typical of most standardized tests: a few very high scores and a few very low scores with much more frequent scores closer to the average.

The frequency of each possible raw score on a commonly used 25-item standardized test is shown in Table 1 for 407 students in one school district. (Other school districts, other tests, or a norm based on a national sample would yield different distributions of frequencies; however, they would share some of the general characteristics of the one shown in Table 1.) In particular, there are many more scores near the average (14.67) for the distribution shown in Table 1 than there are scores well above or well below the average. For example, 33 students had scores of 14 while only 2 students had a score of 4, and only 5 students had a score of 25. Where the frequencies are high in the distribution, a single additional

PACE ABILITY DEFINITIONS

Verbal Comprehension
Ability to understand and interpret complex reading material and to use language where precise correspondence of words and concepts makes effective oral and written communication possible.

Judgment
Ability to make decisions or take action in the absence of complete information and to solve problems by inferring missing facts or events to arrive at the most logical conclusion.

Induction
Ability to discover underlying relations or analogies among specific data where solving problems involves formation and testing of hypotheses.

Deduction
Ability to discover implications of facts and to reason from general principles to specific situations as in developing plans and procedures.

Number
Ability to perform arithmetic operations and to solve quantitative problems where the proper approach is not specified.

DESCRIPTION OF PACE QUESTION TYPES

Ability	Question Type	Description
Verbal Comprehension	Reading Comprehension	Reading comprehension questions require the examinee to read a given paragraph and to select an answer on the basis of comprehension of the conceptual content of the paragraph. The correct answer is either a reworded statement of the main concepts in the paragraph or a conclusion so inherent in the paragraph content that it is equivalent to a restatement.
Verbal Comprehension	Vocabulary	Each vocabulary question contains a key word and five alternative choices. The examinee is to select the alternative word that is closest in meaning to the key word. The incorrect alternatives may have a more or less valid connection with the key word. In some cases the correct choice differs from the others only in the degree to which its meaning comes close to that of the key word.

FIGURE 5 A description of the contents of the PACE test.
SOURCE: Trattner et al. (1977:2-4).

Ability	Question Type	Description
Judgment	Comprehension	Comprehension questions require the examinee to determine the most plausible or reasonable alternative which might explain or follow from a given statement. Selection of the best alternatives requires general knowledge not included in the original statement. While more than one alternative may be plausible, the correct answer is the most plausible of the alternatives.
Induction	Letter Series	Letter series questions consist of a set of letters arranged in a definite pattern. The examinee must discover what the pattern is and determine the letter which should occur next in the series.
	Figure Analogies	Figure analogy questions each consist of two sets of symbols where a common characteristic exists among the symbols in each set and where an analogy is maintained between the two sets of symbols. A symbol is missing from one of the sets. The examinee must discover which alternative fits the missing symbol in such a way as to preserve the characteristics common to the second set and to preserve the analogy with the first set.
Deduction	Tabular Completion	Tabular completion questions present charts or tables in which some entries are missing. The examinee must deduce the missing values.
	Inference	The inference question type presents a statement which is to be accepted as true and should not be questioned for purposes of the test. The correct alternative must derive from the statement without drawing on additional information not presented. Incorrect alternatives rest, to varying degrees, on the admission of new information.
Number	Computation	Computation questions require straightforward calculation and may include decimals, fractions, and percentages.
	Arithmetic Reasoning	Arithmetic reasoning questions are word problems which require quantitative reasoning processes for their solution.

FIGURE 5   *(Continued)*

TABLE 1   Illustrative Frequency Distribution with Associated Percentile Ranks and Standard Scores for a Sample of 407 Students on a 25-Item Test

Raw Score	Frequency	Percentile Rank	Standard Score[a]	T-Score[a]
25	5	99	2.05	70
24	7	97	1.85	68
23	14	94	1.65	66
22	15	90	1.45	64
21	21	85	1.25	62
20	21	80	1.06	61
19	21	74	.86	59
18	27	68	.66	57
17	19	63	.46	55
16	29	56	.26	53
15	23	50	.07	51
14	33	42	− .13	49
13	30	35	− .33	47
12	18	30	− .53	45
11	34	22	− .73	43
10	20	17	− .92	41
9	16	13	−1.12	39
8	16	9	−1.32	37
7	21	4	−1.52	35
6	9	2	−1.72	33
5	5	1	−1.91	31
4	2	0.2	−2.11	29
3	0	0.2	−2.31	27
2	0	0.2	−2.51	25
1	1		−2.71	23
0	0		−2.90	21

[a] See discussion in text.

right answer, i.e., a 1-point increase in the raw score, is associated with a large increase in percentile rank, but where the frequencies are small, an additional right answer produces a smaller change in percentile rank. Thus, an increase in the raw score from 14 to 15 corresponds to an 8-point increase in percentile rank whereas an increase in the raw score from 5 to 6 corresponds to only a 1-point increase in percentile rank.

Standard Scores

Standard scores also are based on results from a norm group, but, unlike percentile ranks, they do not alter the relative magnitude of the differences between the raw scores at different points in the distribution. Standard scores are expressed in terms of (standard) deviations from the mean.[2]

Standard scores are computed by first setting the mean equal to a standard score of zero. Other scores are then expressed as the number of standard deviations above the mean (positive numbers) or below the mean (negative numbers). A raw score equal to the mean plus 1 standard deviation is converted to a standard score of +1.0. Standard scores corresponding to each raw score are listed in Table 1. A raw score of 20 is converted to a standard score of 1.06 (20 equals the mean 14.67 plus 1.06 standard deviations). Even without knowing the distribution of scores or the number of items on the test, more information is conveyed by stating that a person has a standard score of 1.06 than by reporting a raw score of 20.

In order to avoid negative scores and the need for decimal places, standard scores are frequently converted to some other scale. One common conversion, called T-scores, sets the mean at 50 and the standard deviation at 10. T-scores are obtained by multiplying the standard scores by 10 and adding 50. Thus, as can be seen in Table 1, a standard score

---

[2] The standard deviation of a distribution is a statistic that describes the degree to which scores vary. Mathematically, it is the square root of the sum of the squared deviations from the mean divided by the number of observations minus 1:

$$\frac{\sum_i (x_i - \bar{x})^2}{N - 1} .$$

For the example in Table 1, the standard deviation is 5.05 points. Part of the descriptive value of the standard deviation may be seen by using it to describe score intervals. In the distribution in Table 1, the mean plus 1 standard deviation is 14.67 plus 5.05, which is 19.72, or approximately 20. Approximately 15 percent of the students had scores higher than 20. Similarly, the mean minus 1 standard deviation is approximately 10 and about 17 percent of the students had raw scores lower than 10. The remaining 68 percent of the students had raw scores between 10 and 20 (inclusive). The exact percentage of scores that fall between −1.0 standard deviation and +1.0 standard deviation will vary depending on the shape of the distribution. But distributions of scores on standardized tests almost always have between 60 and 75 percent of the scores within 1 standard deviation of the mean, and more than 90 percent of the scores within 2 standard deviations of the mean. (See the discussion of normal curve, below.)

44

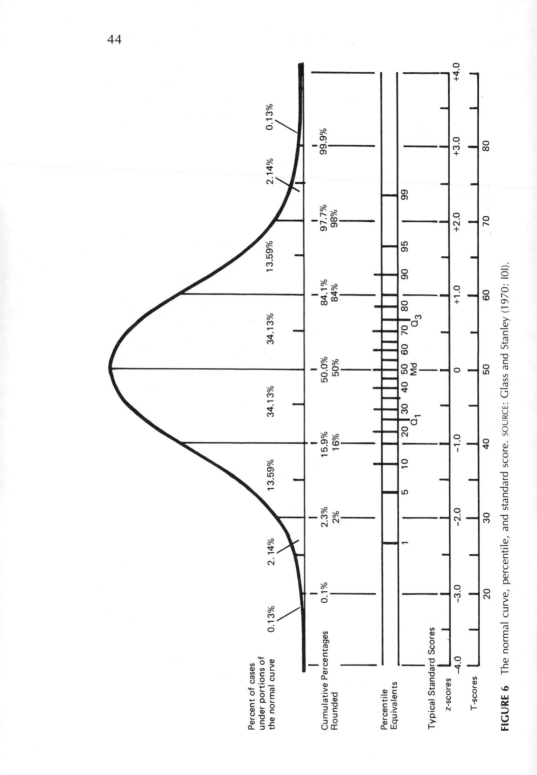

FIGURE 6 The normal curve, percentile, and standard score. SOURCE: Glass and Stanley (1970: IOI).

of 1.06 corresponds to a T-score of 61 (10 times 1.06 plus 50, 60.6, which is rounded to 61).

Normalized T-Scores

The normal distribution is a theoretical distribution with great importance in statistics, and it is often used in defining test scores. Although it is never observed in practice, the normal distribution is very useful mathematically and provides a reasonable approximation to many distributions that are observed in practice.

A curve depicting the normal distribution is shown in Figure 6. The area under the curve represents the proportion of the distribution that falls between any two score points on the horizontal axis. The exact proportion of the distribution that lies in any interval can be computed from the mean and standard deviation. About 68 percent of the area falls within one standard deviation of the mean (i.e., between standard scores of −1.0 and +1.0), and about 95 percent falls within two standard deviations of the mean. Although these proportions are not precisely the same as would be found for an actual distribution, they provide an approximation that is reasonably close for some tests. The normal distribution is the basis for defining the scales that are used to report scores for a number of standardized tests. One such example is a normalized T-score.

Normalized T-scores are obtained by transforming the original raw scores so that the distribution of the transformed scores is as normal as possible and setting the mean equal to 50 and the standard deviation equal to 10. As can be seen in Figure 6, about 2.3 percent of a normal distribution lies below −2.0 standard deviations. Hence a raw score below which 2.3 percent of the cases in the norm group fall would be converted to a normalized T-score of 30 (i.e., the mean of 50 minus 2 standard deviations of 10). Similarly, raw scores below which 15.9 percent, 50.0 percent, 84.1 percent, 97.7 percent, and 99.9 percent of the cases fell would be converted to normalized T-scores of 40, 50, 60, 70, and 80 respectively (see Figure 6).

Normalized T-scores are similar to standard scores in that they are expressed in standard deviation units for a normal distribution. Using the assumption of a normal distribution also allows ready conversion back and forth between T-scores and percentile ranks. It should be recognized, however, that the use of normalized scores is a convenience, not a principle. The shape of a raw score distribution depends on the way a test is constructed. Many, but by no means all, standardized tests are constructed in a way that the distribution has a shape at least roughly similar to a normal distribution for the population for which they are intended to be used. It is quite possible to select items for a test that will yield distributions of raw scores with radically different shapes, and this is sometimes done.

Normal Curve Equivalent

There are a number of variations of normalized scores in addition to T-scores; one example is the normal curve equivalent (NCE). The NCE is a normalized standard distribution of scores with a mean of 50 and a standard deviation of 21.06. This seemingly unusual number for the standard deviation was selected so that the NCE and percentile ranks have the same numerical value at l, 50, and 99. Other NCE values do not correspond to the same numerical percentile rank.

The NCE is the scale that is used for the evaluation and reporting system that is mandated for programs funded under Title I of the Elementary and Secondary Education Act of 1965. Because of the adoption of the NCE for this purpose, publishers of some of the more commonly used tests for elementary and secondary school students now provide NCE scores.

Age-Equivalent Scores

Age-equivalent scores are sometimes used, but they are not considered valuable because of difficulties in interpreting them. The age equivalent was popularized as the so-called mental age with early IQ tests. A child with a "mental age" of 9 is one who earns as many points on the test as the average 9-year-old. But a 13-year-old with a mental age of 9 will have quite different skills than a 7-year-old with a mental age of 9. For these and other reasons, most publishers no longer depend on mental-age scores either as a primary means of reporting or for purposes of computing IQ scores.

Grade-Equivalent Scores

Grade-equivalent scores, though somewhat controversial, are widely used and apparently quite popular with educators. They bear some similarity to age-equivalent scores, but are based on performance of normative samples of students by grade level rather than age. If the average raw score on a test for 5th-grade students in the norm group is 20, then a student with a raw score of 20 would receive a grade-equivalent score of 5. Actually, there is usually some smoothing across grades, and the month of the school year is taken into account, but the principle is straightforward.

Proponents of grade-equivalent scores often emphasize their ease of interpretation. Telling a teacher that a student has a grade-equivalent score of 5.5, for example, provides the teacher with a reference point. The teacher's familiarity with what an average student can do by the middle of the 5th grade gives the teacher a basis for understanding some of the implications of the score. Also, a comparison of students' grade-equivalent scores with their current grade levels provides an immediate indication of whether their performances are above or below the average for the norm group at that grade level.

Opponents of grade-equivalent scores emphasize limitations and typical interpretations that are misleading. A high-scoring 5th grader and a low-scoring 12th grader, for example, might both have grade-equivalent scores of 8.0. However, they are apt to have correctly answered quite different kinds of questions, so the educational implications of their scores will be quite different. The 5th grader is probably unfamiliar with a number of items covered in 7th-grade lessons, but scored well because of speed and accuracy on content taught through the 5th grade and because of her ability to use knowledge to solve new problems. The 12th grader, on the other hand, though having been exposed to more topics, might not have scored so well because of inefficiency and confused understanding.

Another frequently mentioned problem with grade-equivalent scores stems from the notion that children should advance one grade-equivalent unit per year. Technically, the average student does advance at that rate, but one unit may represent considerable growth in one subject and little in another. The score distributions of 8th graders and 12th graders overlap markedly in reading, which is not a regular subject in high school curriculums. In science or history the distribution for grades 8 and 12 overlap much less because students are taught these directly in high school.

Grade-equivalent scores tend to have a wider spread for students in higher grades than those in lower grades. This is not true of other popular scales, such as standard scores. Consequently, investigators who use different score conversions can arrive at different conclusions, as was shown by an analysis in *Equality of Education Opportunity* (Coleman et al. 1966) that used two conversions. That famous survey collected data in several grades in various parts of the country and tabulated average scores for various ethnic groups. In the metropolitan Northeast, 6th-grade students in one minority group were found to average 1.8 grade-equivalent units lower than whites in that region. For 12th-grade students, the difference was 2.9. Focusing on differences of this kind, the authors argued that the relative position of some minority groups "deteriorates over the 12 years of school" (p. 273). But standard scores tell a different story. On a standard score scale with a mean of 50 and a standard deviation of 10, the same minority group was 8 points behind in both grades 6 and 12. Thus, standard scores show that the relative position of the two groups was the same at the 6th and 12th grades.

Scales Used with College Admissions Tests

Several different scales are used to report scores on the tests most widely used for purposes of admission to college and to graduate and professional schools. The SAT is reported on a scale of 200 to 800, and the ACT battery is reported on a scale that ranges from 1 to 36. Both scales are maintained by equating new forms of the test to previous forms. In this way, unintended differences in difficulty from one test form to the next are taken into account, and scores obtained from different forms of the test are as nearly comparable as possible.

The SAT scale was established in 1941 so that the mean for the somewhat more than 10,000 students who took the SAT in April of that year was 500 and the standard deviation was 100. The scale has been maintained by means of statistically equating new forms to old forms; however, the current mean and standard deviation are no longer 500 and 100 respectively. In the 1976-77 academic year, the mean score for the approximately 1.4 million students who took the SAT was 429 for the SAT-V and 471 for the SAT-M.

The ACT score scale was established in 1959 and based on the score system used for the Iowa Test of Educational Development. In 1973 the 25th, 50th, and 75th percentile ranks for the nation's high school seniors were estimated as 11, 16, and 20, respectively, on the 1-36 scale of the ACT composite. The corresponding percentile ranks for first-semester college-bound seniors taking the ACT battery were 16, 20, and 23, respectively (ACT 1973:51). As with results for the SAT, the average scores of students taking the test in more recent years are somewhat lower.

Graduate and professional schools have their own score scales. Some, such as the Law School Admissions Test (LSAT) and the Graduate Record Examination (GRE), use a 200-800 score scale modeled after the SAT. It should be noted, however, that a 500 on the GRE is not equivalent to a 500 on the SAT or the LSAT, since each of these scales was established on quite different norm groups. Others, such as the Medical College Admissions Test (MCAT), are reported on quite a different scale. MCAT scores are reported on a 15-point scale that was established so that the 30,599 examinees who took the test in April 1977 had an average scaled score of 8.0 and a standard deviation of 2.5 on each of the six content areas for which MCAT scores are reported.

The various scales used for college, graduate, and professional school admission are all arbitrary in the sense that they are based initially on some norm group, and the scale for that group is selected to have convenient properties (e.g., mean and standard deviation with round numbers such as 500 and 100 or a mean of 8 and a standard deviation of 2.5, which allows a 1-15 score range to cover all scores). Once established, however, the scales become less arbitrary with experience through the process of equating, which makes an ACT score of 23 or a SAT score of 550 have relatively constant meaning from year to year despite necessary changes in the forms of the test.

Domain-Referenced Tests

Much has been written in recent years about tests that have been variously labeled "criterion-referenced," "domain-referenced," or "objective-referenced." These labels have been used in a variety of ways by different authors. Some definitions of criterion-referenced tests emphasize absolute interpretations of what a person with a particular score can and cannot do. Others emphasize clarity of the definition of the test content and procedures used to select items and are similar to definitions of domain-referenced tests used by other authors. Yet another type of definition of a criterion-referenced test involves the use of an absolute standard or critical level used to distinguish "masters" and "nonmasters." No attempt is made here to discuss all the meanings that have been attached to the above labels. They can all generally be considered as approaches to developing and interpreting tests rather than as distinct types of tests.

In idealized form, a domain-referenced or criterion-referenced test does not require a comparison to the performance of other test takers, as is implicit in all of the scales discussed above. By clear definition of the task, the score would describe what a person can do without saying it is less or more than most of his or her peers can do. Thus, if the domain of the test is all the words in a specified spelling book, a score that estimated the proportion of words that a person could spell correctly would have meaning independent of whether or not most people could spell correctly a larger or smaller percentage of the words in the book.

Discussions of criterion-referenced and domain-referenced tests frequently stress the virtue of interpretations that do not depend on comparison of one person's performance to the performances of others. Indeed, discussions often start with criticisms of "norm-referenced tests" and contrast them with criterion- or domain-referenced tests. The latter are said to require an emphasis on competency and content, while norm-referenced tests are said to depend on the statistical properties of items and test scores and on the distribution of the scores.

The emphasis on competencies and content in discussions of domain-referenced tests is valuable. It forces attention to what a test is attempting to measure. It is a mistake, however, to assume that such attention to content is lacking if norms are provided for a test or because statistics are used to select items. In practice, the distinction between "norm-referenced" and "domain-referenced" tests is not as sharp as much of the discussion has implied. Few content domains are as clear-cut as the example of the list of words in a spelling book. It is the exception rather than the rule when the proportion of items that a test taker answers correctly can be interpreted as an estimate of the proportion of a clearly defined domain that the person knows. And norm-referenced tests are not constructed purely on statistical grounds; content considerations are crucial for a norm-referenced test as well as for a domain-referenced test. In considering domain-referenced and norm-referenced tests, a continuum, extending from tests designed primarily to provide discrimination among people and tests that are designed to describe what a person can and cannot do without regard to the performance of other people, better reflects reality than does a dichotomy.

For any particular test, the location on the continuum that is most desirable—whether it is desirable to base item selection on statistical considerations or on content considerations only—depends on the purpose of the test. If the objective is to estimate the proportion of words on a spelling list that a child can spell correctly, it does not make sense to eliminate items from the test because they do not help in discriminating good spellers from poor spellers. On the other hand, if the goal is to select the most able applicants for a limited number of jobs, then items that do not discriminate among individuals will not be helpful.

Some decisions based on test results involve a quota, as in the latter example. In such cases, discrimination among individuals is important and the use of statistical procedures, commonly associated with norm-referenced testing as an aid in item selection, can be helpful in ensuring that the test provides the desired discrimination. A number of other types of decisions, however, do not involve a quota. For example, a decision that a student has mastered a skill or domain of knowledge and is ready to move on to a new segment of instruction does not require discrimination among individuals. In such cases, the statistical selection of items for purposes of ensuring discrimination may not only be unnecessary, it may also be counter-productive because it may result in a test that is less representative of the skill or domain of knowledge being tested. This issue of content coverage rather than the existence of norms per se is central to the debate of domain-referenced versus norm-referenced tests.

HOW WELL TESTS MEASURE ABILITY

The evaluation of a test involves many considerations. The choice of which test to use, or whether to use any test to provide information for a particular decision, involves considerations about the importance of the decision to the individual and to the institution involved. The choice also depends on the cost, practicality, and technical quality of the test. Two psychometric concepts that are particularly important in judging the quality of a test are validity and reliability. Although these concepts are most frequently applied to tests, they also are applicable when using alternatives or supplements to ability tests.

Validity

Validity is generally regarded as the touchstone of educational and psychological measurement. Questions of validity are concerned with what a test measures and how well it measures what it is measuring. According to the *Standards for Educational and Psychological Tests* (American Psychological Association et al. 1974:25): "validity refers to the appropriateness of inferences from test scores or other forms of assessment." Sometimes the inferences amount to simple predictions and the process of validation focuses on evidence regarding the accuracy of those predictions. For example, predictions regarding first-year grades in law school are made from scores on the Law School Admissions Test (LSAT). The validity of this prediction is investigated by examining the relationship between scores on the LSAT and first-year grades in law school.

Other inferences require different evidence. In the case of the LSAT, a prediction that people with high scores are better lawyers would require different evidence than the inferences regarding first-year grades. Or an inference that LSAT scores are highly dependent on a test taker's test-wiseness or that scores can be significantly altered by short-term coaching would also need different evidence for validation. That is, evidence of score changes as the result of coaching or as a function of test-wiseness would need to be accumulated. In the latter example, evidence refuting the inference would be supportive of the main use of the LSAT as would, in the former example, evidence of a high degree of accuracy in predicting better lawyers. Both types of evidence would contribute to validity claims for the test.

Some important features of validity are illustrated by the above example. What is validated is a particular use or interpretation of a test score for a particular group of people; validity is not a static characteristic of a test score. Just as a test may have many uses and interpretations, so may it have many validities. Even for a particular inference, the validity may change with time. For example, predictions of success in a remedial program may be altered by changes in the instructional method even though the test and the criterion used to judge success remain unchanged. It should also be clear in the above example that validity is always a matter of degree. The predictions will not have perfect accuracy, but they may be better than could be done without knowledge of the test score. For example, the effect of coaching may be small but not zero.

Several types of validity are traditionally distinguished, and the kinds of evidence that are needed to support the different types of validity are discussed separately. This separation is sometimes convenient since there are many different types of inferences, and the kind of evidence that is most appropriate for one inference may differ from that which is most useful for another, as noted by Cronbach (1971). However, "validation of an instrument calls for an integration of many types of evidence. The varieties of investigation are not alternatives, any one of which would be adequate . . . *in the end* [validation] *must be comprehensive, integrated evaluation of the test*" (Cronbach 1971:445, emphasis in original).

Usually, all three "types of validity" that are officially recognized in the *Standards* (American Psychological Association et al. 1974) and in the *Uniform Guidelines for Employee Selection Procedures* (Equal Employment Opportunity Commission et al. 1978) are needed in the validation of an ability test. But because the labels for these types of validity are widely used and because they do emphasize approaches to accumulating evidence that correspond to particular inferences, they are briefly described here. The three types are criterion-related, content, and construct validity.

Criterion-Related Validity

As the name suggests, criterion-related validity is concerned with evidence regarding the degree of relationship between a test and what in testing terminology is called a criterion. Simply put, a criterion is some other measure of performance that is closer to the focus of interest. Two criteria were suggested in the law school example above: first-year grades in law school and quality of performance, "success," as a lawyer. The former is a clearly defined set of numbers for each student completing the first year of law school, which can be associated with students' test scores. But the latter criterion is not clearly defined. Before a validity study could be conducted with success as a lawyer as the criterion, "success" would have to be defined and measured. Even after this were done, however, there would still be a need to be concerned about the match between the criterion as it is measured and the criterion as it is conceptualized. For example, yearly income might be proposed as a measure of quality of performance as a lawyer, but such a criterion measure would certainly do violence to at least some conceptions of professional excellence. A distinction could also be made between first-year grades and degree of success as a student. In either case, it is important that the criterion measure be justified. That is, reasons for being interested in the criterion that is used should be provided, and the correspondence between the criterion as it is measured (e.g., first-year grades or yearly income) and the quality of real interest (e.g., academic or professional success) should be considered. Too often a criterion measure is used simply because it is convenient rather than because it is the best indicator of the quality of interest that is feasible.

A basic summary of a criterion-related study is an expectancy table. Such a table reports the estimated probability that people with particular values on a test, or on a combination of predictors, will achieve a certain score or higher on the criterion. For example, an expectancy table might report that people with a test score of 60 have a probability of .85 of achieving a "minimally acceptable" level of performance on the criterion and a probability of .45 of achieving an "excellent" level. In contrast to the above, the corresponding probabilities for people with a test score of 40 might be .50 and .10 for minimally acceptable and excellent, respectively.

Expectancy tables are based on experience with people who have been previously selected and have records on both the predictor and the criterion. The proportion of people with a given value on the test (or combination of predictors when there are several) who achieve any particular value on the criterion can be computed and used as the estimate of the expectancy for a new group of applicants.

Since an expectancy table is developed from data about one group of individuals (e.g., the freshman class of 1980) and used for another group (e.g., the 1981 applicants), there are always questions about the comparability of the two groups and the constancy of the system in which they are functioning. Thus, uses of expectancy tables are most defensible when applied in a relatively stable setting to a group that is similar to the one used to derive the table. Major changes in the criterion (e.g., increased stringency of grading), in the conditions on the job or in the school, or in the applicant populations can all decrease the accuracy of predictions based on expectancy tables.

In constructing expectancy tables, information about the relationship between the predictors and the criterion and about their distributions, together with a theoretical distribution, are used to compute the probabilities. It is usually assumed that the predictor and criterion have a bivariate normal distribution. Just as the proportion of scores in any score interval can be computed directly from knowledge of the mean and standard deviation when the scores are assumed to have a normal distribution, the proportions used for constructing an expectancy table can be computed from knowledge of a few summary statistics with the assumption of a bivariate normal distribution. But the bivariate normal distribution is a theoretical distribution and may or may not be adequately approximated by the observed distribution of predictor and criterion scores. Yet without the theoretical distribution many of the observed proportions may be quite unreliable because very few people in a sample used for the criterion-related validity study will happen to have a particular value on the predictor. For example, if only five people have a test score of 30, then the proportion of that group who achieve at least some specified level on the criterion will not provide a very dependable estimate of the probability that other people with test scores of 30 will achieve that level. The assumption of a bivariate distribution makes it possible to use information from the entire criterion-related validity study sample rather than from just the five people with test scores of 30 to make the estimate.

Table 2 is an example of an expectancy table that relates college grades to a composite of test scores and high school grades. Knowledge of the score on the composite can be used to determine the probability that people with that score will achieve any particular grade average or better.

TABLE 2   Sample Expectancy Table: Probability that a Freshman Will Achieve a Particular Grade Average Given a Particular Composite Score

Grade Average	Predictor Score							
	50–54	55–59	60–64	65–69	70–74	75–79	80–84	85–89
A− or better	−1	−1	1	3	6	13	23	37
B− or better	4	8	16	28	41	57	72	84
C− or better	32	47	62	76	86	92	96	99
D− or better	80	89	95	98	99	99+	99+	99+

NOTE: This table is based on the report for a particular college. Results were obtained by an indirect method assuming a bivariate normal distribution, rather than by simple tabulation; from *Indiana Prediction Study* (1965:46).

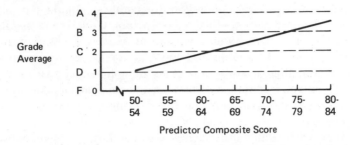

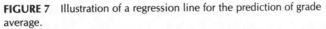

Predictor Composite Score

FIGURE 7 Illustration of a regression line for the prediction of grade average.

Clearly, on the average, people with high composite scores have a better chance of getting a high grade average than those with low composite scores. Thus, the expectancy table provides evidence that the composite has validity, albeit far from perfect, for predicting grades. A similar table could be constructed for a single test or any other predictor.

The trend shown in the expectancy table can be described by the average grade within each column using a 4-3-2-1-0 scale for grades. The average is 1.74 at 60-64, 2.91 at 80-84, etc. A further simplification produces the graph shown in Figure 7. The slanted line in Figure 7 is a regression line: the regression line represents a prediction formula (regression equation) that can be used to convert any score on the test, or other predictive composite, into a predicted grade.

Either the expectancy table or the formula permits predictions about applicants. Sometimes a cutoff score is set that represents the minimum acceptable risk. If, for example, a college wishes to admit students who have at least one chance in four of achieving at least a B − average, the cutoff score would be set close to 65. However, decisions are not usually made by a hard-and-fast division of a group of applicants at a single cutoff point. Most often, people well above the cutoff level are accepted, those well below it are not, and those in the neighborhood of the cutoff score are studied individually—partly to recognize special experience and handicaps that the test score does not adequately take into account and partly to increase the diversity of the group selected. The proportion of applicants selected is referred to as the selection ratio. Even though judgment enters into actual decisions, statements about effectiveness of selection are usually based on the assumption that everyone above the cutoff score is accepted and everyone below is rejected.

Criterion-related validity studies are frequently summarized by a single number, the correlation coefficient, often simply referred to as "the validity coefficient." This number is used to express the relationship between the predictor variable and the criterion variable. A correlation coefficient can range from − 1.0, representing a perfect inverse relationship, to + 1.0, representing a perfect positive relationship. A value of 0.0 indicates no relationship between the test and the criterion measure.[3] The correlation for the expectancy table shown in Table 2 is .55. Correlations between ability tests and grades in college or between tests and training outcomes in employment settings are often around .3 to .5, and correlations of only about .2 are fairly common for occupational performance measures (see Linn in Part II).

A difficulty in judging the predictive value of a test from correlations obtained in routine studies is caused by the fact that criterion data are collected only for persons accepted. Ideally, one wants a correlation coefficient applying to all applicants. When the accepted group is a select subset of the applicant group, the correlation with the criterion is lower than it would be for all applicants. In extreme cases the reasons for a lower correlation in a selected group are easy to see. In a basketball league that was limited to people with heights of 5'10" or 5'11", height would not be expected to be a good predictor of a player's average number of rebounds per game. If player heights vary greatly, however, the correlation between height and average number of rebounds would be expected to be higher. Fricke (1975) described a similar example based on actual experience. He noted that before weight classifications were introduced for boxers, weight was a relatively good predictor of the outcome of a match. But weight is not now a good predictor since the introduction of a classification system where people only box others of similar weight.

The effects of selection on correlations between tests and criterion measures are usually less extreme than in the above examples, but they can be substantial. Schrader (1971), for example, found that the median correlation between the SAT-V and first-year grades in college was .44 for 113 colleges with standard deviations on the SAT-V of 85 or more compared to a median correlation of only .31 for 105 colleges with SAT-V standard deviations less than 75. With more extreme selection the effects can be even greater. For example, based on results from 726 validity studies involving the LSAT, Linn (1980) estimated that the typical

---

[3] Technically, the usual product-moment correlation of zero rules out only a linear relationship and not the possibility of a more complex but systematic relationship.

correlation with first-year grade average is .51 for schools with a standard deviation on the LSAT of 100 compared to only .22 for schools with a standard deviation of 50. Thus, it is important to estimate not only the correlation for the accepted group but also what the correlation would be for the whole applicant group.

The estimate of correlations of all applicants depends on theoretical assumptions that, as was true of assumptions discussed above, cannot be expected to hold precisely in practice. If the assumptions do not hold, there will be inaccuracies in the estimates for the applicant group (Novick and Thayer 1969, Greener and Osburn 1979). Nonetheless, estimates for applicant groups, which are commonly referred to as "corrections for range restriction," are needed, and there is some evidence that the corrected estimates are more accurate than the uncorrected ones (e.g., Greener and Osburn 1979). Even after correction, predictive correlations for ability tests very rarely exceed .7. Values of .4–.6 are more usual for academic criteria or training criteria in employment settings and lower values for occupational performance criteria.

The magnitude of the correlation between an ability test and a criterion measure found in one study may differ substantially from that found in another study even though the same test may have been used and the situation and criteria appear to be quite similar. For example, for a group of 312 colleges, the correlation between the best composite of ACT scores and freshman grades was .35 or less in 10 percent of the colleges; for another 10 percent of the colleges, the correlation was .61 or greater (see Linn in Part II). Such variation in correlations has led many people to think in terms of situational specificity and to believe that criterion-related validity study results cannot be generalized from one institution to another. Recent work by Schmidt, Hunter, and their colleagues (e.g., Pearlman et al. in press, Schmidt and Hunter 1977, Schmidt et al. 1979), however, has provided support for the proposition that a good deal of the variability can be attributed to sampling variability and the effects of selection on correlations.

Some of the variability in correlations is caused by differences in the degree of selectivity from one study to another. Still greater variability is caused by small sample sizes often used in criterion-related validity studies. Schmidt and Hunter (1977) have concluded that, when these and other lesser artifacts (e.g., variation in reliability of criterion measures from study to study) are taken into consideration, there is strong support for the notion that correlations between an ability test and a criterion measure are quite generalizable for large categories of jobs. For example, an analysis of 144 studies led Pearlman et al. (in press) to estimate that the correlation between a test of general ability and proficiency in clerical work is .51. Almost all the variation from that figure in the 144 studies analyzed was attributed to artifacts of effects of selection, to effects of unreliability of criterion measures, and to sampling fluctuations.

Questions about the situational specificity and the generalizability of validity study results are far from resolved. The work of Schmidt and Hunter and their colleagues indicates that results may be more generalizable across situations and groups than previously thought, albeit possibly not to the extent that these authors seem to suggest. But much remains unknown about the degree to which results can be generalized across institutions and the factors of job similarity that determine the limits of generalizability.

Interpretation of a validity coefficient, whatever its degree of specificity or generalizability, depends on many considerations. As a first step, it is useful to consider the degree of predictive accuracy that is implied by a correlation of a particular magnitude. This information can then be used, along with information about the availability of applicants, the number of people to be selected, and the importance that is attached to differences in criterion performance, in arriving at a judgment about the value of a test.

One approach that is useful for understanding the degree of predictive accuracy that is associated with a particular correlation is to determine the probability that persons who rank high on a test will also rank high on the criterion. With a correlation of .50, for example, the chances are 44 in 100 that someone who is in the top fifth on the predictor will also be in the top fifth on the criterion, while the chances that someone in the bottom fifth on the predictor will be in the top fifth on the criterion are only 4 in 100 (Schrader 1965); these values assume a bivariate normal distribution. Without knowledge of the predictor, the chances, of course, would be 20 in 100. Thus, a predictor with a correlation as high as .50 clearly allows improved accuracy in prediction. When the correlation is only 2.0, the utility of the predictor is less obvious; then the chances of being in the top fifth on the criterion are 28 in 100 for those in the top fifth on the test and 13 in 100 for those in the bottom fifth on the test. Whether the latter is a strong enough relationship to be useful depends on the situation.

In deciding whether a test predicts well enough to be useful for selection, three factors should be considered together: the correlation coefficient or regression line, the judgments of utility or importance of various outcomes on the criterion, and the selection ratio (see Chapter 4 and Cronbach and Gleser 1965). The benefit of testing is greatest when applicants vary widely in test scores, the correlation is high, small differences on the criterion have substantial differences in utility or value, and the selection ratio is small (see Chapter 6 and Linn in Part II).

Questions of utility require a focus on the criterion and judgments about the costs and benefits associated with differences on the criterion. The fact that criterion performance can be predicted quite accurately is of little consequence if high performance on the criterion is valued only slightly more than low performance. For example, those who attach little value to grades and see little, if any, greater value derived from the admission of an A student than a C student would consider the use of a test, even one with good predictive validity, to have little utility. On the other hand, predictors need not have a high correlation with the criterion to be useful. In a task where failure can be costly (e.g., an airline pilot), a test with a low correlation is worth using in selection if no better one is available. The availability of applicants is also an important determinant of utility. A test that has a low correlation with a criterion is useful when a small fraction of the applicants can be selected; the utility is much less when most of the applicants must be hired. In the extreme, there is obviously no gain in utility as the result of a test if all applicants must be accepted, at least not with regard to selection, since there is no selection decision to be made.

Content Validity

Content validity is evaluated by demonstrating how well the items in a test sample a clearly defined domain of subject matter or situations. Claims regarding content validity are usually supported by logical analysis and judgments of experts in the field of knowledge or skill area that a test is intended to assess. In rare instances, definitions of content domains are explicit enough to allow random sampling of items from the domain. More often, item selection is based on a combination of statistical and content considerations, and the adequacy of the sample must be judged on the basis of rational argument.

Tests designed to measure achievement in specific subject matter areas are most commonly evaluated largely in terms of content validity. Tests of job knowledge and work sample tests are also frequently evaluated, at least in part, in terms of content validity. For a test to be justified for use in selection on the basis of content validity, the task on the test must be so close to major tasks on the job that there is a necessary assumption that if the person can do it on the test he or she can do it on the job. The road test for a driver's license is a sample of such a test: it includes pulling into traffic, steering, responding properly at intersections, and parallel parking. Since a driving test is not apt to include controlling the car at highway speeds or on ice-covered roads, it would be judged relevant but incomplete.

If the performance to be measured is well specified, it is possible to design a good sample. The spelling required for the job of an insurance clerk, for example, may be specified by a list of words and their frequency of use in insurance. The test that covers general office vocabulary appropriately has content validity for the ordinary office job. As is almost always the case, however, the validation of the measure will be improved by the addition of evidence of other forms of validity (e.g., does the test predict quality ratings of performance as a secretary).

For general ability tests such as the SAT, content validity may appear less salient, but it is still an important part of the overall evaluation of the test. The claim, for example, that the SAT-M measures the "ability to solve problems involving arithmetic reasoning, algebra and geometry" (College Entrance Examination Board 1978:3) partly depends on a logical analysis of the content of the test items. Simply knowing, for example, that recent test forms have had 16 or 17 geometry questions of a total of 60 questions is relevant. Inspection of the items and comparisons to geometry problems in high school textbooks would provide additional information about the content validity of the test.

Construct Validity

Construct validity is addressed to the question of what it is that ability tests measure. Construct validation involves a process of research intended to illuminate the characteristics of ability by establishing a relationship between a measurement procedure (e.g., a test) and an unobserved underlying trait. Typical constructs that have been the basis of particular ability tests are "leadership," "intelligence," and "scholastic aptitude."

Construct validity is the most comprehensive of the three types of validity that are generally distinguished; it is also the most difficult to define. For some test theorists it is *the* validation approach since it encompasses information from criterion-related validity studies and from analyses of content validity. At the same time, construct validity has generated the most controversy and confusion among testing specialists and between specialists and laymen who are concerned with testing and such matters as regulation.

Part of the confusion and controversy springs from philosophical differences. Some test specialists may be characterized as behaviorists: they see no need for constructs or postulated human traits. They eschew the introduction of any unobservable characteristics to explain test performance; their concern is only with "ability" as it is operationally defined by responses to items. In contrast, some psychologists believe that one needs theory to understand the meaning of empirical evidence, that the relevance of observed variables (the measured performance) becomes clear as it is tested against a theoretical construct that provides possible explanations. The desire for explanations, it must be added, has become more pressing in recent years as the focus of public policy has shifted from those selected (e.g., merit scholarships, merit hiring) to those screened out. The judicial doctrine of job-relatedness gives added prominence to the question of what test questions measure.

Among those who embrace construct validity as the most fundamental, if not the only, type of validity, a distinction may also be made between two views. There are those who think in terms of real traits, unobservable characteristics of people, that are manifested in certain consistencies of behavior in test (and nontest) situations. The traits are viewed as the mechanisms that cause certain behaviors. Others are reluctant to attach reality to an unobservable trait, preferring instead to speak of hypothetical constructs that have reality only in the theoretical system of the researcher.

Another part of the confusion about construct validity is that no simple prescription can be given for investigating it. Construct validity involves a continuing process of marshalling evidence to support or refute inferences and interpretations of test results (Cronbach 1971, Messick 1975, Messick in press). The process involves many possible types of logical analysis as well as empirical investigations, including correlational studies and experimental studies. Both content validation and criterion-related validity may contribute to the construct validation process, but they do not exhaust the process.

The emphasis in construct validation is as much on finding faults with test interpretations and on finding the absence of relationships as it is on showing that a test predicts results on other measures as accurately as hypothesized. Investigations that pit one hypothesis as to what a test measures against a rival hypothesis are often an important part of construct validation. Alternative interpretations are considered and refuted or the interpretation is altered. For example, a charge that an ability test designed to measure mechanical reasoning is really a measure of reading skill and vocabulary for some people could be evaluated. The evaluation might involve the collection of new data, additional analysis of existing data, a review and analysis of results of previous studies, or a judgmental review of the test items. If scores are not increased by having an examiner read aloud the questions for the test takers, if evidence is presented to show that the vocabulary is familiar to the test takers, and if test scores are found to correlate more highly with a nonverbal test of spatial relations than with scores on a vocabulary test or on a reading test, then the charge would not be given much credence; other patterns of evidence would make it plausible.

As noted by Cronbach (1980:102), the justification of an interpretation of a test "has to take the form of plural, converging arguments, plus a refutation of counterinterpretations." The justification is never complete and will be more compelling to some people than to others. There is always more to justification than the presentation of empirical evidence. The evidence must be embedded in a logical argument. Cronbach (1980:102) describes validation as a "rhetorical process" in which:

A defender of the interpretation tries to spell out an argument compatible with what most of his hearers believe. The defender of an alternate interpretation does the same. Whoever accepts either conclusion acts as if the statements in the argument describe reality. Some links in any responsible argument rest on substantial evidence and are widely believed, and some links are debatable. The listener has considerable freedom of choice [italics in original].

Construct validition is, in sum, a scientific dialogue about the degree to which an inference that a test measures an underlying trait or hypothesized construct is supported by logical analysis and empirical evidence.

Reliability

Although the first and most important questions about the quality of a test are those of validity, it is also important to recognize that test scores are subject to many sources of error; it is necessary to be able to estimate the magnitude of the effects of those errors on test scores. Just as an athlete may be up for one game but not for the next, a person taking a test may try harder and do better on one occasion than on another. A person's score may also depend on the particular questions on the test form. Thus, if one form of a history test happens to have two or three questions about a historical figure whose biography the test taker has just read while an alternate form of the test has questions about an equally prominent figure who is unfamiliar to the test taker, then the person would probably have some advantage if given the first form of the test. The lack of perfect consistency in performance on different occasions or from one form of a test to another is part of what is called measurement error.

The purpose of reliability studies is to estimate the size of the effect of various sources of measurement error, or conversely, to estimate the degree of consistency, or reliability, of test scores. Just as there are several sources of measurement error that can be identified, there are several kinds of reliability coefficients that are used. Each kind of reliability coefficient, however, provides an index of the degree of consistency of scores, or the proportion of variability in the scores that is due to systematic differences among the test takers (i.e., to differences in true ability rather than errors of measurement).

One useful way of estimating reliability is to administer two forms of a test that are intended to measure the same ability and are as nearly equivalent as possible. The correlation between these alternate forms is one kind of reliability coefficient. For high-quality ability tests, the correlations between alternate forms are often close to .90. (A summary of 28 alternate-form reliability estimates for the SAT, for example, showed values ranging from .88 to .91 for the SAT-V and from .86 to .89 for the SAT-M (Donlon and Angoff 1971). A reliability of .90 is interpreted to mean that 81 percent $(81\% = [.90]^2)$ of the variability in observed test scores is due to true variability and the remaining 19 percent is due to errors of measurement, which in the above case of alternate-form reliability would include variability due to differences between forms.

Another commonly used approach to estimating reliability depends on only a single form of a test. Estimates of reliability are obtained either from the relationship between halves of the test (split-half reliability) or from consistency among individual items. These estimates of reliability are referred to as internal-consistency estimates and involve different sources of error that alternate-form reliability estimates.

A reliability coefficient can be used to obtain estimates of the standard error of measurement, which is generally more useful than the reliability coefficient itself. The standard error provides an estimate of the amount of variation in scores that can be expected from a particular source of error. A test that has a parallel-form reliability of .90 and a standard deviation on observed test scores of some norm group of 10 would have a standard error of measurement of 4.4. The latter value is interpreted to mean that if a person were measured many times with many alternate forms of the test his or her scores would spread around a true value with a standard deviation of 4.4. Thus, assuming a normal distribution, there would be about 2 chances in 3 that any particular observed score would be within 4.4 points of the true value for that person, and there would be about 19 chances in 20 that it would be within twice that many points of the true value. In other words, the standard error of measurement provides information about the degree of dependability of the observed test scores. It can be used to estimate the likelihood that a person's score would be different by a given amount if retested with an alternate form.

As they have traditionally been estimated, reliability coefficients and their associated errors of measurement are dependent on the norm group on which the statistics are based. The working assumptions have been that these group-based indices are applicable to individual test takers and that they are equally accurate across the whole range of scores. Both assumptions have been subjected to serious question in recent years, and alternative approaches to reliability have been proposed (Lumsden 1976, Weiss and Davison 1981). New developments in test theory promise to provide a means of estimating the amount of measurement error at each score level. With such techniques, it will be possible to determine if the likely margin of error is larger in some score regions than in others. Another potential advantage of the newly emerging techniques is that the reliability coefficients that are used to describe test qualities will not depend on the population used to develop and standardize the test. While reliability as traditionally estimated may change greatly from one population of test takers to another, coefficients from the newer approaches should not (Journal of Educational Measurement 1977, Traub and Wolfe in press).

Limits on Information in Test Results

In any situation in which one is interested in assessing people—whether for purposes of selection, guidance, instructional planning, or some other purpose—there are many more potentially important characteristics than can be measured by ability tests. Tests can provide reasonably good indications of whether an individual can read and comprehend certain material or whether he or she can solve certain types of mathematical, mechanical, or other problems. But they do not assess an individual's honesty, willingness to work hard, interpersonal skills, or social concerns.

For example, the MCAT measures medical school applicants' knowledge of biology, chemistry, and physics and their ability to solve science problems and quantitative problems and to draw conclusions from written material. It does not measure and does not purport to measure personality attributes that may be important to effective functioning as a clinician or researcher. It is not that the latter attributes are considered unimportant by members of the Association of American Medical Colleges (AAMC) concerned with admission to medical school. On the contrary, the AAMC has supported efforts to develop the means of assessing important characteristics not measured by the MCAT. However, such efforts have generally borne little fruit. Dependable measures, which cannot be faked, of such desirable characteristics as honesty or compassion for others have not been developed.

Test scores can provide some information that is relevant for particular decisions, but the information is limited. An LSAT score is useful to an undergraduate student in deciding whether or not to apply to a particular law school that publishes the proportion of applicants by LSAT score bands that were admitted in a previous year. The score is also useful to the student in determining the likely difficulty that he or she will have in doing the academic work at a law school. But the test score does not provide a reasonable basis for deciding whether the student should become a lawyer.

Extraneous Factors Influencing Test Scores

Any event or characteristic that affects a person's test score but is not a part of the interpretation of that score is a source of error in that interpretation. For example, if a person is not motivated to do well or is so anxious that he or she cannot do well, then the interpretation that the individual has low ability may be seriously in error. There are many possible events or characteristics that can interfere with performance on a test. Four of the more salient ones and evidence regarding their effects on test scores are briefly discussed here. These factors are motivation, test anxiety, test-wiseness, and coaching.

Motivation

As was discussed above, ability tests are intended to measure the upper limit of what a person can do. It is obvious, however, that if a person is not motivated to do well on a test, then the score will not reflect his or her best performance. An individual cannot fake a higher score on an ability test than he or she deserves. But it is easy to get a lower score by not trying very hard or even by purposefully giving answers to questions that are known to be incorrect. The latter sometimes occurs in testing situations when low scores are seen as advantageous. For example, when the military draft was in effect, some individuals attempted to avoid the draft by intentionally doing poorly on military selection tests.

Usually the effects of poor motivation are less extreme than the situation just described. The draft example illustrates that motivation to do well on the test can vary with the situation and intended use of the test scores. In most selection situations high test scores can facilitate desired outcomes, and it can reasonably be assumed that most people are motivated to do well. Even in these situations, however, the perceived importance will vary from one person to another. The differential effects of motivation are apt to be greater, however, when high scores are of less direct and obvious benefit to the student. Lack of motivation may pose a particularly serious problem when tests are administered in schools for purposes of program evaluation without any clear use of the scores for or by individual teachers or students (see Cole in Part II).

Arousing suitable motivation is not easy. Those who administer tests are advised to establish rapport and give encouragement. The advice works well with most students from middle-class families and with job applicants accustomed to meeting the demands of teachers or employers. But, paradoxically, strong motivation may not be optimum motivation. As is elaborated below in the discussion of test anxiety, the fear of failing or falling short of a person's aspirations can interfere with performance. In other cases, some people who are well motivated on everyday intellectual tasks back off from a tester's artificial tasks. Black youths in Harlem were described as deficient in language ability when interviews in school evoked only monosyllabic responses. A quite different impression emerged when a black interviewer went to one of their homes, gathered a group around a heap of potato chips on the floor, and set the stage for free expression by uttering a few taboo words. Speech was fluent and well elaborated (Labov 1972).

Many aspects of the testing situation can make a difference in a person's acceptance of the task. Age, sex, race, and other characteristics of the test examiner affect test scores in some cases: an aloof and formal examiner may get different results from one who is natural and approachable (Anastasi 1976:39). But research results do not support simple generalizations, such as that blacks' scores consistently go up when a black examiner administers the test or when the test directions are given in black English.

Test Anxiety

Anxiety may be viewed as one aspect of motivation. It is considered separately only for convenience. Individual differences in reactions to evaluative situations can influence test results. People with low test anxiety benefit from a certain amount of stress and the prospect of being evaluated; it leads to concentration on the task and their best effort. But for people with high test anxiety, stress and the prospect of evaluation can result in maladaptive responses; rather than focusing increased attention on the task, it tends to lead to a focus on themselves and the prospects of failure. They feel ill-equipped to cope with the situation, and their somatic reactions and focus on those reactions interfere with performance on the task.

Research indicates that the debilitating effects for people with high test anxiety are greatest under conditions of extreme time pressure and high emphasis on the evaluative aspects of the test. Efforts to reduce the effects of test anxiety have focused on desensitization through frequent experience with tests. Nonevaluative test directions and increased time limit have been shown to facilitate the performance of children with high test anxiety. However, evidence of enduring positive effects of efforts to reduce test anxiety as reflected in results on standardized tests given under standard conditions is limited.

As suggested by Cole (see Part II) test anxiety is a reflection of a fairly enduring characteristic that is manifested in a variety of situations and might better be labeled evaluation anxiety. Such anxiety can also interfere with school performance or performance on the job. Thus, anxiety effects on tests do not necessarily reduce the relationship between test scores and the outcomes observed on certain criterion measures. Indeed, the common effects of evaluation anxiety may actually enhance the predictive value of tests in some situations.

Test-Wiseness

As the term is generally used, test-wiseness refers to the ability of an individual to use characteristics of the test items or testing situation to obtain a high score on the test. For example, knowing to respond to all questions when there is no penalty for wrong answers, or avoiding multiple-choice options that do not fit the question stem grammatically, may enhance a person's score without regard to his or her knowledge of the subject matter of the test. Most of the research on test-wiseness has focused on the use of flaws or cues in multiple-choice questions. There is evidence that people can be taught to recognize and use to their advantage certain flaws in multiple-choice items. The effects of instruction on tests specially designed to have flaws are clear and substantial.

Efforts are made in the development of standardized tests to avoid flaws or irrelevant cues that can be used to eliminate wrong answers. But a number of studies have found positive effects of instruction in test-wiseness on performance on standardized test. The effects seem to be larger in the early elementary school grades than for older students.

Coaching

Coaching, especially for college admission tests, recently has been the focus of considerable attention and controversy. Included under the label of coaching is a wide variety of activities that are intended to prepare people to take tests and to improve their scores. Some coaching activities are largely directed toward the reduction of anxiety and the teaching of test taking strategies (test-wiseness). Commercially available coaching schools for tests such as the SAT, the LSAT, or the MCAT usually attempt to provide more than test familiarization and instruction in test-taking strategies: they may also involve fairly lengthy instruction in the knowledge and skill areas that the test is intended to measure. Thus, some aspects of coaching are indistinguishable from instruction as it takes place in school or college.

The admission tests for which most of the coaching takes place all measure developed abilities. The knowledge and skills that are important for these tests are learned. Thus, evidence that coaching can lead to improved test performance is neither surprising nor does it necessarily imply that the test is less valid or useful because of these effects. It is important, however, to distinguish different types of effects.

To the extent that coaching improves the abilities being tested and thereby improves not only the test scores but also other indicators of those abilities, then coaching is the cause of no special concern as far as test interpretations are concerned. Indeed, it may simply be viewed as a desirable form of instruction, one that might usefully be applied in traditional educational settings and made widely available. Of course, the differential availability of coaching opportunities as a function of the affluence of a student's family would remain a concern even if coaching were shown to be an effective form of instruction rather than an inflator of test scores. But the latter concern is not fundamentally different from ones regarding other differences in opportunities such as access to private preparatory schools, to tutors, to books and other educational aides in the home, or to a variety of other resources.

On the other hand, coaching effects that increase test scores but not the abilities they are intended to measure (or performance based on those abilities outside the testing situation) affect the validity of a test. Such effects, if large, would be the cause of special concern because of the added advantage given to those who are already better off and in a better position to have the money and ready access to coaching schools. Interpretations of tests, such as the SAT, that are purported to measure abilities that are developed gradually over many years, to have content drawn from a wide variety of areas, and not to be overly sensitive to curriculum variations would also be called into question by evidence of large effects of short-term coaching.

Strong statements suggesting that coaching effects are very large as well as statements suggesting that they are trivial can be readily found. The evidence in support of either claim, however, is rather ambiguous. Interpretation of the results of several of the studies showing large effects is problematic because of the lack of adequate controls or a suitable basis for estimating what part of score gains were due to coaching and what part to other factors such as self-selection, natural growth, or differences in testing conditions before and after coaching. Some of the better con-trolled studies that have shown relatively small effects, however, may not have used the most effective coaching techniques. In particular, the latter studies have not involved the best-known commercially available coaching schools. A recent analysis of the available results of coaching for the SAT suggests that the amount of student contact time is an im-portant determinant of the likely magnitude of the size of coaching effects (Messick 1980). For a fixed amount of time, the effects tend to be larger for the mathematical section than for the verbal section of the SAT. The effect of coaching may also vary for different individuals. Relatively little is known, for example, about the importance of motivation in the coach-ing situation.

Research on coaching leaves many questions unanswered. A better understanding is needed not only of the likely magnitude of the average score gain for different kinds of coaching, but of many other issues. For example, does coaching alter the predictive meaning of test scores? What individual differences in background, motivation, and other aptitudes affect the likely size of the gains of various types of coaching? What are the key components to most successful coaching programs? Questions such as these cannot be answered from the available research on coach-ing, but they are vital to certain interpretations and uses of test results.

GROUP DIFFERENCES AND BIAS

Group Differences in Test Results

When ability tests are taken by different groups in the population (e.g., men, women, children of parents with different socioeconomic status, blacks, Indians) differences in *average* performance are usually found. The differences in average performance vary depending on the ability tested. In addition, the size of the differences between group averages is usually small compared to the variability among individuals within a single group. Thus, a person who ranks high in a group with a low average will have a higher score than most of the people in a group with a high average, and conversely, the low-scoring person in a group with a high average will be outperformed by most people in a group with a low average.

Despite the substantial overlap in distributions of scores for different groups, differences in average performance may have important impli-cations for test use. If group differences on tests used for selection do not reflect actual differences in practice—in college or on the job—then using the test for selection may unfairly exclude a disproportionately large number of members of the group with the lower average test scores. Furthermore, even when the groups differ in average performance on the job or in college as well as in average performance on the test, the possible adverse impact on the lower-scoring group should be considered in evaluating the use of the test.

Group differences in average test scores cannot be taken as evidence of innate differences. They may, however, reflect differences in probabilities of success in school or on the job that need to be understood in order to develop sound educational or social policies. Therefore, it is important to consider the kinds of differences in average performance of groups that have been found on ability tests and the degree to which these differences reflect differences in nontest performance. The latter issue is considered as part of the section on bias in tests, the next major part of this chapter. The rest of this section briefly summarizes the kinds of differences in average test scores that have been observed for men and women, for people of different socioeconomic status, and for different racial and ethnic groups.

Socioeconomic Status

From the earliest studies to recent ones, children of the well-to-do have been found to score higher, on average, on tests of general ability than children of the poor. These findings hold regardless of which indicator of socioeconomic status (SES)—parental occupational status, education, or income—is used. Correlations between SES and ability test scores run about .30 (Speath 1976). Translated into mean differences, the average test performance of children from families in the top 20 percent of the socioeconomic distribution is at about the 65th percentile of the general population. Average scores for children whose families are in the bottom 20 percent of the socioeconomic distribution is at about the 35th percentile. Differences of this kind are found with a wide variety of general ability and educational achievement tests. The relationship is somewhat higher for verbal ability than for quantitative or spatial abilities.

Sex Differences

The mean test differences for males and females are smaller than those for socioeconomic status, and the direction of the difference varies with the type of ability measured. Males tend to score higher on tests of spatial and quantitative abilities; females score higher on tests of verbal ability. It should be emphasized again that these are only *average* differences;

the within-sex variability is much greater than that between sexes. Some females will score higher than most males on spatial and quantitative tests; some males will score higher than most females on tests of verbal ability.

The test differences change as a function of age. Differences in quantitative scores usually are not found with young children; they begin to appear at adolescence and increase throughout high school. Sex differences in spatial abilities begin to appear at about ages 6-8 and increase with age through high school. Onset of differences in verbal ability is debated. Some studies find females showing verbal superiority from toddlerhood on—speaking earlier than male children and showing greater facility in reading and writing throughout the primary grades. Other studies report little difference until adolescence, when females surge ahead.

The norm group for the DAT illustrates the magnitude of the sex differences that are found on tests of different abilities. A score that is better than that attained by 50 percent of the 12th-grade boys on the numerical ability test is better than that of 55 percent of the 12th-grade girls. On verbal reasoning, a score that is better than 50 percent of one sex is also better than 50 percent of the other group. On language usage, however, a score that is better than 50 percent of the 12th-grade boys would exceed that of only 35 percent of the 12th-grade girls. The largest sex differences are found on the more specialized tests. Thus, a mechanical reasoning test score that exceeded the 85th percentile of the girls would be only at the 50th percentile for boys while a score at the 30th percentile for girls on clerical speed and accuracy would be at the 50th percentile for boys. These figures, while saying nothing about the cause of the difference, do enable one to determine the amount of adverse impact that the use of a test for purposes of selection would be expected to have. For example, a selection from the DAT norm group on the basis of numerical ability test scores that excluded half the boys would exclude 55 percent of the girls. Much greater adverse impact on girls would result if selection were based solely on the mechanical reasoning test. The greater the magnitude of the adverse impact, the greater is the need to determine if differences on the test reflect differences in performance in school or on the job.

Racial and Ethnic Differences

Many studies have shown that members of some minority groups tend to score lower on a variety of commonly used ability tests than do members of the white majority in this country. The much publicized Coleman study (Coleman et al. 1966) provided comparisons of several racial and ethnic groups for a national sample of 3rd-, 6th-, 9th-, and 12th-grade students on tests of verbal and nonverbal ability, reading comprehension, mathematics achievement, and general information. The largest differences in group averages usually existed between blacks and whites on all five tests and at all grade levels. In terms of the distribution of scores for whites, the average score for blacks was roughly one standard deviation below the average for whites. Differences of approximately this magnitude were found for all five tests at 6th, 9th, and 12th grades. The differences at 3rd grade were somewhat smaller, especially on the verbal and nonverbal general ability tests, but were still about two-thirds of a standard deviation or more. The roughly one-standard-deviation difference in average test scores between black and white students in this country found by Coleman et al. is typical of results of other studies.

If it is assumed that the test scores are normally distributed, that the groups have equal standard deviations and means that are one standard deviation apart, then the degree of adverse impact to be expected by selecting from the two groups solely on the basis of test scores may be readily calculated. Proportions in the two groups for several cutoffs are listed in Table 3. As can be seen in Table 3, a rule that would select 20 percent of the group with the higher average would select only 3 percent of the group with the lower average. Regardless of the degree of selectivity, short of selecting almost everyone in both groups, the proportions that would be selected differ markedly for the two groups.

The numbers in Table 3 are based on a theoretical situation and do not correspond exactly to the proportion that would result from actual

TABLE 3   Proportion of People in Two Groups That Would be Selected by Various Cutoffs Assuming Both Groups Have Normally Distributed Scores with Equal Standard Deviations but Means That Differ by One Standard Deviation

Group with Higher Mean	Group with Lower Mean
.10	.01
.20	.03
.30	.06
.40	.11
.50	.16
.60	.23
.70	.32
.80	.44
.90	.61

distributions on any particular test for whites and blacks. But they do provide a good indication of the order of magnitude of the adverse impact on blacks that would result from strict reliance on test scores for selecting from random samples from the two groups. With adverse impact of such magnitude it becomes very important to determine the degree to which differences on tests reflect differences in performance that the tests are designed to predict and to determine the predictive power of the tests. Long-term consequences and outcomes broader than performance on the job or in school also need to be considered in evaluating test use in light of such potential for adverse impact.

The potential for substantial adverse impact is not limited to blacks. Some other racial and ethnic minority groups have average test scores well below that for whites. Though generally not quite as large as the black-white average differences, Coleman et al. (1966) found differences large enough to result in considerable adverse impact for Mexican Americans, Puerto Ricans, and Indian Americans when compared with whites. Smaller differences were found between Oriental Americans and whites, with whites having lower average test scores. Although there is a great deal of overlap in the distribution of scores for all groups, some of the differences are large. With the exception of Oriental Americans, a rule that selected high-scoring people from the Coleman et al. sample on any of the five tests at any of the four grades would select a considerably smaller proportion of persons from each of the minority groups than from the white majority.

Bias

In light of the differences in the test score averages for some groups and the implications of those differences for adverse impact, it is important to determine the degree to which the differences reflect differences in performance in school or on the job. This is usually done by means of comparing the predictive meaning of a test for particular criterion measures for separate groups. One would like to know, for example, whether an expectancy table would be different if it were based on experience with black employees than if it were based only on experience with white employees. Would the same or different regression lines be found for men and women or for blacks and whites? Studies designed to investigate such questions are referred to as differential prediction studies. Results from a variety of such studies are briefly summarized below. Before doing so, however, we review in general some questions of test bias.

Differential prediction studies are often described as studies of test bias, but this terminology is misleading. Differential prediction studies do provide information about whether or not members of a particular group tend to perform better or worse on the criterion than would be predicted using test scores in a single prediction formula for members of all groups. And it is quite reasonable to define as "bias" such a systematic difference between actual criterion performance and that predicted from the test scores. But the bias refers to the predictions and to a particular use of a test, not to the test itself. (Use of the test scores in other prediction formulas, e.g., in a formula developed specifically for each group, would not lead to the tendency for actual performance to be systematically better or worse than predicted.)

More importantly, "test bias" has many meanings other than a statistical definition based on notions of differential prediction. Consequently, the test specialist who uses test bias to mean differential prediction, and the nontest specialist, who uses test bias to mean group differences in average test scores, culture dependent tests, or test content that is expressed in standard English rather than black English often talk right past each other.

Ability tests clearly are culture dependent. This is obvious for verbal tests that depend on familiarity with a particular language. It is also apparent that numerical operations and mathematical concepts are largely taught in school, and quantitative tests could hardly be expected to be free of educational experiences. Attempts to develop culture-free tests have not met with success. Neither have efforts to develop tests based only on experiences that are equally familiar to all groups or that are balanced such that for each item that is more familiar to the experiences of one group there is a comparable item for which the reverse is true.

Efforts to develop culture-free tests have fallen short of the goal in two important ways. First, the tests that have been developed as supposedly culture free have not proven to be as good predictors—of academic performance and performance on the job—as the ability tests they were intended to replace. This result is not surprising in view of the fact that nontest criteria are also culture dependent. The second shortcoming of efforts to develop culture-free tests is that group differences on such tests have often been found to be of a magnitude similar to that observed for many of the tests they were intended to replace.

The simple existence of group differences in average performance on tests is often taken to imply that the tests are biased. It is assumed that one group is not inherently less able than the other and that the tests are supposed to measure inherent ability. Even if the first of these assumptions is correct, the second is certainly not. As we have already emphasized, a test can only measure developed ability at a given point in time, and the level of development depends on a combination of many factors, including heredity and experience. No statement about the heritability of group differences can be justified because the experiences of the members are not equivalent, and there is no feasible way of either equating them or allowing for the experiential differences.

It is clear that there are many inequalities in society. On average, poor children and children in some minority groups are not provided the same opportunities to develop the abilities that are measured by standardized tests as white, middle-class children. This difference may be reflected in average test scores. A test that reflects such unequal opportunity to develop is not, strictly speaking, biased. Precise use would restrict the term "test bias" to systematic differences in the predictive power of tests related to group identity. Interpretations of the test results that assume that opportunities have been equal, however, are incorrect.

A typical type of interpretation of test scores is the prediction of nontest behavior, i.e., performance. Such predictions do not assume equality of opportunity. But if the same predictive interpretation is given to a test score regardless of whether the test taker is black or white, male or female, etc., then one must assume or have evidence that, among people with the same score, the accuracy of prediction does not depend on group membership. It is this, and only this, issue that is addressed by differential prediction studies.

Although differential prediction studies often involve several predictors, they are most readily conceptualized by considering the simple case where predictions are based on a single test and there is only one criterion of interest. A prediction equation converts the test score into an estimate of the performance on the criterion for people with a particular test score. The prediction equation is usually estimated from previous data for a sample for which both test scores and criterion measures (scores) are available. The prediction equation involves two coefficients, a and b, the intercept and slope, respectively, and the prediction equation is called a linear regression equation. The predicted criterion score is obtained by multiplying the test score by b and adding a to the resulting product.

Regression equations developed separately for two groups (e.g., blacks and whites) could differ in slope or intercept or both. In addition, the variation between actual criterion scores around predicted scores might differ from one group to the other. Thus, differential prediction studies are generally designed to compare the variability of observed criterion scores around their predicted values, the slopes, and the intercepts obtained for different groups. If differences in variability of observed scores around predicted criterion scores are found, it implies that predictions can be made with greater accuracy for members of one group than for

members of the other. It does not necessarily imply any differences in
the predicted value associated with particular test scores. Differences in
slopes imply that the predicted criterion scores change more rapidly as
the test score changes for members of one group than they do for the
other. Equal slopes but unequal intercepts imply that for a given test score
the average score on the criterion is higher for one group than the other.

When the regression lines for two groups differ in slope or intercept
or both, it means that the use of a single prediction equation for everyone
will result in systematic errors of prediction for at least one of the groups.
That is, the predicted criterion scores will tend to be higher (or lower)
than the actual criterion scores for members of one of the groups with
certain test scores. Underprediction, i.e., predictions that tend to be lower
than actual criterion performance may be considered a bias against members of a group since they tend to perform better on the criterion than
predicted by using the test score. Overprediction, on the other hand, can
be considered predictive bias in favor of the members of a group. Thus,
it is important to determine the direction and magnitude of the differences
between predicted and observed criterion scores for members of a given
group when predictions are made using a single equation for all test
takers.

Differential prediction studies have been conducted in a variety of
contexts, including undergraduate colleges, law schools, private and public employers, and the military. Most frequently, the differential prediction
for blacks and whites has been investigated. Studies have also been
conducted for men and women, whites and Mexican Americans, people
of lower and higher socioeconomic status, and a few other groups. In
college and law school settings, the criterion usually has been first-year
grades. In employment settings, studies have sometimes used training
criteria and sometimes used job performance criteria. Only a brief summary of the results of these studies is attempted here; a more detailed
summary is found in Linn in Part II.

Sex Differences

The prediction equations for men and for women have usually been found
to differ for undergraduate college performance. The differences in the
equations are such that the use of the equation that is appropriate for
men tends to result in predicted grades that are lower than women actually
achieve. Thus, such predictions are biased against women. The amount
of the underprediction of the grade point averages (GPAs) of women tends
to be about a fifth of a point on a 4-point GPA scale. (This figure is an

average for studies using the equation for men with both high school grades and test scores as predictors.)

The equations from differential prediction studies conducted in law schools, unlike those conducted at the undergraduate level, have generally been found to be quite similar. In about a third of the studies, a common equation would result in predicted grades for women that are somewhat higher than actually achieved. In the remaining studies, the predictions for women tend to be somewhat lower than actual grades, but the differences were usually small: the median underprediction for 29 studies was only about .04 standard deviations.

Minority and Majority Group Differences

At the undergraduate college level, the equation for white students has usually been found to result either in predicted grades for blacks that tend to be about equal to the grades they actually achieve or that tend to be somewhat better than the grades they actually achieve. The tendency for predicted grades to be higher than actual grades is somewhat greater for black students with high test scores than for those with low test scores. The results of studies at law schools are generally consistent with those at the undergraduate level. That is, a single equation based on the combined group of black and white students produces predicted grades that tend to be slightly higher than the grades actually achieved by black students. Thus, using a single prediction equation tends to give some advantage to black applicants to college or law school in comparison with the predictions that would be made based only on data from black students or in comparison with actual performance.

The differential prediction study results for black and white employees and with air force personnel are generally consistent with the results in academic settings. That is, predictions based on a single equation (either the one for whites or for a combined group of blacks and whites) generally yield predictions that are quite similar to, or somewhat higher than, predictions from an equation based only on data for blacks. In other words, the results do not support the notion that the traditional use of test scores in a prediction equation yields predictions for blacks that systematically underestimate their actual performance. If anything, there is some indication of the converse, with actual criterion performance being more often lower than would be indicated by test scores of blacks. Thus, in the technically precise meaning of the term, ability tests have not been proved to be biased against blacks: that is, they predict criterion performance as well for blacks as for whites.

The research on other minority groups is much more limited. But similar results have been obtained for differential prediction studies involving whites and Mexican Americans in employment and law school settings. At the college level, the findings are more mixed. Underprediction and overprediction occurred about equally often.

Although differential prediction studies provide strong evidence against the contention that blacks or Mexican Americans tend to do better on criterion measures than is indicated by test scores, those results must be placed in context. The implications of the results depend on the degree of acceptability of the criterion measures used. Interpretations of evidence of predictive bias depend on assumptions that the criterion measure is itself unbiased. It should be clear that lack of differential prediction, or even evidence that what differential prediction there is tends to be in favor of rather than against minority group members, does not refute the claim that society discriminates against them. Unequal opportunity may result in lower scores on tests and on the criterion measures used to validate the tests.

As was noted above, a cutoff score designed to fill the available places with those having the best chance of success may exclude many persons who would succeed and whose chances of success are not much less than those of the last persons selected, the ones who just scrape by the cutoff score. This obviously holds for majority and minority groups considered separately. Among members of the minority group who are not selected when ranking and prediction are based purely on predicted performance, many would be satisfactory workers or students, and some would be excellent.

REFERENCES

American College Testing Program (1973) Assessing Students on the Way to College: Technical Report for the ACT Assessment Program. Iowa City, Iowa: American College Testing Program.

American Psychological Association, American Education Research Association, and National Council on Measurement in Education (1974) Standards for Educational and Psychological Tests. Washington, D.C.: American Psychological Association.

Anastasi, A. (1976) Psychological Testing. New York: Macmillan.

Anastasi, A. (1980) Abilities and the measurement of achievement. Pp. 1-10 in New Directions for Testing and Measurement. San Francisco, Calif.: Jossey-Bass.

Braswell, J. S. (1978) The College Board Scholastic Aptitude Test: an overview of the mathematical portion. The Mathematics Teacher 71:168-180.

Coleman, J. S., Campbell, E. Q., Hobson, C. J., McPortland, J., Mood, A. M., Weinfeld, F. D., and York, R. L. (1966) Equality of Educational Opportunity. Washington, D.C.: U.S. Department of Health, Education, and Welfare.

College Entrance Examination Board (1978) Taking the SAT. New York: College Entrance Examination Board.

Cronbach, L. J. (1971) Test validation. In R. L. Thorndike, ed., *Educational Measurement*, 2nd ed. Washington, D.C.: American Council on Education.

Cronbach, L. J. (1980) Validity on parole: how can we go straight? Pp. 98-108 in *New Directions for Testing and Measurement*. San Francisco, Calif.: Jossey-Bass.

Cronbach, L. J. and Gleser, G. C. (1965) *Psychological Tests and Personnel Decisions*, 2nd ed. Urbana, Ill.: University of Illinois Press.

Donlon, T. F. and Angoff, W. H. (1971) The Scholastic Aptitude Test. In W. H. Angoff, ed., *The College Board Admissions Testing Program: A Technical Report on Research and Development Activities Relating to the Scholastic Aptitude Test and Achievement Tests*. New York: College Entrance Examination Board.

Equal Employment Opportunity Commission, Civil Service Commission, Department of Labor, and Department of Justice. (1978) Adoption by four agencies of uniform guidelines for employee selection. *Federal Register* 43(3):38290-38315.

Fricke, B. G. (1975) Grading, Testing, Standards, and All That. Report to the faculty, Ann Arbor, Michigan: Evaluation and Examinations Office, University of Michigan.

Glass, G. V., and Stanley, J. C. (1970) *Statistical Methods in Education and Psychology*. Englewood Cliffs, N.J.: Prentice-Hall, Inc.

Greener, J. M., and Osburn, H. G. (1979) An empirical investigation of the accuracy of corrections for restriction in range due to explicit selection. *Applied Psychological Measurement* 3:31-41.

Guilford, J. P. (1967) *The Nature of Human Intelligence*. New York: McGraw-Hill.

Indiana Prediction Study: Manual of Freshman Class Profiles for Indiana Colleges (1965). Princeton, N.J.: Educational Testing Service.

Journal of Educational Measurement (1977) Special Issue: Applications of Latent Trait Models. 14(Summer):2.

Labov, W. (1972) *Language in the Inner City: Studies in the Black English Vernacular*. Philadelphia: University of Pennsylvania Press.

Linn, R. L. (1980) Admissions Testing on Trial. Paper presented at the annual meeting of the American Psychological Association, Montreal, Canada.

Lumsden, J. (1976) Test theory. *Annual Review of Psychology* 27:251-280.

Messick, S. (1975) The standard problem: meaning and values in measurement and evaluation. *American Psychologist* 30:955-966.

Messick, S. (1980) *The Effectiveness of Coaching for the SAT: Review and Reanalysis of Research from the Fifties to the FTC*. Princeton, N.J.: Educational Testing Service.

Messick, S. (in press) Test validity and the ethics of assessment. *American Psychologist*.

Novick, M. R., and Thayer, D. T. (1969) *An Investigation of the Accuracy of the Pearson Selection Formulas*. RM-69-22. Princeton, N.J.: Educational Testing Service.

Pearlman, D., Schmidt, F. L., and Hunter, J. E. (in press) Validity generalization results for tests used to predict job proficiency and training success in clerical occupations. *Journal of Applied Psychology*.

Resnick, L., ed. (1976) *The Nature of Intelligence*. Hillsdale, N.J.: Lawrence Erlbaum Associates.

Schmidt, F. L., and Hunter, J. E. (1977) Development of a general solution to the problem of validity generalization. *Journal of Applied Psychology* 62:529-540.

Schmidt, F. L., Hunter, J. E., Pearlman, K., and Shane, G. S. (1979) Further tests of the Schmidt-Hunter Bayesian validity generalization procedure. *Personnel Psychology* 32:257-281.

Schrader, W. B. (1965) A taxonomy of expectancy tables. *Journal of Educational Measurement* 2:29-35.

Schrader, W. B. (1971) The predictive validity of College Board Admissions tests. In W.

H. Angoff, ed., *The College Board Admissions Testing Program: A* Technical Report on Research and Development Activities Relating to the Scholastic Aptitude Test and Achievement Tests. New York: College Entrance Examination Board.

Spaeth, J. L. (1976) Characteristics of the work setting and the job as determinants of income. In W. H. Sewell, R. N. Hauser, and D. L. Featherman, eds., *Schooling and Achievement in American Society.* New York: Academic Press.

Technical Report on Research and Development Activities Relating to the Scholastic Aptitude Test and Achievement Tests. New York: College Entrance Examination Board.

Thorndike, R. L., and Hagen, E. P. (1977) *Measurement and Evaluation in Psychology and Education*, 4th ed. New York: John Wiley & Sons.

Trattner, M. H., Corts, D. B., van Rijn, P. O., and Outerbridge, A. M. (1977) *Research Base for the Written Test Portion of the Professional and Administrative Career Examination (PACE): Prediction of Job Performance for Claims Authorizers in the Social Insurance Claims Examining Occupations.* TS-77-3, Personnel Research and Development Center. Washington, D.C.: U.S. Civil Service Commission.

Traub, R. E., and Wolfe, R. G. (in press) Latent trait theories and the assessment of educational achievement. *Review of Research in Education.*

Weiss, D. J., and Davison, M. L. (1981) Test theory and mehods. *Annual Review of Psychology* 32:629-658.

3

Historical and Legal Context of Ability Testing

HISTORICAL PERSPECTIVES

Two themes characterize the development of standardized ability testing in the United States from its beginnings in the late nineteenth century: a search for order in a nation undergoing rapid industrialization and urbanization, and a search for ability in the sprawling, heterogeneous society that emerged from those processes. During the Progressive era early in this century, testing seemed to promise social efficiency for institutions that faced problems of unprecedented scale—by selecting the right person for the job, by monitoring the success of classroom instruction, and by sorting students according to ability. From the 1920s on, and especially from 1940 to the early 1960s, testing was increasingly looked upon as an objective means to identify talent in a democratic society, to ensure individual opportunity regardless of race or class, and to mobilize America's human resources for national survival in the Cold War.

Since their use began, ability tests probably have, overall, allowed more impartial selection of candidates for jobs and better guidance of students. What effect they have had on expanding the pool of eligible job applicants or on broadening opportunities for students or workers is not so clear. Obviously, ability tests exclude as well as include. Tools constructed to identify talent sometimes served to restrict opportunity—for example, when they were used to assign students to vocational tracks in schools or to justify restrictionist immigration policies. The content of tests has, to an extent not always realized by users, reflected the social structure of the society within which they were given. As a result, although tests have been the means of crossing social barriers for some people, the widespread use of tests has also helped to strengthen some of those barriers. Some historical analysts believe that tests were used intentionally to restrict opportunity for groups that were powerless or out of favor.

The Search for Order

Psychological testing is of comparatively recent origin: the widespread use of objective and standardized tests in the United States to classify students and to select employees is closely tied to the emergence of industrial society in the late nineteenth and early twentieth centuries. The remarkable growth of the U.S. economy and of the nation's population in the years between the Civil War and World War I put extraordinary strains on a society characterized by local autonomy, dispersed power, and informal social, political, and economic arrangements. The signs of strain were obvious, at least to some contemporary observers: corruption at all levels of government, unrestrained competition in business, the plundering of the nation's resources, the growth and increasing radicalism of labor unions, the political threat of Populism, and high rates of crime and delinquency. All suggested that society had grown too fast for traditional bonds to hold it together.

These signs of disintegration spawned what Robert Wiebe (1967) has called a "search for order." Many Americans came to regard the development of integrated standards, whether in the width of railroad tracks or in the content of school curricula, as the key to forging a national community. Businessmen, educators, politicians, and Progressive reformers alike championed social efficiency as a prerequisite to economic progress. America could achieve this efficiency, many argued, only if the ad hoc social arrangements of the past were replaced with carefully planned systems of organization. Science and expertise were to be enlisted in organizing the nation's human, as well as its natural, resources. One tool that appeared particularly promising in organizing society—and one that was promoted particularly aggressively by its practitioners—was the new technique of educational and mental testing, which emerged at the turn of the century. Enthusiasts claimed that testing could bring order and efficiency to schools, to industry, and to society as a whole by providing the raw data on individual abilities necessary to the efficient marshaling of human talents.

Civil Service Examinations

Standardized testing gained its first foothold in the federal government. In the years following the Civil War, the spoils system was at its height. By the 1860s, every election of a new president signaled a complete turnover of government employees. The spoils system, by this time almost 50 years old, had staunch supporters who justified it as democratic: it affirmed the truth that the operations of government required no special skills, it kept government within the hands of ordinary people, and it prevented the development of an entrenched bureaucracy. The spoils system, however, also brought with it a high price in inefficiency and corruption during years in which the federal government grew dramatically, both in number of employees and in level of responsibility.

Discontent with the spoils systems precipitated a civil service reform movement in the postwar years, spearheaded primarily by a small but vocal group of patrician reformers. One goal of these reformers, many of whom felt dispossessed by the new urban and often immigrant electorate, was to curb what they regarded as the excesses of democracy. To do this, they suggested the establishment of a federal personnel system, organized on the merit principle rather than by patronage. The movement achieved success in 1883 with the passage of the Civil Service Act (5 USC 3304) in the wake of President Garfield's assassination by a disappointed office seeker. The act set up a bipartisan Civil Service Commission, which was given the responsibility to administer open, competitive examinations for certain federal positions.

The act initially covered slightly more than 10 percent of the federal service. In the next few years, New York and Massachusetts, leading centers of the reform movement, passed their own civil service acts, and the federal system was slowly extended until it covered 60 percent of government workers in 1908. In the 1880s and 1890s, several major cities also adopted civil service systems, but no state followed the lead of Massachusetts and New York until the twentieth century.

Many reformers, looking to the British civil service system, envisioned a set of examinations that would ensure government by the educated. Congress, however, feared the creation of such an elite bureaucracy, and the Civil Service Act specifically required that the tests be "practical in character." They were to be designed so that candidates with an 8th-grade education could compete successfully with college graduates on the basis of experience. The Civil Service Commission, as a result, adopted a common-sense standard of testing: it tested for job-related skills in a standardized setting, and it developed standards of relevance that could be defended to the public and that conformed to everyday notions of how a test should be constructed. In their common-sense character, the Civil Service examinations differed radically from the indirect mental tests that were soon to be developed by psychologists and applied in the schools and the workplace.

Employment Testing, 1900-1915

By the turn of the century, the larger and more technologically advanced American businesses had committed themselves to rationalizing the management of personnel. Central personnel bureaus—staffed not by foremen but by management experts—introduced time cards, job clocks, and other innovations; industrial managers hired efficiency experts like Frederick Taylor to streamline production.

High rates of labor turnover and industrial accidents in the first two decades of the century, however, suggested that efficiency in the workplace was not enough; a successful business had to hire suitable "human material" to begin with. Indeed, it was soon to become a tenet of personnel management that the disorders that attended modern industry would evaporate "when a scheme has been devised which will make it possible to select the right man for the right place" (Link 1919:293). Among the schemes available were systems of character analysis, standardized interviews, and application forms (especially for those who found graphology a useful tool). Another increasingly popular tool was testing.

Mental testing had emerged in the 1880s from the experimental psychology of Wilhelm Wundt in Leipzig and the anthropometric observations of Francis Galton in London. Early psychologists had approached their science as an adjunct to philosophy, and they had concentrated their efforts on unfolding the processes of the mind in the abstract. By the 1890s, however, many experimentalists in the United States, England, France, and Germany had shifted their attention to measuring sensory and motor skills and more complicated functions like memory, suggestibility, and judgment. In an age that placed a high value on quantification, it seemed that any trait that could be identified could also be measured. "Whatever exists at all exists in some amount," the educational psychologist Edward Thorndike asserted in 1918 (quoted in Cremin 1964:185): "To know it thoroughly involves knowing its quantity as well as its quality." And to know the quantity of the various mental traits of an individual meant to be able to judge his abilities and to predict his success in one walk of life or another.

By the 1910s, a small number of psychologists were enthusiastically promoting the use of mental tests in the selection of personnel. Often at the suggestion of Progressive reform groups or individual businessmen, they experimented with tests to select workers for positions as typists, telephone operators, trolley drivers, and salesmen, and for other skilled and semiskilled jobs in the new bureaucratic and industrial world. The tests, for the most part, differed sharply from Civil Service examinations and from the educational and physical examinations already in use by some businesses because they were only indirectly related to the job to be filled. The Civil Service Commission might ask a prospective trademark examiner what the characteristics of a trademark were, or how he would treat a specific trademark application; the psychological tester might ask the prospective telephone operator to sort cards into piles or to memorize nonsense syllables. The testers tried to make tests that could be used with inexperienced and untrained applicants—after all, in 1915 virtually no prospective telephone operators or typists had previous experience—and that would identify aptitude for learning the skills required by the job. Armed with new statistical techniques, the tester could correlate scores on the test with success on the job, defined perhaps by longevity in the position or by a supervisor's rating. If the correlation was high, the test that did not, on the surface, resemble the job could be considered an indicator of talent for the job.

By 1915, according to the psychologist H. L. Hollingworth (1916:79), tests for twenty types of work had been developed and, to one extent or another, tried out. By this time, too, several large businesses, including the American Tobacco Company, the National Lead Company, Western Electric, and Metropolitan Life, were using tests to select employees. Before World War I, however, employment testing was confined to a few industries and businesses; it remained for the U.S. Army testing program developed during the war to stimulate widespread use of employment testing.

Testing in the Schools, 1900-1915

The American educational system at the turn of the century faced many problems of unrestrained growth that were similar to those of American industry, and, like many businessmen, educational reformers adopted efficiency and central control as a credo. With the increased effectiveness of laws on child labor and on mandatory school attendance, the public schools, particularly high schools, grew rapidly around the turn of the century. In 1870, there were approximately 80,000 students in American high schools, almost all of them in private schools; in 1910, there were approximately 1,000,000 students, 90 percent of them in public schools. Looked at another way, between 1890 and 1918 the high school population grew 711 percent compared with a total population growth of 68 percent. It was generally agreed that the traditional college preparatory courses did not suit most of the new students. To complicate the situation, in the cities many of the new students were the children of immigrants and spoke English only as a second language. In 1908, for example, a Senate Committee reported that 72 percent of all public school students in New York had fathers born abroad; in most other large cities, the figure was around 50 percent (Tyack 1974:230,183).

According to educational muckrakers, the rapid growth of schools and their changing composition was accompanied by chaos. The accomplishment of students differed greatly from one locality to another. Standards were declining, students were learning less and disobeying more, and failure rates were overwhelming. The schools, critics argued, were failing to educate American citizens and, in particular, were failing to introduce lower-class and immigrant children to American ways. The fault, according to most of the critics, lay in lack of expertise in the schools and in political corruption in the cities.

To meet this problem, Progressive reformers, who included educational specialists, university presidents, and leading businessmen, sought to bring efficiency to local school systems by centralizing school administration and by restricting the power of ward school boards. This movement for administrative efficiency was similar, both in its nature and in the type of people who supported it, to the civil service reform movement in the 1880s. And it overlapped a renewed call for civil service reform in the Progressive years that brought merit systems, including competitive examinations, to Wisconsin, Illinois, Colorado, and New Jersey, as well as to several large cities.

Locally made tests had long been used to standardize classroom practices and to compare the efficiency of instruction in different schools within a locality. Tests designed for comparisons across localities and communities became a major weapon in the educational reformers' arsenal. From 1895 to 1903, for example, Joseph Rice publicized the plight of the schools in a series of immensely popular articles by citing the results of arithmetic and spelling tests that he had given over the years to thousands of schoolchildren. Reformers and school administrators came to advocate standardized tests as a means of introducing the principles of scientific management in the schools and of improving the instruction of students. In 1911 the National Education Association established its influential Committee on Tests and Standards of Efficiency, and from 1908 to 1916 Edward Thorndike and his students at Columbia developed tests for achievement in arithmetic, handwriting, spelling, drawing, reading, and language ability. In the 1910s and 1920s, encouraged by outside experts from the universities, school system after school system adopted the use of such tests. According to one contemporary, the schools during these years were engaged in "an orgy of tabulation" (Rugg, quoted in Cremin 1964:187).

In the 1910s, educators acquired a major new tool to complement the standardized achievement test: the Binet intelligence scale. Psychologists had long sought tests that could measure general intelligence, defined as the capacity to learn, but most attempts failed to give credible results. Alfred Binet achieved a breakthrough when, from 1905 to 1908, he developed and refined a mental test that measured school children against a standard of "normal" development. Binet's test, which he put together to assist the French Ministry of Public Instruction in identifying retarded schoolchildren, combined a series of questions testing for a variety of mental processes that successfully differentiated children by age. Retarded children were those who performed several years below the normal for their age level. In Binet's last (1911) revision of his intelligence scale, for example, the normal 8-year-old could count backwards from 20 to 0 and knew the date; the normal 12-year-old could put words arranged in a random order into a sentence; the normal adult could give three differences between a president and a king. A retarded child or adult could not answer most of the questions at his age level.

Henry Goddard, Lewis Terman, and others quickly adapted the Binet scale for American use, introducing the concept of an intelligence quotient, which was found by dividing the level reached on the scale ("mental age") by actual age (for children and adolescents). The IQ was considered to be a measure of intelligence that would remain constant throughout a person's life. The American adaptations of the Binet test were immediate successes: in 1911, according to one survey, the Binet scale was used by 71 of the 84 cities that administered psychological tests to verify the classification of a child as "feebleminded" (Wallin 1914). By 1914, Binet-type tests had been used, at least experimentally, to assist psychiatrists at Ellis Island in screening out and turning back "imbecile" and "feebleminded" immigrants (Knox 1914). The Binet and similar tests, however, were of limited use in situations in which large numbers of people were to be tested because they could be administered only to individuals and, in theory, only by trained psychologists.

World War I and Nativism

The first major experiment in group intelligence testing took place during World War I, when American psychologists devised tests—the famous Army Alpha and Beta examinations—that by 1918 had been given to almost 2,000,000 recruits. European nations had already tested soldiers for specific positions, for example, in transport and telegraphy, but the United States alone developed a broad "intelligence" testing program. The Army psychologists, who included most of the leaders of the profession, developed a pencil-and-paper test consisting of multiple-choice and true/false questions that could be scored with a key. The results of the tests, they reported, correlated as well with the judgment of superior officers as did scores on individualized tests.

The Army testing program was primarily experimental: most of its organizers agreed that it had little effect on the outcome of the war or indeed on the placement of personnel. Of the nearly 2,000,000 men tested, 8,000 were recommended for immediate discharge and 10,000 for assignment to labor battalions. On the whole, however, test scores played, at most, a secondary role in personnel assignment. But the impact of the Army program on testing in the postwar period was extraordinary. It led to a flurry of testing activity in the 1920s in both schools and industry, and it trained a corps of psychologists who were to have a profound influence. In addition, the results of the Army tests, presented to the public in a massive study by the National Academy of Sciences (Yerkes 1921), fell in with the growing nativist sentiment of the 1920s and triggered a national debate on the relationship of ethnic background, environmental influences, and intelligence.

The Academy study, conducted under the leadership of Robert M. Yerkes, exhaustively analyzed the test scores of more than 160,000 recruits, randomly selected. One of the most striking correlations drawn by the study was between ethnic background and test scores. According to the analysis, native whites scored highest on the tests. Of the immigrants, the scores were highest for groups from northern and western Europe and lowest for groups from southern and eastern Europe.

The study's findings were picked up by anti-immigrationists, partly because many Americans, including a number of psychologists, assumed that mental tests revealed genetically determined ability and that low intelligence was associated with crime and unemployment. Southern and eastern Europeans, the argument went, polluted the American gene pool, created a mass of unemployable and marginally employable people, and fed high rates of crime and delinquency. (See Gould 1981 for a description of the racial theories that were part of the intellectual atmosphere in which testing was developed.) In fact, test scores on the Army Alpha also correlated very closely with the length of time of residence in the United States and with years of schooling. This fact, however, did not stop some of the leading psychologists who had participated in the Army program from supporting eugenics and immigration restriction with arguments based on the study. Those psychologists included Yerkes and Carl Brigham, soon to be the chief architect of the College Entrance Examination Board Scholastic Aptitude Test. Brigham, however, who in 1923 had advanced a theory of racial determinism in his widely quoted *Study of American Intelligence*, soon recanted, at least to the extent of realizing that the measurement of "intelligence" was far more complicated than he had realized. He concluded his 1930 review of the status of intelligence testing of immigrant groups: "This review has summarized some of the more recent test findings which show that comparative studies of various national and racial groups may not be made with existing tests, and which show, in particular, that one of the most pretentious of these comparative racial studies—the writer's own—was without foundation" (Brigham 1930:165).

Statements by well-known psychologists about group differences lent scientific respectability to the xenophobic sentiments that flourished in the United States after World War I. These sentiments culminated in the restrictionist National Origins Act of 1924, which based severely limited nationality quotas on the percentages of each national group in the U.S. population in 1890—before the influx of eastern and southern Europeans had begun. By the 1930s, after restrictionist policies had come close to shutting off immigration, most psychologists had come to accept the position that the Army tests measured such factors as schooling, quality of home experience, and familiarity with English along with innate endowment. Yet most of them also remained committed to the belief that the Army experiment, for all its flaws, had demonstrated that group tests could predict performance.

Testing in Education and Industry, 1920-1970

The years after World War I saw a rash of testing in industry and schools as psychologists applied their skills in the civilian world. Shortly after the war, for example, a group of psychologists put together the National Intelligence Test, based on the Army Alpha test, and sold 400,000 copies to schools in six months. By 1921, according to Lewis Terman, 2,000,000 children a year were being tested with one or another of the dozens of group tests that were then available (Tyack 1974:207). Before World War I, educators had used individual tests to assess exceptionally gifted and retarded children. In the 1920s, however, group intelligence tests served a new function in schools: dividing high school students between college-bound and vocational tracks and grouping younger students into several instructional levels.

There had been a strong movement for vocational education and tracking by ability in American high schools since the late nineteenth century. On one hand, systems of tracking reflected the expectation that, in an age of rapidly expanding high school enrollment, most students would not go to college. On the other hand, tracking expressed the progressive philosophy that the purpose of education was to foster the talents of each student rather than to force all students into a common mold. For the most part, students were assigned to tracks by school grades and by teachers' assessments. In the 1920s, however, testing was added as a more objective measure of students' aptitude.

The Army tests had been designed to identify the exceptional at both ends of the spectrum of ability, but, according to Yerkes' analysis, they did more than that: they proved a striking correlation between intelligence and status in the military. The higher a soldier's rank and the greater the prestige of his previous civilian position, the higher his score tended to be. For many educational psychologists, the implications were obvious. Schools could use intelligence tests not only to identify the retarded and the gifted, but also to arrange students in a hierarchy of ability groupings. By the mid-1920s, the use of tests for guidance and tracking was commonplace, and in 1932, according to one survey, 75 percent of 150 large cities in the United States used intelligence tests, to some extent, to assign elementary school children to ability groups (Tyack 1974:208).

For many educational leaders, these tests provided an efficient way to divide students into homogeneous ability groups and thereby to meet the problems of size in postwar schools. Some pilot studies indicated that guidance based on tests reduced dropout and failure rates in high school. Mental tests also ensured, according to some educators, the extension of "true democracy" into the classroom; they made it possible to offer "the same general type of training to all who can take it," and to "provide special opportunities for those who cannot take our standard course and for those who can accomplish more" (Dickson 1924:89).

Many testers recognized that test results correlated with social background. According to Lewis Terman and colleagues (Terman et al. 1917:99), for example, there was "a correlation of .40 between social status and intelligence quotient." Many testers assumed further that the cause of this correlation was primarily innate endowment: "From what is already known about heredity," Terman and his coworkers wrote (1917:99) "should we not naturally expect to find the children of the well-to-do, cultured, and successful parents better endowed than the children who have been reared in slums and poverty?" Not surprisingly, critics of testing charged that tracking students by mental tests led to the recapitulation of the American social and economic structure in the school rooms. In 1924, the Chicago Federation of Labor expressed the point sharply: "The alleged 'mental levels,' representing natural ability, it will be seen, correspond in a most startling way to the social levels of the groups named. It is as though the relative social positions of each group are determined by an irresistible natural law" (quoted in Tyack 1974:215).

In the immediate postwar years, colleges also turned to mental tests to rationalize admissions procedures. By 1920, 200 colleges in the United States were using mental tests to determine whether prospective students could do college work: many reported that the scores on these tests correlated better with college grades than did high school records or scores on essay examinations. Some institutions used the tests to guide the admission of "special students"—older students whose high school careers had been interrupted by World War I. But tests were sometimes used in an attempt to exclude certain kinds of students.

One revealing story comes from Columbia University, which during the war had given the Thorndike Tests for Mental Alertness to candidates for officer training. In 1919, Columbia adopted the tests for general admission, ostensibly to measure applicants' "capacity to do college work." There is evidence that some administrators also hoped, however, that the tests would screen out "objectionable" candidates who had done well in high school and on the New York State Regents examination, but who had not had "the home experiences which enable them to pass these tests as successfully as the average American boy" (Synott 1979:290). Specifically, Columbia was concerned about Jewish students, who, before the war, made up 40 percent of the student body. The Army Alpha tests had disproved—as Carl Brigham put it—"the popular belief that the Jew is highly intelligent," and so Columbia's administrators assumed that the Thorndike test could be used to eliminate "the lowest grade of applicant," who turned out in many cases to be "New York Jews" with "ambition but not brains" (quoted in Wechsler 1977:160-161). The exact part that the Thorndike tests played in shaping Columbia admissions is hard to measure, but, combined with new application forms, photographs, and interviews, the psychological tests contributed to a new selective admissions policy that soon reduced the number of Jewish students at Columbia to 20 percent. Columbia was not, of course, alone in instituting such policies. Most Ivy League schools restricted the percentage of Jewish students by one means or another in these years. A different set of impulses led the College Entrance Examination Board to develop the SAT.

The College Board had been founded in 1900, as one of its early leaders put it, "to introduce law and order into educational anarchy" (Fuess 1950:3). As the number of secondary schools increased at the turn of the century, colleges had found it more and more difficult to evaluate school transcripts; at the same time, the variety of college entrance requirements and examinations presented a formidable obstacle to high school counselors and students. To bring order to the process, the College Board developed essay examinations in several academic subjects, which it used with candidates for member colleges. By World War I, a small group of elite colleges in the East either required College Board examinations or accepted them as substitutes for their own examinations. The majority of American colleges, however, continued to accept students on the basis of high school certification.

Before World War I, colleges had used the College Board examinations to check that candidates had the necessary background and skills for college; they generally admitted all qualified students. By the 1920s, however, many colleges, especially the best, were faced with more qualified applicants than they were willing to accept; for the first time, colleges rejected applicants whom they judged capable of doing the work. In this sense, college admissions assumed a new selective function.

In 1926, the College Board introduced the SAT, which became a major tool in the selection process, particularly at the most prestigious colleges. In theory, the SAT was more democratic than achievement tests, because it purportedly tested for the ability to learn, rather than for information learned. But, as one critic has written, colleges used the tests "to choose students from among the existing applicant pool—not to expand that pool" (Wechsler 1977:248). This policy was to be broadened only in the late 1930s, during the Depression years of falling enrollments, when at the urging of Harvard, Yale, and Princeton, the College Board offered the SAT and objective achievement tests at more than 100 locations throughout the country to facilitate the awarding of scholarships to excellent candidates.

World War I demonstrated that testing on a mass scale was possible; World War II fulfilled the promise of World War I by transforming Americans into the most tested people in the world. During the war, more than 9,000,000 recruits took the Army General Classification Test, a general aptitude test that was used to divide them into five broad categories of ability. At the same time, the Army and Navy developed and administered tests for a wide range of skills and aptitudes, and the College Board, at the military's request, gave objective tests to select officers. Unlike the situation in World War I, military leaders were convinced that the tests were effective—indeed, it was estimated that the pilot testing program of the Army air forces saved the taxpayer $1,000 for every dollar spent on testing (Lawshe and Balma 1946:7). As a result, the military expanded and developed its testing programs in the postwar years, as did American businesses and schools.

Educational and industrial testing continued to increase from 1940 to 1970. During the war, the College Board switched entirely to the SAT combined with objective achievement tests, and it never returned to essay examinations. As the number of college students grew in the 1950s and 1960s, the use of these and rival tests increased accordingly. By the 1970s, millions of students were taking objective entrance examinations for colleges, graduate schools, and professional schools every year. Testing in industry, spurred on in part by the availability of inexpensive tests from private test producers and from the U.S. Employment Service, increased just as dramatically until in the 1960s almost all American businesses of at least moderate size gave some kind of employment test.

The Search for Ability

At the beginning of the century, tests were adopted to achieve efficiency; by World War II, the search for order had given way to a search for ability. This search for ability, of course, was not new. Early in the century, people like Nicholas Murray Butler of Columbia and Charles W. Eliot of Harvard expressed a concern for identifying talent in the lowest ranks of society. Although testers recognized a wide range of ability within classes, people then tended to believe that talent was concentrated in the upper ranks of society. An objective system of testing, therefore, might make it possible for society to uncover and reward "the natural history 'sport' in the human race," as Eliot called the gifted poor (quoted in Tyack 1974:129). But such a program, overall, only appeared to confirm the natural divisions of society that had evolved in history. The Army Alpha tests, which showed that officers were more "intelligent" than the average draftee, and the tests given at Ellis Island in the 1910s, which showed that most immigrants were "retarded," seemed to many to support the view that talent was rare in the lower classes. Given the assumptions that underlay that view, testing programs could easily serve to preserve the existing social order.

By the 1930s, the basic assumptions of many American social scientists and, by extension, American policy makers had changed from hereditarian to environmentalist in their explanation of group differences (see Cravens 1978:238-241 and Myrdal 1944:1003). Talent and intellectual ability were no longer considered the genetic endowment of select classes, races, or nationalities;[1] they were seen, instead, to be distributed without

---

[1] See, for example, Thomas Pettigrew (1964), which cites public opinion survey data showing that in 1942, 2 out of 5 white Americans regarded blacks as their intellectual equals, while in 1956 the figure was 4 out of 5.

regard to human groupings. Within this frame of reference, which came to be pretty much the conventional wisdom by the 1950s, testing seemed a liberating tool that could circumvent the privileges of birth and wealth to open the doors of opportunity to Americans of all kinds. Tests had a potential for democratizing American society.

Talent, Democracy, and the Cold War

A corollary to the assumption that talent could be found in all segments of society was the assumption that talent, and particularly talent for leadership, had not been adequately developed in America. A striking feature of testing in the years after World War II was the increased use of diversified batteries of tests (rather than just IQ tests with their emphasis on verbal and mathematical reasoning) to identify leaders in a heterogeneous society. This point emerges clearly in the development of industrial testing. Most testing in industry was—and still is—for clerical positions or for positions requiring specific skills. Since World War II, however, industrial psychologists have become increasingly concerned with ways to identify managerial talent. From the fad of personality inventories in the 1950s to the remarkable growth of managerial assessment centers in the last 15 years, the message has been the same: in a world of increasing complexity, human talent is at a premium.

Changes in the structure of industry have created a rapid expansion in the executive and managerial ranks—with the result that managerial specialists have come to consider the shortage of qualified managerial personnel the most pressing problem facing industry.[2] Such specialists encouraged businesses to enlist the entire array of psychological tools, including testing, in the effort to identify competence. Because most of the testers by the 1950s believed that talent was no respecter of family, class, or race, it was felt that effective managerial talent searches would democratize the corporate world and, by extension, American society.

The search for managerial talent suggested a second theme of postwar testing: the conviction that ability tests could fulfill the American promise that each citizen should have the opportunity to express his or her talent to the fullest. Once again, the theme was not a new one, but it received new meaning in a nation transformed by the New Deal and World War

---

[2] One researcher found an average increase of 32 percent between 1947 and 1957 in two-thirds of the companies he studied (Spencer 1959); see also Hinrichs (1969) and Lopez (1970).

II and caught in the grips of the Cold War. For millions of Americans—veterans, farmers, women, blacks—the postwar world promised opportunities that were undreamed of a generation earlier. At the same time, many Americans argued, the challenge of the Soviet Union demanded that the nation repair its democratic fences and mobilize its human resources to the fullest.

Testers, benefiting from new sophistication gained in the war as well as from new computerized scoring methods, suggested that they held in their hands—in the words of the president of the Educational Testing Service in 1956—America's "secret weapon" in its contest with the Russians (quoted in Goslin 1963:191). John Stalnaker, who set up the National Merit Scholarship program in the mid-1950s, made the point clearly: "The power which recognizes talent and develops it to the productive stage, quickly and in quantity, has the best chance in winning the race" (Stalnaker 1969:161). The National Merit Scholarship examinations were intended to foster American talent and to spur the nation on in the contest. The remarkable growth of ability testing in the postwar years, often actively encouraged by the federal government, must be seen in this context.

A related conviction that came out of wartime years was that Americans were far brighter than had been thought. After World War I, the National Academy of Sciences study (Yerkes 1921:785) on the Army testing program reported that the average draftee had a mental age of about 13 and that this group was probably a little lower in intelligence than the country at large. The Academy study also concluded that distinctly more than average intelligence would be a prerequisite for a college education and was almost as clearly necessary to successful high school work (p. 783). After examining the results of intelligence tests given to military personnel in World War II, President Truman's Commission on Higher Education came to a very different conclusion: at least 49 percent of the American population had the mental ability to complete 14 years of education and, if they chose, to pursue advanced liberal or specialized studies (President's Commission on Higher Education 1947:41). Both human justice and the survival of freedom, the Commission argued, required that these vast human resources be tapped. Educational testers and counselors, armed with new batteries of aptitude tests, set out to provide guidance for elementary and high school students and for the returning veterans. Symptomatic of the atmosphere, too, were longitudinal studies, like John C. Flanagan's Project Talent, begun in the late 1950s: 140,000 students in more than 1,000 schools were given a battery of 23 aptitude tests in an effort "to obtain a national inventory of human resources" (Flanagan 1973).

The Role of the Federal Government

As far back as the mid-1930s, the U.S. government actively promoted and, in some cases, required testing as a means of ensuring both national efficiency and individual opportunity, regardless of class or race. In the Social Security Act amendment of 1939 (and in other legislation), for example, Congress required that state and county employees administering federal grants-in-aid be hired under a merit system. From the 1940s the federal government offered assistance to the states in developing testing programs for selecting their employees. The results were predictable: in the mid-1930s, only nine states had merit systems; by the 1950s, all had some sort of system, even if the system applied only to employees in federal programs. In the same period, the U.S. Employment Service became a leading source of employment and vocational tests used by state employment services and schools. In the 1960s, under the National Defense Education Act, the U.S. Office of Education (USOE) financed guidance and testing programs in schools throughout the country. In 1965-1966, for example, testing agencies under contract to USOE gave 2,000,000 standardized tests in public elementary schools and 7,000,000 in public secondary schools (U.S. Congress 1967).

Because it was assumed that merit was equally the property of all groups, it followed that testing could be a tool for opening up American society to groups that were traditionally the target of discrimination. Evidence accumulated in the 1960s, however, that indicated that, whatever the distribution of merit in society, the ability to do well on specific tests was not equally divided among different segments of society. When the federal government undertook, in a series of major civil rights statutes, to ensure that all groups share equally in the benefits and participate fully at all levels of society, testing entered a new phase.

THE LEGAL CONTEXT

As we have seen, the success of psychological testing in America has been due in part to its adoption in the federal government—by the armed forces in the two world wars and by the Civil Service Commission in carrying out its mandate to establish a merit system for the selection of government employees. In recent years, however, governmental policy has given rise to significant restrictions on the use of tests.

The civil rights initiatives of the 1960s brought with them the first real challenge to unfettered use of tests. Public concern with the intrusiveness of so-called personality tests and psychologist-guided selection methods culminated in the spring of 1965 in House and Senate hearings on the use and abuse of psychological tests. The debate at this point focused on the invasion of the constitutional right of privacy threatened by test items concerned with sexual preference, religious beliefs, family relationships, and other intimate subjects.[3]

In the long run, however, federal prohibitions against discrimination in employment and educational practices have had far more significant effects on testing. The emerging doctrine of fair employment law, most particularly judicial and regulatory construction of Title VII of the Civil Rights Act of 1964 (P.L. 88-352), has produced a complex set of constraints on an employer's actions in hiring, placing, promoting, or dismissing employees. Since ability tests are frequently the most visible part of the decision process, they have been the focus of a great deal of regulatory activity. (For a fuller discussion of litigation on employment testing, see Wigdor in Part II.)

The Prohibition Against Discrimination in Employment

The goal of Title VII of the Civil Rights Act was twofold: to assure equal treatment of all individuals and to improve the economic position of blacks. The Act sought to achieve the latter goal, which is redistributive in nature, by enforcing the former. The central obligation of an employer under Title VII is to refrain from using race, sex, color, national origin, or religion as the basis of employment decisions. While some people doubted that equal treatment would result in fair treatment for blacks in a situation produced by conditions of severe, long-term, and officially sanctioned inequality, the 1964 Act did not attempt to do more than eliminate discrimination.[4] Indeed, it reserved to the employer the authority to set standards for his work force, both by specifically excepting from the enumeration of unlawful employment practices the use of "any professionally developed ability test," provided it is not used to discriminate (§703h), and by stating that nothing in the title should be interpreted to require any employer to grant preferential treatment to individuals in the protected classes on account of any imbalance in his workforce (§703j).

---

[3] So unaccustomed was the psychological profession to this sort of attention that *The American Psychologist*, in November 1965, devoted an entire issue (20) to the congressional hearings and public controversy.

[4] President Johnson gave voice to such doubts in 1965: "You do not take a person who for years has been hobbled by chains . . . [bring] him up to the starting line of a race and then say 'You're free to compete' and justly believe that you have been completely fair." Quoted in "Labor Department Regulations: Affirmative Action is Under a New Gun," *The Washington Post* (March 27, 1981:A8).

The rationale of fair employment laws, including Title VII of the Civil Rights Act, involved a set of assumptions, both constitutional and economic, that lent credence to the antidiscrimination approach. Chief among these was the merit principle, defined as selecting the most able candidate, which would promote simultaneously the national interest in high productivity and the national sense of fairness. A further assumption was that characteristics such as race, color, ethnic origin, and sex are irrelevant to productivity and, therefore, contrary to merit selection.

This line of reasoning led naturally to the conclusion that nondiscriminatory selection would produce more merit-oriented selection. Theoretically, at least, Title VII would have the beneficial effect of increasing national productivity, improving the economic position of blacks and other groups formerly kept from full participation in society, and revitalizing the constitutional principle of equality. And it would do so by prohibiting employers from basing hiring decisions on criteria that were as inimical to their own economic well-being as to the larger interests.

Early formulations of the theory of fair employment practices law emphasized the limited nature of the benefits conferred by Title VII. Fiss (1971:265) speaks of the law's commitment to a "symmetrical stricture against preferential treatment based on race: prefering a black on the basis of his color is as unlawful as choosing a white because of his color."

After 15 years of enforcement activity, however, it is now being recognized that there has been a dramatic shift in government policy from the requirement of equal treatment to that of equal outcome. Bureaucratic and judicial interpretation of Title VII has turned increasingly toward a notion of equality based on group parity in the work force or what has come to be called a "representative work force." This policy makes the redistributive impulse in Title VII much more immediate, and it is accompanied by a good deal of tension and confusion inside and outside of government as to rights, obligations, and permissible social costs.

Regulatory Definition of the Obligation of the Employer

Throughout most of the period since 1964, four federal agencies have shared major responsiblity for the administration and enforcement of Title VII. Preeminent among them is the Equal Employment Opportunity Commission (EEOC), created by the Civil Rights Act for the purpose of promoting compliance. In addition, the U.S. Department of Labor has been charged by Executive Order 11246 with ensuring compliance among federal contractors through its Office of Federal Contract Compliance and Programs, and the Civil Service Commission (CSC), until recently, has had oversight of equal employment opportunity in the federal government. The role of the U.S. Department of Justice has been to represent the agencies in court as well as to initiate suits against federal contractors and governmental units whose employment practices give evidence of a pattern of systematic discrimination.

In the process of working out the implications of Title VII, the implementing agencies quickly converged on testing (which is defined broadly enough to cover any selection procedure that involves choice among candidates) as the most important locus of discriminatory employment practices. Each of them developed a separate set of guidelines on employment testing procedures; in the process of successive reiterations, these guidelines became more and more complicated statements of technical validation methods (see Novick in Part II).[5] Significant policy differences among the agencies have developed, differences expressed in their separate guidelines and in the tenor of their compliance activities. The failure to develop a uniform federal posture on the obligation of the employer under Title VII, although mitigated by the adoption in 1978 of *Uniform Guidelines on Employee Selection Procedures* (hereafter, *Uniform Guidelines*) by all four agencies, has created untold confusion and irritation, for even the most willing employer cannot respond to conflicting requirements.

A recent case, involving the New York State Police examination, illustrates the problem. The position of state trooper is covered by New York civil service laws, which prescribe competitive examination, the ranking of candidates according to test scores, and selection strictly by numerical order. These are typical requirements in merit systems. The examination was developed with the help of the U.S. Civil Service Commission—and officials of the agency later testified on behalf of the de-

---

[5] There are seven such guidelines: Equal Employment Opportunity Commission (1966) Guidelines on employment testing procedures. *Federal Register* 31:6414; Office of Federal Contract Compliance, Department of Labor (1968) Validation of employment tests. *Federal Register* 33:14392; Equal Employment Opportunity Commission (August 1, 1970) Guidelines on employee selection procedures. *Federal Register* 35(149):12333-12336 (reissued, *Federal Register* 41:51984, 1976); Office of Federal Contract Compliance, U.S. Department of Labor (1971) Employee testing and other selection procedures. *Federal Register* 36(192):19307-19310; Office of Federal Contract Compliance, U.S. Department of Labor (1974) Guidelines for reporting criterion-related and content validity. *Federal Register* 39(12):2094-2096; U.S. Department of Justice, Department of Labor, Civil Service Commission (1976) Federal executive agency guidelines on employee selection procedures. *Federal Register* 41(227):51734-51759; Equal Employment Opportunity Commission, U.S. Civil Service Commission, U.S. Department of Labor, U.S. Department of Justice (1978) Uniform guidelines on employee selection procedures. *Federal Register* 43(166):38290-38315.

fendant at the trial. The U.S. Department of Justice, at the request of the EEOC, brought suit against the state of New York, alleging that the examination was not constructed in such a manner as to fulfill the requirements of the *Uniform Guidelines*, and that, in the light of its adverse impact on minorities, it was unlawfully discriminatory. The judge remarked that even the most casual reader of the decision would notice the "friction and conflict" between the two agencies and would not blame the state defendants if they felt misled by the federal government, given the conflicting positions of the representatives of the two agencies.[6]

This conflict within the government is not essentially a matter of bureaucratic rivalry or political aggrandizement. Rather, it reflects an ambivalence about the nature of equality. The Civil Service Commission and the Equal Employment Opportunity Commission, for example, are both committed to enforcing fair employment practices. But they have had very different conceptions of their mission.

The Civil Service Commission (now, the Office of Personnel Management) looks back on a history of almost 100 years in which its mission has been to develop and implement a competitive system for staffing the civilian bureaucracy. The merit principle provided the rationale for the agency's activities, and tests have been its major selection instrument. The CSC has long employed a staff of psychometricians to produce tests that purport to rank candidates on the basis of ability. Without getting into the question of how well the CSC tests actually fit worker to job on the basis of ability, the principle itself can be considered to embrace a reasonable definition of equal opportunity, and one that satisfies a sense of fairness. The only discrimination involved is discrimination on the basis of ability, which is neither against the law nor contrary to basic American values.

For its part, the Equal Employment Opportunity Commission is not interested in tests, nor even primarily in merit (see Robertson 1976). Its mission is to ameliorate the economic condition of blacks, females, Hispanics, and certain other ethnic minorities by ensuring that more of them are hired and promoted than have been in the past. To that end, the EEOC has interpreted Title VII discrimination to consist not merely of employment practices for which the intent was to discriminate, but also of those practices for which the result was to reject black candidates in greater proportions than white.

The first set of EEOC *Guidelines on Employment Testing Procedures*

---

[6] *United States* v. *State of New York*, slip opinion #77-CV-343, Sept. 6, 1979. The Justice Department won its case; see Wigdor (in Part II) for a fuller discussion of the case.

issued in 1966, was used as the vehicle for announcing the EEOC's definition of discrimination; if an employer, union, or employment agency uses a test or other selection device that results in proportionally lower selection rates for minorities and females than for white males, the procedure will be considered discriminatory and declared unlawful, unless the employer can "validate" the test in accordance with the requirements laid out in the *Guidelines*. The definition indicates how quickly the EEOC came to the view that testing was the major barrier to its goal of redressing the racial and gender imbalance in the work force. It became the basis for the formula for federal oversight of personnel selection.

There is some irony in the fact that an agency with no intrinsic interest in tests has come to be the arbiter of what constitutes technical adequacy. However, given the mission of the agency and the continued failure of blacks and Hispanics to equal the test scores of their white counterparts, it is not surprising that relatively few employment testing programs have been able to survive an EEOC compliance review or legal challenge. If testing technology improved so that tests routinely withstood legal challenge, the agency would have to seek other means of fulfilling its mission. (This view was expressed by the EEOC chair, Eleanor Holmes Norton, at a Commission meeting in 1977.) In the meantime, the EEOC's validation requirements are demanding enough to discourage all but the larger firms from using testing programs, if their overall selection ratios show differential impact. Even the Professional and Administrative Career Examination (PACE), the major test used by the Civil Service Commission, has apparently failed to survive legal challenge; by the terms of a consent decree negotiated between the Justice Department and the plaintiffs, but not yet formally ruled on by the court, the PACE will be phased out of existence over the next three years.[7]

The policy of the Equal Employment Opportunity Commission is clearly to make the justification of test use as demanding as possible whenever tests result in differential selection.[8] And, as we discuss below, the agency has received a good deal of backing for this policy from the courts, which are the final arbiters of the meaning of Title VII discrimination.

Over the years, EEOC's position vis-à-vis the other implementing agen-

---

[7] The consent decree was negotiated in *Luevano* v. *Campbell*, Civil Action No. 79-0271 (D.D.C. 1979) Feb. 24, 1981.

[8] See, e.g., memorandum of David Rose (1976), chief, Employment Section, Civil Rights Division, U.S. Department of Justice. Rose remarked that the thrust of the EEOC Guidelines was to "place almost all test users in a posture of noncompliance; to give great discretion to enforcement personnel to determine who should be prosecuted; and to set aside objective procedures in favor of numerical hiring."

cies has been enhanced, so that it is significantly more than one among several agencies with equal employment opportunity jurisdiction. This primacy was formally recognized by Executive Order 12067 (issued June 30, 1978), which gave the EEOC the authority to coordinate all federal equal employment opportunity programs, which by one count involve 18 different agencies enforcing some 40 equal employment opportunity laws.

Administration backing of the EEOC mission was made even clearer in the Civil Service Reform Act of 1978, which gave the Civil Service Commission a new name, the Office of Personnel Management, as well as a new statutory mandate to combine the principle of merit selection with the goal of achieving a representative work force. The role of testing in a selection system responsive to this dual mandate will no doubt emerge only slowly. In the meantime, the Reform Act empowers the Office of Personnel Management to delegate many of its functions with regard to administering the competitive service to the individual agencies. EEOC is to regulate the agencies' employee selection procedures.

Tests on Trial

The judicial standards for applying Title VII to employment tests were laid out by the Supreme Court in 1971 in *Griggs* v. *Duke Power Co.* (401 U.S. 424). By this opinion, the central policy determination of the Equal Employment Opportunity Commission concerning the nature of discrimination under Title VII was accorded the status of law. The Court adopted an operational definition of discrimination: it focuses judicial attention on the consequences of a selection process rather than on intent or motive. If tests are shown to have an exclusionary effect—which EEOC calls adverse impact and the courts tend to call disparate impact—then it can be inferred that discrimination has taken place, for one result of discrimination will indeed be imbalance in the make-up of the work force.[9]

The *Griggs* decision established the basic two-step procedure of Title VII litigation on testing. First, the plaintiff bears the burden of presenting evidence strong enough to support an inference of discrimination. Since the emphasis is on consequences, the evidence will normally be a com-

---

[9] There is some ambiguity in the doctrine of Title VII discrimination with regard to motive or intent. See *Board of Education* v. *Harris* (48 LW 4035), in which the reasoning of the majority opinion (by Justice Blackmun, joined by Chief Justice Burger and Justices Brennan, White, Marshall, and Stevens) differs in significant respects from the minority opinion (by Justice Stewart, joined by Justices Powell and Rhenquist).

parison of the categories of people actually present in the employer's work force with those in a population representing the potential pool of applicants form which he might be expected to draw. Second, upon the plaintiff's having established the prima facie case, the evidentiary burden shifts to the defendant, the employer. To rebut the inference of discrimination, the employer must demonstrate that the challenged test (or other selection device) is a "reasonable measure of job performance." Showing the test to be a measure of job-related qualifications establishes, unless rebutted, that the basis of the selection decision is a legitimate, nondiscriminatory purpose, such as productivity, and not race, color, sex, or other forbidden considerations.

Like the Civil Rights Act, the Supreme Court opinion in *Griggs* firmly denied any legal requirement for preferential treatment: "Congress has not commanded that the less qualified be preferred over the better qualified simply because of minority origins." Indeed, the opinion states repeatedly that the whole purpose of Title VII is to promote selection on the basis of job qualifications. Yet this defense of selection on the basis of ability is rendered ambiguous by another line of argument. In declaring that "basic intelligence must have the means of articulation to manifest itself fairly in a testing process," the Court would seem to place upon employers the burden of overcoming or bypassing with their tests (or other assessment devices) any disadvantage that might have been produced by past discrimination, as if disadvantage is a garment that can be cast off to reveal the core of unaffected productive capacity beneath.

The seeming simplicity of the *Griggs* formula was belied by subsequent litigation, for it left two basic questions largely undefined: What constitutes a persuasive showing of adverse impact upon protected classes? What evidence will satisfy the employer's burden of proving that the challenged test is a legally sufficient measure of job qualifications?

As it turns out, the first question has absorbed much of the energy and attention of the advocates in employment discrimination litigation. Because of the emphasis on consequences, statistical proofs have increasingly become the means by which plaintiffs seek to establish, and defendants to rebut, a finding of adverse impact.

A basic assumption underlying *Griggs* was that, in an entirely neutral marketplace, people will be selected for employment in roughly the same proportion as they are represented in the population. In 1977, the Supreme Court gave voice to that assumption: ". . . absent explanation, it is ordinarily to be expected that nondiscriminatory hiring practices will in time result in a workforce more or less representative of the racial and ethnic composition of the population in the community from which employees are hired" (*Teamsters* v. *United States*, 431 U.S. 324, 329). Such comparisons between the general population and an employer's work force almost invariably show great disparities, and they rarely provide much information about the talent pool from which an employer must actually draw, particularly for positions requiring long training or special skills. Consequently, lawyers for the defense have become prime movers in developing refinements in the statistical comparisons of the composition of the employer's work force and the relevant labor pool. In spite of the increased sophistication of the statistical argument in employment discrimination cases, however, no clear definition of what constitutes adverse impact has emerged since 1971, and it is left to a court to determine the proper statistical norm in each case. It remains very difficult, therefore, for employers, even if they have instituted all of the record-keeping procedures recommended by the EEOC and other compliance agencies, to know whether or not their employment procedures will be judged to have a legally questionable differential impact.

Once the attention of a court shifts to the test itself, an employer's problems increase. For a number of reasons, relatively few specific uses of tests have passed judicial muster. Fiss (1971) noted that the mechanism adopted in the *Griggs* case—using statistics on race to shift the burden of proof to the employer—tends to blur the distinction between cause (racial discrimination) and consequence (racial imbalance), leading to the possibility that the distinction will become a merely formal one.

His concern was well-founded, for, more and more, establishing the prima facie case has come to determine the outcome of the suit. Lost from view is the inferential nature of a finding of presumptive discrimination drawn from statistics revealing imbalance: the realization that discrimination is a probable, but not necessarily the correct, explanation of this imbalance. A recent district court ruling, for example, bars New York City from using the results of a civil service entrance examination to hire new police officers unless 50 percent of the recruits are blacks and Hispanics. In his ruling, Judge Robert L. Carter concluded from statistical evidence of a long-standing pattern of differential selection: "This studied adherence to discriminatory procedures at this point must be deemed conscious and deliberate" (quoted in *The New York Times*, January 30, 1980:B4).

More importantly, the courts have interpreted the job-relatedness standard as requiring a demonstration of technical validation in accordance with the EEOC's *Guidelines on Employee Selection Procedures* and professional standards. In the matter of validating the use of a test, the guidelines are formidable. The 1970 version was informed by the testing standards adopted by the American Psychological Association (APA) in

1955 and amended in 1966.[10] The APA is the major professional organization of psychologists who hold doctorate degrees, and the *Standards*
represent the interests and concerns of the academic, research, and test
development community. While the *Standards* reflect the best professional expertise, they are rarefied for the everyday world of employment
testing. By incorporating them into the *Guidelines*, EEOC transformed
what had been a state-of-the-art professional judgment, which the individual psychologist was expected to adapt in the light of particular circumstances, into ground rules for an employer's compliance with the
Civil Rights Act.

The *Griggs* decision paved the way for courts to use the *Guidelines* as
the standard against which a challenged selection procedure should be
judged. Although it did not give specific guidance as to what would
satisfy the obligation of the employer, it did specifically endorse EEOC,
saying that the administrative interpretation of the Civil Rights Act by the
enforcing agency was entitled to "great deference." The oft-repeated
phrase lent tremendous authority to the EEOC's *Guidelines*, even though
the Court has subsequently gone out of its way to emphasize that guidelines are not legally binding regulations.[11]

Since *Griggs*, a significant body of precedent has made it clear that
some sort of formal validation study is necessary to establish the job-
relatedness of a test under Title VII. There is no easy answer to the question
of what constitutes a sufficient validation study. The striking fact is that
most of the decisions have ruled against the challenged tests; no selection
program seems to have survived when the *Guidelines* were applied in
any detail. A catalogue of the deficiencies of specific test applications
drawn from opinions delivered in the 1970s includes: failure to conduct
a differential validity study; an inadequate job analysis; failure to justify
the use of a content-validity or construct-validity strategy by showing the
infeasibility of a criterion-related validity study as recommended by the
1970 EEOC *Guidelines* (no longer a requirement); use of unvalidated cutoff scores; failure to validate ranked scores; absence of significant statistical correlations; the use of weak or inappropriate criteria; weakness of
correspondence between the skills tested and the domain of job skills;
inadequate attempt to identify an alternative with less adverse impact.
But in none of these cases is there much in the way of a working model

---

[10] The 1966 version is entitled *Standards For Educational and Psychological Tests and
Manuals* (American Psychological Association et al. 1966). The *Standards* bear on educational tests as well as employment tests.
[11] *General Electric Co. v. Gilbert*, 97 S. Ct. at 410-411 (1977).

for employers to look to as a legally defensible testing program under Title VII.

In the early litigation, employment testing cases usually involved very weak testing programs, often introduced just as Title VII went into effect and with little or no attempt to evaluate the usefulness of the instrument for the jobs in question. That is no longer true. Carefully constructed and researched tests are now the subject of litigation, and they, too, seldom withstand legal challenge. Judges are requiring, in the face of evidence of differential impact, a degree of technical adequacy that tests and test users apparently cannot provide.

The Current Situation

Given the repeated failure of tests and other modes of selection to withstand challenge, as well as the pressure from the compliance authorities to achieve a representative work force, it seems probable that many employers will quietly begin to select on the very bases that Title VII disallows (race, color, sex, or national origin) but now for the purpose of eliminating the work force imbalances that make them vulnerable to litigation. Yet such numerical hiring is illegal under Title VII and other fair employment laws and raises the possibility of reverse-discrimination suits brought by individuals or affected classes. (Presumably the government would not initiate such an action.) The legal obligation of employers has not been sufficiently clarified by judicial construction of the Civil Rights Act. The weight of the case law certainly indicates that employers who wish to use tests or other assessment techniques for selecting employees from a pool of applicants will have to formally validate the instrument or choose an instrument that has been validated elsewhere for the same job.

On the question of test security, that is, ensuring that applicants have not had prior access to test questions, a recent decision upheld, on very narrow grounds, the interests of the employer in the integrity of the instrument.[12] But the question is likely to arise again, and the quest for visibly fair employment practices will perhaps seem more meaningful to the courts than will psychometric necessities.

The institutionalization of compensatory practices as part of formal affirmative action programs may emerge as the most practicable course among the competing claims of merit and group parity in employment selection, but to date the legal status of such programs is largely unde-

---

[12] *Detroit Edison* v. *N.L.R.B.*, 99 S. Ct. 1123 (1979).

fined.[13] Early in the last decade, the affirmative action concept seemed to one prominent legal scholar "either meaningless or inconsistent with the prohibition against discrimination" (Fiss 1971:313). Since affirmative action has become a central equal opportunity policy of the government, it is increasingly clear that traditional legal doctrines do not resolve the inconsistency between affirmative action and nondiscrimination obligations.

In the present confusion, employers, white males, and members of the protected groups all feel that they are being treated unfairly. And in some sense, each of them is. It is disingenuous to impose test validation requirements that employers, even with the best will and a sizable monetary investment, cannot meet. It is misleading to define a fair ability test as one on which members of disadvantaged groups perform as well on the average as members of the majority group (although one might well define a fair selection strategy in terms of equal outcome).

Employment testing is being subjected to a degree of governmental scrutiny that few human contrivances could bear. Many interests may be served by testing: efficiency or productivity; the sense of fairness that results from cloaking the allocation of scarce positions with the mantle of objective selection; better matching of people and jobs; the identification of talent that might otherwise go undetected and unrealized. But these interests are not at present strong enough to compete with the commitment of the government to finally break the pattern of economic disadvantage and estrangement that has characterized the position of blacks, women, and members of other specific groups in the society. Hundreds of cases and a decade and a half later, the dilemma remains unchanged. Until a constitutional principle evolves that incorporates into the idea of equality an acceptable rationale for compensatory treatment of the disadvantaged, national perceptions of fairness and national interest in productivity will continue to suffer.

Educational Testing and the Law

Federal judicial involvement with testing practices developed more slowly in education than in employment. There is, however, a fundamental similarity between the two: most of the constitutional and statutory protections afforded to test takers in either setting relate to members of groups considered vulnerable to discriminatory practices based on color, race, ethnic origin, gender, or handicapping condition. As a result, most con-

---

[13] See *Steelworkers Union* v. *Weber*, 99 S. Ct. 2721 (1979).

troversies over educational decisions based on test scores also involve minority plaintiffs; they are being cast in the analytical framework provided by employment testing cases, often triggering standards like those developed in the course of Title VII litigation. (For a detailed description of the case law, see Hollander in Part II.)

Rights and Remedies

Various legal remedies have been called on in challenging the use of standardized tests in school settings, some of them based on constitutional rights, others based on rights created by statute. The protections brought into play by state action (for example, when a state or school district mandates testing for the purpose of ability grouping or institutes a minimum competency testing program) are found primarily in the constitutional guarantees of equal protection and due process of law. The equal protection clause of the Fourteenth Amendment to the Constitution bars the state from intentionally treating classes of citizens differently, unless such action can be shown to be rationally related to a legitimate state purpose. Moreover, in the case of certain classes of people—particularly, those who, because of their race or ethnic identity, have been subject to unequal operation of the laws in past generations—something more is required: the state must show a "compelling state interest" in such course of action, a far more difficult level of proof.

The due process clause prohibits the state from depriving an individual of liberty or property without due process of law. This protection from arbitrary governance has been called on in challenging minimum competency testing programs when passing the test is tied to receiving a high school diploma. Courts have recognized a student's property right in a diploma, which right might be infringed, for example, by failing to make the standards of competence known to students or failing to allow for a sufficient phase-in period (Tractenberg 1979.)

A number of statutory protections are available to test takers in school districts that receive federal financial aid, which is almost universally the case among public school systems and frequently so among private institutions. Here it is the power of the purse (rather than the Constitution) that enables federal policy to influence school practices. Although federal funds on average make up only 8 or 10 percent of spending in support of public education (in comparison with approximately 50 percent in state funds and 40 percent in local funds), acceptance of federal funds under an educational program brings with it an obligation to conform to federal antidiscrimination policies in the conduct of education. The most important federal statutes in encouraging or shaping school testing practices include Title VI of the Civil Rights Act of 1964, the Elementary and Secondary Education Act of 1965, Section 504 of the Rehabilitation Act of 1973, and the Education for All Handicapped Children Act of 1975.

Since most of our discussion will focus on legal challenge to the use of standardized tests in the schools, challenges that are usually brought under the authority of federal law, it is important to emphasize at the beginning that federal educational policy has not been characterized by opposition to testing. Indeed, many funding programs encourage testing, albeit indirectly, by requiring school districts to submit annual reports indicating how participants in special programs benefited from the supplementary services. One frequently used measure of program effectiveness is the comparison of scores of tests given in the fall and spring. (See, for example, the section on programs under Title I of the Elementary and Secondary Education Act of 1965 in U.S. Department of Health, Education, and Welfare 1978:107-133.)

In addition, the "mainstreaming" statutes, the Rehabilitation Act of 1973 and the Education for All Handicapped Children Act (EHA) of 1975, in effect encourage testing. They mandate that each handicapped child shall be provided with an "appropriate" public education in the least restrictive environment. Under the EHA regulations, each such child is to be provided with an individualized education program based on an assessment of the child's learning problems and educational needs. Both statutes assume that testing will be among the evaluation methods used and provide rules for test use. Among the rules are the requirements that assessment procedures, including testing, not be culturally discriminatory; that they be expressed in the child's native language or mode of communication; and that tests be validated for the specific purpose used. Federal policy may thus be said to extend to handicapped students the right to accurate assessment so that they may be placed in appropriate tracks, special classes, and suitable schools.

As is often the case with testing, policy makers are rather too optimistic about what tests, in their present state of development, can accomplish in the pedagogical attempt to overcome disadvantage or to neutralize the effects of handicaps on school performance.[14] As a result, the schools are witnessing with increasing frequency the anomaly of federal courts striking down uses of tests that were encouraged or required by federally funded or state mandated educational programs.

---

[14] The report of the Panel on Testing of Handicapped People explores this subject in detail; see Sherman and Robinson (1982).

Testing Litigation

The 1954 Supreme Court decision in *Brown* v. *Board of Education* (347 U.S. 483) ruled that the maintenance of dual, segregated school systems denied the equal protection of the law to black children. As a consequence, dual educational systems were gradually abolished, though not without a great deal of pressure from the federal government. Dismantling the dual system did not automatically bring about racial integration in the schools, however. Many formerly segregated school systems introduced testing programs to track students into ability groups with the effect of continuing patterns of racial segregation within school buildings. Despite the general reluctance of the courts to intervene in matters of school policy, the federal courts have, since the late 1960s, repeatedly struck down this use of apparently neutral mechanisms to recreate all black classes in formerly segregated systems.[15] The Fifth Circuit, for example, which covers much of the South, prohibited all testing for purposes of ability grouping until such time as meaningful integration of the schools had been achieved (Rebell and Block 1980:5.64).

The use of tests for ability grouping has also come under legal attack in school systems outside the South. The leading case is *Larry P.* v. *Riles*,[16] which spanned much of the 1970s. The central complaint in *Larry P.* concerned the use of IQ tests as a basis for determining whether black pupils should be placed in special classes for the educable mentally retarded (EMR classes). Plaintiffs charged that the tests in question were racially and culturally biased against black pupils and did not reflect their experience as a class, with the result that some of them were wrongfully removed from the regular course of instruction and placed in dead-end, nonacademic classes. The case initially concerned placement practices in the San Francisco area, but ultimately affected the entire state of California.

One of the most interesting things about *Larry P.* was the court's attention to the analysis and precedents developed in *Griggs* and other employment testing cases.[17] Equally important, however, was the court's

---

[15] See, e.g., *Singleton* v. *Jackson Municipal Separate School System*, 419 F.2d 1211 (1969), rev'd in part on other grounds, 396 U.S. 290 (1970); *Moses* v. *Washington Parish School Board*, 330 F. Supp. 1340 (1971); *Lemon* v. *Bossier Parish School Board*, 444 F.2d 1400 (1971); *United States* v. *Gadsden City School District*, 508 F.2d 1017 (1978).

[16] 343 F. Supp. 1036 (1972), 502 F.2d 963 (1974); 495 F. Supp. 926 (1979), 48 LW 2298 (1979). See also, *Diana* v. *State Board of Education*, Civil Number C-70-37 RFP (1973); *Hobson* v. *Hansen*, 269 F. Supp. 401 (1967).

[17] Rebell and Block (1980:5.64-5.69) present a useful analysis of *Larry P.*

recognition that the function of public education placed limits on the applicability of those precedents. *Larry P.* was the first federal case to require scientific validation of tests used for EMR placement (p. 989). When the case began in 1972, black children and their parents sued for an injunction against the use of the WISC, the Stanford-Binet, and other intelligence tests used in the San Francisco Unified School District until a full trial could be heard. The court enjoined the use of the tests, reasoning from precedents established in employment discrimination case law that the use of standardized tests must be shown to be valid for the purpose at hand (in this instance the identification of mild mental retardation in black children) to avoid the inference of discrimination. Absent such showing, the court said, the use of tests that have adverse impact cannot be considered substantially related to a legitimate state purpose, and thus constitutes a denial of the equal protection of the laws.

By the time the case was tried on the merits (beginning in October 1977), two statutes had been passed that added some definition to the validation requirements: the Rehabilitation Act of 1973 and the Education of All Handicapped Children Act of 1975. At trial, the case was argued and the opinion reasoned very much in the mold of Title VII litigation. The analytical formula for apportioning the burden of proof established by *Griggs* was applied (see Wigdor in Part II). Plaintiffs presented statistical evidence that black children were placed in EMR classes in numbers much greater than their representation in the general student population. The court accepted this evidence of unequal selection as establishing the prima facie case, shifting the burden of proof to the school officials to rebut the presumption of discrimination.

As in the earlier proceeding, the court followed the employment testing guidelines requirement for an empirical showing of test validity; it found reliance on the general reputation of a test insufficient in the face of disproportionate impact. This holding is rather important, since schools have, by and large, relied upon commercially produced tests and have seldom undertaken local validation studies. Most school officials probably have not, until recently, thought to question the adequacy of the producer's validation research for their situation.

The crucial—and puzzling—conceptual question concerned the nature of the empirical showing: what, in the context of educational testing, takes the place of the job-relatedness doctrine in employment testing litigation? *Larry P.* did not provide clear guidance. The defendants attempted to establish the predictive validity of the intelligence tests by showing the correlation of those test scores with two criterion measures, achievement test scores and grades. (See Chapter 5 for a discussion of the merits of validating one sort of standardized test against another.) The court rejected this approach of translating the notion of predicting job performance to the educational context:

If tests can predict that a person is going to be a poor employee, the employer can legitimately deny that person a job, but if tests suggest that a young child is probably going to be a poor student, the school cannot on that basis alone deny the child the opportunity to improve and develop the academic skills necessary to success in our society. (p. 969)

The limited academic instruction in the special education classes, which emphasized social adjustment and economic usefulness, would make this a self-fulfilling prophecy.

One weakness of the defendants' (the schools) line of reasoning lies in their failure to distinguish between the role of business in a generally capitalist economy and the function of public education in a democratic society, which the Supreme Court in *Brown* v. *Board* described as "the very foundation of good citizenship" (347 U.S. 483, 493). The doctrine of job-relatedness includes the principle of business necessity, by which the courts have recognized that an employer's interest in productivity outweighs any particular individual's interest in getting a job (see *Larry P.*, p. 969). In education, there is no other interest competing with the educational needs of each child (except, perhaps, the educational needs of all children, which might, for example, justify the removal of an obstructive child from the classroom). Thus, while validation in the employment context has been understood by the courts to mean showing the relationship of the test to the job (or test scores to job performance), in *Larry P.* it is defined as showing the appropriateness of the test and placement decision to the specific educational needs of the child. The evidence of high correlations between intelligence test scores and school performance did not, in the eyes of the trial judge, justify placing the child in an environment in which the attempt at academic education would, for all practical purposes, cease.[18]

Had the defendants presented convincing evidence that there is in fact more mild mental retardation among black students, they might have rebutted the prima facie case, as indeed they could have by showing that the tests in question had been validated for the specific use on the specific population. But nothing in the evidence convinced the court that the tests were not culturally biased against black students and, therefore, differentially valid for black and white students. Since the meaning of the test

---

[18] He suggested that construct validation might be a more appropriate strategy than predictive or content validation (fn. 84).

scores was unknown for black children, the placement decisions were of necessity "irrational," and could not produce an "appropriate" education for them. In *Larry P.*, the school officials did not argue strenuously against the allegation of cultural bias; indeed, the court remarked that the cultural bias of the tests was hardly disputed in the litigation (p. 959). The opinion of the court is largely devoted to the question of what legal consequences flow from a finding of racial bias in the tests.[19]

A second major case involving the use of intelligence tests for placement of black pupils in special classes for the educable mentally retarded centered directly on the question of test bias. Contrary to the finding in the California case, in 1980 the trial court in *Parents in Action on Special Education* v. *Hannon* (Civil Number 74 C 3586) found the Wechsler tests and the Stanford-Binet substantially free of cultural bias. After examining the test item by item, the judge decided, on a common-sense basis, that only nine questions were troublesome on that account. Since the test scores were interpreted by masters-level school psychologists, a good number of whom were black, and since test scores were only one of the criteria for the placement decision, the court found it unlikely that those few items would result in misplacement of black children in the Chicago school system. The judge held that the tests, used in this manner, did not discriminate against black children in the Chicago public schools (p. 115).

Judicial interpretation of the obligations of school officials with regard to testing practices is still largely uncharted. It seems likely that the assessment of handicapped students will continue to be subject to close judicial scrutiny, given the special statutory protections afforded such students, but the standards for compliance with the law are not yet clear. At the very least, school officials are on notice that they must address questions of validation and impact. The unthinking or naive use of intelligence tests or other assessment devices to place children of linguistic or racial minority status in special education programs will not be defensible in court.

It is not clear that the federal courts will take on the same level of involvement in general school testing policies or move to extend the validation requirements of *Larry P.* to the use of standardized tests in making decisions about nonhandicapped students. Rebell and Block (1980:5.70) suggest that the use of intelligence tests to track students

---

[19] The judgment enjoined California from using any standardized intelligence tests without securing the prior approval of the court.

would be invalidated on a wide-ranging basis if the courts were to examine these practices as closely as they have scrutinized employment testing practices. But they have not done so, and they continue to show reluctance to interfere with educational policy. In *Berkelman* v. *San Francisco Unified School District* (501 F.2d 1264) in 1974, for example, the court upheld admission to the special academic high school on the basis of grades despite the adverse effect of the selection system on certain minority groups. It accepted the decision rule on the basis of its common-sense reasonableness (what in psychometric language is called face validity), pointing out that the situation was unlike *Larry P.* in that those not admitted to the academic high school suffered no harm.

The major case involving minimum competency testing, *Debra P.* v. *Turlington*,[20] suggests that some middle ground might be found with regard to test validity. This case was a class action suit brought by black Florida high school students challenging the state-mandated functional literacy test, which students had to pass as one condition for graduating. Plaintiffs based their charge on the disproportionate numbers of black students adversely affected by the test: 78 percent of black students failed the first time in comparison with 25 percent of white students.

Neither the district nor the appeals court took issue with the state plan to test for basic skills, to provide separate remedial instruction for a number of hours each day, and ultimately to tie graduation to passing the test. The circuit court opinion affirmed the traditional reluctance of the federal courts to get involved in state educational policy:

At the outset, we wish to stress that neither the district court nor we are in a position to determine educational policy in the State of Florida. The state has determined that minimum standards must be met and that the quality of education must be improved. We have nothing but praise for these efforts. (p. 402)

On the question of establishing the validity of the test, however, the district and circuit courts reached somewhat different conclusions. The district court found that the State Student Assessment Test II (SSAT II), which had been developed by the Educational Testing Service in accordance with objectives drawn up by the Florida Department of Education, was both valid and reliable. The court held that the state of the art in testing and measurement is not to be equated with the constitutional standards for Fourteenth Amendment due process and equal protection review; it restricted its probing to the limited question of whether the test

---

[20] 474 F. Supp. 244 (1979), 644 F. 2d 397 (1981).

"reasonably or arbitrarily evaluates the skill objectives established by the Board of Education" (p. 28).

On appeal, the circuit court accepted the finding that the test had adequate construct validity, saying that it does test functional literacy as defined by the Board of Education; it also affirmed the trial court's ruling that the functional literacy examination bears a rational relation to a valid state interest. But the appeals court did not find these holdings sufficient to satisfy equal protection considerations. The court ruled that the

. . . state administered a test that was, at least on the record before us, fundamentally unfair in that it *may* have covered matters not taught in the schools of the state. . . . (p. 404)

and sent the case back to the district court for investigation of that point. To be judged fair, the test would have to be demonstrated to be a test of material that was in fact taught in the classroom. This decision thus placed on the state of Florida the burden of proving what the court termed the "curricular validity" of the test.

While the requirement of curricular validity broadened somewhat the span of judicial oversight, the circuit court opinion was not cast in language that suggested a highly technical approach to the question of validity. The deference of the federal courts to the states' plenary powers over education and the constitutional standard under which most educational testing cases will be argued may well mean that the validation requirements imposed by the courts will not be as difficult to meet as has been the case in litigation involving employment tests. Most of the employment cases are tried under the standards of Title VII of the Civil Rights Act, which places a heavy burden of proof on the test user while relieving the plaintiff of the need to establish the user's intent. Since the Civil Rights Act was extended to governmental units in 1972, few employment cases have been argued under the less rigorous validation standards required of the test user by the Constitution.[21] As a result, *Washington v. Davis*, the leading constitutional case (see Wigdor in Part II) has had limited precedental value in employment testing cases.

It is possible, however, that the Davis case may be influential in many

---

[21] In *Washington* v. *Davis*, the Court rejected the claim that the constitutional standard for adjudicating claims of racial discrimination is identical to the standards applicable under Title VII. Title VII, "involves a more probing judicial review of, and less deference to, the seemingly reasonable acts of administrators and executives than is appropriate under the Constitution where special racial impact, without discriminatory purpose, is claimed. We are not disposed to adopt this more rigorous standard for the purpose of applying the Fifth and the Fourteenth Amendments in cases such as this." 426 U.S. 229, 247-8.

educational testing cases. It suggests that plaintiffs in such cases will have to make a showing of intent to discriminate; statistical evidence of disproportionate effects will not suffice to establish the prima facie case as it would under Title VII of the Civil Rights Act. School officials will face the burden of showing that a challenged testing program is rationally related to a legitimate state purpose, a burden that might well be satisfied by establishing the validity of a test on the basis of its reasonableness rather than a highly technical demonstration of validity. However, testing practices affecting students with handicaps (including, one suspects, minimum competency testing programs) will be subject to more rigorous statutory standards. Here the case law is contradictory: *Larry P.* portends strict judicial inspection of placement testing, while the Chicago case implies less rigor than has prevailed in most Title VII litigation. In summary, Title VII case law is providing the basic analytical structure for judicial interpretation of legal challenges to school testing programs, but it appears that there will not be judicial oversight of educational policy similar to the scope and intensity in employment cases—unless there is some further legislative mandate.

REFERENCES

American Psychological Association, American Educational Research Association, National Council on Measurement in Education (1966) *Standards for Educational and Psychological Tests and Manuals.* Washington, D.C.: American Psychological Association.

Brigham, C. C. (1923) *Study of American Intelligence.* Princeton, N.J.: Princeton University Press.

Brigham, C. C. (1930) Intelligence tests of immigrant groups. *Psychological Review* 37(2):158-165.

Cravens, H. (1978) *The Triumph of Evolution: American Scientists and the Heredity-Environment Controversy.* Philadelphia: University of Pennsylvania Press.

Cremin, L. A. (1964) *The Transformation of the School: Progressivism in American Education, 1876-1957.* New York: Random House, Vintage Books.

Dickson, V. E. (1924) *Mental Tests and the Classroom Teacher.* New York: World Book Co.

Fiss, O. M. (1971) A theory of fair employment laws. *The University of Chicago Law Review* 38(Winter):235-314.

Flanagan, J. C. (1973) *The Career Data Book: Results from Project Talent's Five-Year Follow-up Study.* Palo Alto, Calif.: American Institutes for Research.

Fuess, C. M. (1950) *The College Board: Its First Fifty Years.* New York: Columbia University Press.

Goslin, D. A. (1963) *The Search for Ability: Standardized Testing in Social Perspective.* New York: Russell Sage Foundation.

Gould, S. J. (1981) *The Mismeasure of Man.* New York: W. W. Norton and Co.

Hinrichs, J. R. (1969) Comparison of "real life" assessments of management potential with situational exercises, paper-and-pencil ability tests, and personality inventories. *Journal of Applied Psychology* 53(October): 425-432.

Hollingworth, H. L. (1916) *Vocational Psychology: Its Problems and Methods.* New York: D. Appleton and Co.

Knox, H. A. (1914) A scale, based on the work at Ellis Island, for estimating mental defect. *Journal of the American Medical Association* 62(March): 741-747.

Lawshe, C. H., and Balma, M. J. (1946) *Principles of Personnel Testing,* 2nd ed. New York: McGraw-Hill Book Co.

Link, H. C. (1919) *Employment Psychology: The Application of Scientific Methods to the Selection, Training and Grading of Employees.* New York: MacMillan Co.

Lopez, F. M. (1970) *The Making of a Manager: Guidelines to His Selection and Promotion.* New York: American Management Association.

Myrdal, G. (1944) *An American Dilemma: The Negro Problem and Modern Democracy.* New York: Harper and Brothers.

Pettigrew, T. (1964) Negro American intelligence. In *A Profile of the Negro American.* Princeton, N.J.: D. Van Nostrand Co.

President's Commission on Higher Education (1947). *Higher Education for American Democracy: Volume I, Establishing the Goals.* Washington, D.C.: U.S. Government Printing Office.

Rebell, M. A., and Block, A. R. (1980) Competence assessment and the courts: an overview of the state of the law. *The Assessment of Occupational Competence.* ERIC Document No. ED 192-169.

Robertson, P. C. (1976) A Staff Analysis of the History of EEOC Guidelines on Employee Selection Procedures. Unpublished document submitted to the General Accounting Office, August 29. Equal Employment Opportunity Commission, Washington, D.C.

Rose, D. (1976) Memorandum. Reprinted in the *Daily Labor Report,* June 22. Washington, D.C.: Bureau of National Affairs.

Sherman, S. W., and Robinson, N., eds. (1982) *Ability Testing of Handicapped People: Dilemma for Government, Science, and the Public.* Panel on Testing of Handicapped People, Committee on Ability Testing, National Research Council. Washington, D.C.: National Academy Press.

Spencer, L. M. (1959) What's the score now with psychological tests? *American Business* 29(October):7-10.

Stalnaker, J. M. (1979) Recognizing and encouraging talent. In D. L. Wolfe, ed., *The Discovery of Talent: Walter Van Dyke Bingham Lectures on the Development of Exceptional Abilities and Capacities.* Cambridge, Mass.: Harvard University Press.

Synnott, M. G. (1979) The admission and assimilation of minority students at Harvard, Yale, and Princeton, 1900-1970. *History of Education Quarterly* 19(Fall):290.

Terman, L. M., Lyman, G., Ordahl, G., Ordahl, L. E., Galbreath, N., and Talbert, W. (1917) The Stanford Revision and Extension of the Binet-Simon Scale. Educational Psychology Monographs #18. Baltimore: Warwick and York, Inc.

Tractenberg, P. L. (1979) State minimum competency programs: legal implications of minimum competency testing: Debra P. and beyond. Prepared for the National Institute of Education, NIE-G-79-0033.

Tyack, D. B. (1974) *The One Best System: A History of American Urban Education.* Cambridge, Mass.: Harvard University Press.

U.S. Congress (1967) *Notes and Working Papers Concerning the Administration of Programs Authorized Under Title V of the National Defense Education Act, As Amended.* Subcommittee on Education, Committee on Labor and Public Welfare, U. S. Senate. 90th Congress, 1st Session. Washington, D.C.: U.S. Government Printing Office.

U.S. Department of Health, Education, and Welfare (1978) *Annual Evaluation Report on Programs Administered by the U.S. Office of Education.* Office of Evaluation and Dissemination, Office of Education. Washington, D.C.: U.S. Department of Health, Education, and Welfare.

Wallin, J. E. W. (1914) *Mental Health of the School Child*. New Haven, Conn.: Yale University Press.

Wechsler, H. C. (1977) *The Qualified Student: A History of Selective College Admissions in America*. New York: John Wiley & Sons, Wiley-Interscience Publications.

Wiebe, R. (1967) *The Search for Order, 1877-1920*. New York: Hill and Wang.

Yerkes, R., ed. (1921) Psychological examining in the United States Army. *Memoirs of the National Academy of Sciences* XV. Washington, D.C.: U.S. Government Printing Office.

4
Employment Testing

INTRODUCTION

The single most important recent development in employment testing has been the involvement of the federal government in defining adequate testing procedures as a consequence of the Civil Rights Act of 1964. The imposition of successive agency guidelines and the hundreds of testing cases litigated attest to the vigor of the governmental interest in employee selection procedures as a major focus of the drive to eliminate discrimination in American society.

In the course of its investigations, the Committee on Ability Testing has seen evidence of widespread discomfort and confusion about federal requirements regarding the hiring and promotion of employees, particularly as that policy affects the use of tests and other assessment devices to distinguish among applicants. The Committee has also heard, although less frequently, that testing practice, when it has not been forced out of existence, has improved substantially since the advent of governmental oversight.

Employers, personnel managers, and industrial psychologists have filled the pages of their respective trade and professional journals in the last 15 years with information, advice, complaints, and queries about this governmental scrutiny. Private employers, the first to have felt the impact of federal involvement in the hiring process, express frustration at trying to respond to ambiguous and changing requirements. Public sector employers, especially police and fire departments, have seen their tests, ostensibly developed with federal equal employment opportunity policy in mind, repeatedly succumb to legal challenge.

The military, which has one of the largest systematic testing programs in the nation, has also felt the pressure of outside scrutiny of its testing and selection procedures, although for slightly different reasons. Congressional interest in the preparedness of the all-volunteer armed forces has raised the question of the technical adequacy of the Armed Services Vocational Aptitude Battery. The reluctance of the Department of Defense to allow outside inspection of its selection and placement procedures, a position made clear to this committee, is perhaps not surprising, given the rapidity and impact with which governmental regulatory activity has penetrated the private and civilian public sectors.

Federal oversight of hiring, promotion, and firing is in many respects well within the twentieth century pattern of regulation of business activity and labor conditions. The societal interest in preventing systematic discrimination in the job market against blacks, women, Hispanics, and other groups seems a logical extension of fair labor practices law. Some commentators have suggested that the extension of federal jurisdiction to selection practices is compelling on economic grounds, since to ostracize large segments of the potential labor pool on economically irrational grounds can only hamper productivity (Becker 1971). And, in today's world, the arduous record-keeping requirements effectively dictated by the compliance policies of the enforcing authorities are an expected product of federal oversight.

Despite this background, many observers feel that the federal entry into the hiring process to promote the integration of minorities and women into the work force has involved, in the years since 1964, a dramatic shift away from the individualism that has long provided the rationale of American economic and political life. They fear that the shift signals the disintegration of what they perceive as a traditional consensus on fundamental national values—equality of opportunity, equal justice, and the promotion of productivity. The substitution of group parity for individual endeavor as the organizing principle of the nation's economic life appears, from this point of view, to pervert the system in a misguided attempt to extend its benefits to all members of society. Furthermore, it seems inconsistent with accepted conceptions of constitutional law, which until recently did not recognize groups, but, defined the relationship of the individual to the polity.

Those who support the federal role—including many, but by no means all, members of the affected racial, ethnic, and gender groups—are impressed with past legal and social barriers to the promise of equality and with the sentiments that generated those barriers. The exclusion of blacks and women from most kinds of jobs was formerly based on their group identity; hence to many of them it does not seem a drastic break with tradition to implement Title VII of the Civil Rights Act of 1964 and Executive Order 11246 in such a way as to accord preferential status on the basis of membership in a particular group, despite the fact that the statutory language continues to refer to individuals. Proponents of this position argue that discrimination can be eliminated and the promise of our constitutional system fulfilled only when the excluded and powerless are drawn into all levels of economic activity in proportion to their numbers in society. That proportional status is viewed by some as the sole and sufficient indicator of equality of opportunity.

Federal involvement in the hiring process, and particularly the emphasis of the Equal Employment Opportunity Commission on compliance with standards for the use of tests and other assessment techniques, has quickened the clash over fundamental values by providing concrete situations for its actualization. One consequence has been to give employment testing a momentary importance far beyond its usual role in hiring and promotions. Another consequence has been to concentrate more and more social resources on tests (from development through litigation), which may or may not be efficient in terms of drawing minorities and women into the economic mainstream. Above all, federal involvement has substantially enlivened and complicated the question of the social effects of employment testing.

TEST USE BY SECTOR AND FUNCTION

Because of the paucity of data available to the committee, particularly for the private sector, it is impossible to do more than sketch in general outlines the use of tests by employers for purposes of personnel management. (For a documented description of current uses of employment testing, see Friedman and Williams in Part II.) Hence, our conclusions about many aspects of the social impact of such testing must be limited or tentative.

The extent of testing in employment situations can be depicted on a matrix combining three sectors—public, private, and joint—with three functions—entry-level selection, promotion, and certification. Table 4 illustrates the coincidence of sector and function. The public sector includes federal, state, and local civilian employers and the military. The private sector includes businesses, retail establishments, and manufacturers. What we call the joint sector is made up of those private trade and professional organizations and public entities that administer tests for the purposes of licensing and certification.

TABLE 4   Function of Testing by Sector

Sector	Entry-Level Selection	Promotion	Licensing and Certification
Private Sector	x	o	
Public Sector			
Military	x	x	
Civil Service	x	o	
Joint Sector			x

NOTE: x, heavy usage; o, light usage

The Public Sector

The Military

The locus of the most comprehensive and systematic testing for selection and placement is found in the federal service. All of the more than 2 million members of the armed forces on active duty, for example, will have taken at least one test battery to gain entry to the system and probably several more at key career points. Aptitude tests, while not the sole element in the selection process, function as the basic screening device in determining applicants' eligibility for enlisted duty, officer training, and flight training.

One of these, the Armed Services Vocational Aptitude Battery (ASVAB), is currently the most used employment test. In 1978, some 600,000 candidates took the test, and it was also administered to nearly 1 million high school seniors in the hope of bringing able candidates and military recruiters together. (The only other tests of comparable size are the SAT and ACT, both used for college admissions. Whatever other distinctions they may have, seniors in high school are certainly the most tested age group in our society.) In addition to its gate-keeping function, the ASVAB is used to channel enlistees into military occupational specialties. Composites drawn from ASVAB subtests, such as numerical operations, word knowledge, space perception, electronics information, mechanical comprehension, general science, and automotive information, are used by the individual services to assign personnel according to institutional needs.

Enlisted military personnel are, if not unique, then unusual in the frequency with which they encounter written tests on the road to advancement. Naval enlistees in grades E4-6, for example, are tested semiannually; in grades E7-9, annually. It is estimated that all the services together administer tests for promotion to about 1 million people per year, most of them in the enlisted ranks. Unlike the entry-level test batteries, the tests for promotion are specific to a job and are based on the Comprehensive Occupational Development and Analysis Program (CODAP), a servicewide job analysis program. By the end of 1981 the Army expects to have instituted 900 separate skill qualification tests.

The Civil Service

Civilian practice differs noticeably from that of the military in the use of tests for promotion. There has been little centralized development of tests for promotion in the civil service, and the committee has seen no evidence that individual agencies make significant use of tests for that purpose. Rather, the thrust of civil service testing has been found to be directed almost exclusively at entry-level screening.

There are approximately 2,800,000 employees in the federal civilian work force. Of that number, more than 90 percent work under some sort of merit system. The U.S. Office of Personnel Management (OPM, formerly the U.S. Civil Service Commission) has examining jurisdiction over a competitive service of 1,700,000 workers. Until the recent decentralization of examining functions instituted by the 1978 Civil Service Reform Act, OPM administered written tests to about 700,000 applicants per year, mostly for clerical and entry-level professional and administrative positions. (Mid-level and upper level professional registers are accessible through a structured rating of a candidate's education, training, work experience, and other background data, rather than through written tests.) The tests are offered at more than one thousand locations around the country at a cost of millions of dollars annually. Table 5 shows the number of written tests administered in six major job categories for 1974-1978, as well as the total number of "examinations," test and nontest.

If ability tests are charted on a continuum, with achievement tests at one end and aptitude tests at the other, most civil service tests would fall on the aptitude end of the line. There are some performance tests, for example, tests of typing skill and accuracy, and a few are job specific and measure prior learning, like librarianship, but most are general tests of cognitive abilities, with various kinds of verbal, arithmetic, and logical exercises. They are intended to predict how a candidate without much job experience will perform in a job that requires no specialized training, but does require relatively high cognitive ability levels.

The Professional and Administrative Career Examination (PACE), an examination for entry-level positions in the federal government, is typical of this sort of test. It is a generalized test in that it attempts to measure

TABLE 5 Workload Report for Federal Examinations: Number of Applications, Selections, and Veterans Selected

Time	Examinations Requiring Written Tests							All Federal Examinations
	Steno-typist	Other Clerical	Summer Employment	Technical Assistant	PACE	Air Traffic Controllers	Total	
Fiscal 1974								
Applications	275,201	184,213	60,788	69,630	187,569[a]	23,898	801,299	1,620,798
Selections	49,650	32,593	11,315	5,198	12,457[a]	1,809	113,022	237,278
Veterans Selected	1,747	2,953	334	1,486	3,988[a]	1,407	11,915	70,644
Fiscal 1975								
Applications	283,675	173,821	80,053	96,824	219,947	15,794	870,114	1,682,046
Selections	42,707	24,639	11,085	10,274	12,562	2,423	103,690	192,818
Veterans Selected	1,609	2,191	303	3,186	4,174	1,812	13,275	56,378
Fiscal 1976								
Applications	260,613	163,248	72,523	56,819[b]	235,333	14,686	931,519	1,676,936
Selections	36,823	23,343	8,967	5,147[b]	9,304	1,853	85,437	156,534
Veterans Selected	1,541	2,405	199	1,565[b]	2,619	1,304	9,633	42,948

Transition Quarter 1976[c]								
Applications	60,051	43,784	1,553	12,920	23,361	4,933	146,612	348,547
Selections	9,090	4,746	3,798	1,351	2,303	390	21,678	39,491
Veterans Selected	460	587	54	407	744	316	2,568	11,039
Fiscal 1977								
Applications	256,789	175,382	65,430	56,236	219,210	18,229	791,276	1,671,119
Selections	34,455	18,724	7,860	5,085	6,748	1,728	74,600	151,614
Veterans Selected	1,672	2,177	151	1,394	2,095	1,213	8,702	44,781
Fiscal 1978								
Applications	253,159	176,520	45,111	34,380	166,440	13,055	688,665	1,616,178
Selections	37,208	21,591	d	5,221	7,587	2,294	73,935	152,771
Veterans Selected	1,853	2,480	d	1,435	2,072	1,615	9,455	41,610

[a] Figures are from the predecessor Federal Service Entrance Exam (FSEE).
[b] Data are estimated.
[c] Fiscal 1976 ended June 30, 1976; fiscal 1977 began October 1, 1976.
[d] Data not available.

SOURCE: Campbell (1979:17).

skills and aptitudes relevant to many occupations—118 in this case—rather than to a single job. OPM describes this approach as "broad-band examining." In developing the test, OPM researchers concluded that there were six abilities or constructs that were important in predicting performance in the professional and administrative occupations covered by the exam: verbal ability, judgment, induction, deduction, number (arithmetical reasoning), and memory. The test was designed to measure the first five of these; memory was dropped because of a lack of sufficient research on how the ability can be adequately assessed (Campbell 1979).

The PACE was designed to measure certain mental characteristics (constructs) of applicants rather than their performance on specific job tasks. But federal compliance efforts for equal employment opportunity have been task oriented. Both the Equal Employment Opportunity Commission guidelines on employee selection procedures and the job-relatedness requirements established by the case law address the tasks or elements that compose a job, not the characteristics of the worker. This disjunction between the design of generalized aptitude tests like the PACE and the performance-oriented expectations of the compliance authorities has not been fully explored by the interested parties, but it seems that the generalized or broad-band approach to employment testing is going to be abandoned.

In 1979, a number of individuals and organizations brought suit against the director of OPM on the grounds that the PACE had an adverse impact on black and Hispanic applicants. The agency had already recognized that the PACE tended to screen out black and Hispanic applicants and had, during the Carter administration, emphasized alternative routes into the entry-level professional and administrative positions covered by the PACE; the agency estimated that only 35 percent of such positions were being filled by competitive examination in 1979, and that the overall hiring statistics were in line with equal employment opportunity goals.[1] Nevertheless, the government did not defend the test in court, and, by a consent decree negotiated late in the Carter administration and concluded in the early months of the Reagan administration in 1981, agreed to eliminate the PACE over a period of 3 years. If the negotiated settlement is accepted by the court, OPM and the hiring agencies will henceforth have to administer separate examinations for most of the current PACE

[1] In discussions with representatives of this committee, Alan Campbell, then director of OPM, emphasized a policy of combining the PACE with alternate routes like internships and upward mobility programs as a means of reaching desired minority employment goals while retaining the benefits of the PACE. The two together, he felt, were producing a qualified professional work force.

job categories (consent decree in *Luevano* v. *Campbell*). While this does not rule out a construct approach, the efficiencies of generalized testing will have been lost to the government and to applicants. Applicants will have to take tests for each type of professional and administrative position that interests them.

The testing programs used by the military and within the federal competitive service are research based. The U.S. Department of Defense and each of the armed services has a research staff carrying on a continuous process of test development and validation. Similarly, the Office of Personnel Management, which until 1979 had jurisdiction over approximately two-thirds of the federal work force, has a staff of 80 at work on the sixty-three standardized tests used to fill entry-level positions in 300 occupations.

This research-based approach stands in contrast to much private sector employment testing. Although a number of companies, including Sears, Roebuck & Co. and EXXON, have traditionally conducted in-house research to develop tests and keep track of their effectiveness, the more common pattern in smaller companies, at least until the Supreme Court prescribed the job-relatedness requirement, was to buy a a commercial product and assume the test's effectiveness in a given situation. In educational testing, too, most users of standardized educational tests buy them from commercial publishers and do not validate them for local use.

State and Local Merit Systems

The major users of tests in the public sector at the federal level have been able to support elaborate psychometric establishments because they are large employers. They are also less tied to the balance sheet than most private employers, which has contributed to the stability of their programs. Neither of these conditions obtains in state and local jurisdictions, where the pattern of test use—and the quality of the instruments—is far more variable. The New York State Department of Civil Service, for example, in administering the state merit system, serves more than 100 state and local jurisdictions. It uses more than 5,000 examinations to test one-quarter million candidates annually (Wright 1978), but has just one Ph.D. level research psychologist in its test development section. There is no research department; rather, the staff makes use of research done by others and for other purposes, usually in an industrial or academic setting. And New York is a large state: it seems safe to assume that not many localities can afford to support a professional staff for test development and research. They must look to the states for assistance or buy tests from private organizations like the International Personnel Management Association, which develops and validates written tests for a number of commonly occurring occupations including fire fighters and police officers.

Information about the use of tests in state and local personnel systems can be gleaned from two studies, one published in 1971 by the National Civil Service League (Rutstein 1971), the other a joint study by the Office of Personnel Management and the Council of State Governments published in 1979. In both cases, the response rate for the states was high and for the localities, very low. Tables 6 and 7, drawn from the two surveys, indicate the incidence of written testing for different occupations and levels of government. They show that written tests are used most often for office and clerical workers and least often for unskilled workers and those in the category of "trades and labor." The surveys reveal the percentage of respondents who use tests to fill at least some jobs in particular categories, but not the percentage of positions for which tests are used within each category.

Most positions in the civilian public sector at the federal, state, and local levels are part of a system of competitive service. Hiring procedures are governed by legislatively mandated merit principles. Although the specifics of the systems vary from jurisdiction to jurisdiction, the principle that is common to all of them is that public employment shall be open to all on an equal basis and that selection of the most able candidate shall take place through fair and open competition.

Typically, merit systems involve a more or less stringent application of the so-called rule of three. The top three candidates, ranked by a test

TABLE 6   Use of Written Tests in State and Local Governments

| | Government Level | | | | | |
| | State Governments | | Local Governments | | Total Sample | |
Kind of Job	Yes	Number Responding	Yes	Number Responding	Yes	Number Responding
Unskilled	48%	(33)	34%	(268)	35%	(301)
Skilled	50%	(40)	68%	(282)	66%	(322)
Office	98%	(43)	84%	(288)	88%	(331)
Administrative, professional, or technical	93%	(43)	61%	(287)	65%	(330)

SOURCE: Rutstein (1971).

TABLE 7   Use of Written Tests in State and Local Governments by
Occupation

	Government Units		
Occupations	States	Counties	Cities
Clerical	89.6% (43)	46% (64)	54% (55)
Trades and labor	52.1% (25)	4% (6)	35% (35)
Professional	79.2% (38)	25% (35)	33% (33)
Technical	83.3% (40)	31% (43)	43% (43)
Management and administrative	58.3% (28)	16% (22)	26% (27)

NOTE: These data represent the percentage of respondents who use tests to fill at least some jobs in each category, but do not reveal the percentage of positions tested for within each category.
SOURCE: U.S. Office of Personnel Management and The Council of State Governments (1979). Additional unpublished data compiled from the survey was made available to the Committee by the Council of State Governments.

score or by a composite rating based on some combination of assessments (written test, oral test, interview, performance appraisal, rating of training and experience, etc.), are taken from the register of all eligible candidates for consideration by the prospective employer. Because such rank ordering of candidates is a legal obligation under most merit systems, the federal pressure to institute a representative work force has created a tension of contrary legal obligations. As a result, the courts are being drawn more and more into the business of overseeing hiring practices.

The Private Sector

There is no body of systematic data on the private sector from which to estimate the nature and extent of its use of tests. A study of private employment practices prepared for this committee (Friedman and Williams in Part II) reports a complete lack of information on such matters as the percentage of jobs filled through testing in any category or in any industry. Moreover, the available evidence on test use reveals little in the way of standard practice, so it is difficult to generalize about validation techniques, modes of job analysis, or other procedures. As in the case of hiring in the public sector at the state and local levels, it is extremely difficult to gauge the quality of the tests or the people who develop, validate, or use them. It is not even possible to determine whether the tests used tend to be aptitude or achievement tests.

Survey evidence indicates that the use of written tests for employee selection is less widespread in the private that in the public sector, although the size of the private sector means that a much larger number of people are tested. The most extensive such survey, that conducted in 1975 by Prentice-Hall and the American Society of Personnel Administrators (hereafter referred to as P-H Survey), reveals that an important variable in the distribution of test use is, as might be expected, size of employing companies. Medium and large companies are more likely than small companies to use tests—and other means of assessment—for purposes of selection, placement, training, or promotion. Size of company is also a significant factor in determining the source of the test ("homemade," commercial, or professionally developed in-house), the qualifications of the people involved in the company testing program, and the presence of on-site job analyses, validation studies, and other checks on the adequacy of the test. Once again, larger firms are more likely to have trained personnel specialists running their testing programs. Small firms, particularly those with less than 500 employees, tend not to test, and when they do, to make up tests according to commonsense rules or to buy tests from commercial publishers. The tests are administered and interpreted by the personnel office staff. Table 8, which is based on several P-H Survey tables as well as further information provided by Prentice-Hall, summarizes the data concerning the amount of test use, the source of the tests, the involvement of trained psychologists, and the extent of validation attempts.

Despite the paucity of data on test use in the private sector, the survey evidence confirms casual observation in showing that testing is most frequently used for personnel decisions in the clerical occupations (secretarial, bookkeeping, typing, cashier). Since clerical workers constitute not only the largest but the fastest-growing occupational group in the work force—a 29 percent increase to a total of 20 million workers is projected for 1976-1985—testing of this range of job skills is likely to become even more commonplace.

The survey data also indicate that tests are more widely used in nonmanufacturing businesses, such as public utilities, banks, insurance companies, retail sales, and communications, than by manufacturers. A survey of testing practices conducted by the Bureau of National Affairs (Miner 1976a:8) revealed that, of the companies that use tests, more than 80 percent use them for office positions, while only 20 percent use them for production jobs and 10 percent for sales and service jobs. In general, then, lower-level white collar workers are most likely to encounter written tests, and within that group, clerical workers experience by far the most testing.

We turn now from limited survey data on the extent of testing in the private sector to the specific example of a single large firm that has made

TABLE 8   Testing (Percent) in the Public Sector by Size of Company

	Number of Employees						
	1-99	100-499	500-599	1,000-5,000	5,000-10,000	10,000-25,000	25,000+
Use tests	39	51	55	60	67	62	61
Source of tests:							
In-house	60.9	23.7	24.3	24.3	20.4	23.1	28[a]
Hybrid	21.7	26.8	26.5	34.7	38.6	30.7	42
Outside	17.4	49.5	49.2	41.0	41.0	46.2	30[a]
Use of specialists[b]							
Fulltime psychologist	11.1	11.4	15.6	11.8	33.3	37.5	55.6
Consulting psychologist	33.3	44.3	39.3	49.1	—	50.0	—
No use of psychologist	44.4	27.8	23.8	22.2	12.8	9.4	7.4
Validate tests	17	20	25	30	40	60	67

[a]Revised figure; published figure was misprinted.
[b]Percentages for this question do not add up to 100 percent; other sources of expertise may be used or no source at all.

SOURCE: Data from Prentice-Hall (1975) and unpublished data from Prentice-Hall.

a serious commitment to objective selection through mental measurement, Sears, Roebuck & Co.[2] Sears uses a great variety of employment tests to measure characteristics ranging from concrete clerical skills (like the ability to alphabetize) to the more elusive "executive personality." The Sears research-based, custom-made testing program dates from the late 1930s, when the company called upon the prominent psychometrician, L. L. Thurstone, to develop a battery of psychological tests to aid in the selection of executives. Convinced that selection was thereby improved, Sears went on in 1950 to establish a psychological research department to handle the selection, placement, and evaluation of all Sears employees. Over the years, the research staff developed test batteries for the selection and placement of employees in the firm's major

[2] Spokesmen from the company participated in the Committee's open hearings. They described the basic functions of the company's psychometric division and submitted research reports on a variety of testing programs. The statement of V. Jon Bentz to the Committee on Ability Testing, November 17, 1978, is available from the Committee.

job categories: retail sales, technical service personnel (auto mechanics: tune up, front end, and brakes), clerical personnel (including 32 catalog merchandise distribution center specialties), data processing, and, moving away from specialized functions, executive and managerial personnel. These batteries normally include both aptitude and achievement tests. The Sears research staff has also undertaken studies of the predictive relationships between general ability tests and later promotions as a means of identifying and channeling capable employees toward higher-level jobs. Most of the testing programs have involved traditional procedures. Of late, however, executive assessment has included some of the newer devices that are frequently suggested as alternatives to written tests, such as simulations of job situations with in-basket routines or group interactions to sample such executive behavior as problem solving, leadership, or creativity.

An elaborate testing program of this kind, involving job analysis, test development, and a continuing process of validation by a resident research staff, requires a substantial commitment of resources and is possible only for large companies. In some instances, it has been found economically advantageous for companies in the same business (for example, insurance) to form consortia for the purpose of developing and validating tests.[3] But, by and large, programs of the extent and quality of the Sears program are beyond the means of most employers. Except for large public and private employers, most test use is not research based. Under pressure of the federal *Uniform Guidelines on Employee Selection Procedures*, more employers are attempting to validate their tests. The typical amount being spent, however, suggests that many of the studies are not comprehensive (Friedman and Williams in Part II).

Finally, in the private sector, tests are also used by the labor unions. As is the case elsewhere, testing practice varies tremendously among the unions. Many do not test at all; others, such as the building trades, have made extensive use of tests to screen entry into apprenticeship programs. These tests have been frequently and successfully challenged on Title VII grounds.

The Joint Sector

Tests used for the purpose of licensing and certification are administered under the auspices of private organizations, public entities, or some com-

---

[3] The legal status of such efforts is not clear, although the use of multijurisdictional fire fighters examinations was upheld in the U.S. Court of Appeals for the Fourth Circuit (*Friend* v. *Leidinger*, 1978).

bination of the two (as in the case of bar examinations). Whatever the source of regulation, the result is that access to certain occupations is limited to those who fulfill the requirements set by the certifying body.

Occupational licensing is largely the province of the states, although there is some local and federal involvement. Theoretically, states control occupational and professional licensing as an exercise of their police power, that is, for the protection of the public health, safety, or welfare. Actually, the reasons are very complicated and involve a number of factors beyond the fairly obvious consumer interests or guild impulses that bring pressure to bear on legislatures. The explosion of licensing laws in the health fields, for example, is a response not only to the multitude of new technologies requiring workers with new skills, but to the insurance companies' policy of requiring that a practitioner be licensed as a condition for reimbursement for medical services (Hogan 1978).

The health field has not been alone in experiencing a proliferation of licensing laws in the last 20 years or so. In 1950, 73 occupations were licensed in one or more states; by 1969, the number had risen to more than 500. A recent U.S. Department of Labor study (Hogan, n.d.) puts the figure today at 800 occupations, and it suggests that in some states 25 percent of the work force is composed of licensed practitioners. Entry to about 500 of these occupations depends on passing a written examination, among other requirements.

In California for the year 1978-1979, some 30 licensing boards and bureaus reported administering written tests to 110,000 examinees in such fields as cosmetology, behavioral science, embalming, pharmacy, and small appliance repair. In 1979, the state of New York tested 55,473 candidates for entry into 30 occupations, and Florida, about half that many (Friedman and Williams in Part II).

Nongovernmental certifying bodies also use written tests for certification. Although the total number of certification tests given each year is unknown, the following figures for 1979 give some sense of the range of activity: 75,000 tests for automobile mechanic; 12,000 for respiratory therapists/technologists; 4,000 for shorthand reporters; 600 for placement counselors; and 450 tests for computer programmers (Friedman and Williams in Part II).

The quality of the tests used for licensing and certification is difficult to ascertain, but clearly is highly variable. The tests are usually prepared by licensing board members, most of whom are members of the licensed profession who have been appointed to board membership by a state official, with the recommendation of their professional organization. Such tests are not likely to satisfy the technical standards of psychometricians,

TABLE 9 Washington, D.C., Licensing Board Requirements

Board	Testing Required	Use Nationwide Test	Origin of Test
Certified Public Accountants	yes	no	American Institute, N.Y.
Architects	yes	no	Educational Testing Service (ETS)
Barbers	yes	no	homemade
Cosmetologists	yes	no	homemade
Dentists and dental hygienists	yes	no	Northeast Regional Exam
Electricians	yes	no	homemade
Funeral directors and embalmers	yes	no	Conference of Funeral Service Examining Boards
Healing arts and medical doctors	yes	yes	Federal Licensing Examination Board
Nursing home administrators	yes	no	Professional Examining Service (PES)
Optometrists	yes	no	homemade
Pharmacistss	yes	no	Nat'l Assoc. of Boards of Pharmacy
Physical therapists	yes	no	PES
Plumbers	yes	no	homemade
Podiatrists	yes	yes	homemade
Practical nurses	yes	no	Nat'l League for Nursing
Professional engineers	yes	no	Nat'l Council of Engineering Examiners
Psychologists	yes	no	PES
Real estate salespersons and brokers	yes	no	ETS
Refrigeration and air conditioning mechanics	yes	no	homemade
Registered nurses	yes	no	Nat'l League for Nursing
Steam and other operating engineers	yes	no	homemade
Veterinarians	yes	yes	PES

NOTE: This table includes all occupations regulated by the District of Columbia Occupational and Professional Licensing Division.

although they might well be carefully crafted from a commonsense point of view. It is impossible to judge their adequacy except on a case-by-case basis.

A few professions use nationwide tests developed by commercial testing companies. A survey by one testing company of nearly 100 licensing officials in 30 states found national tests psychometrically superior to locally prepared tests. Because national tests are prepared by testing specialists, they are more likely to be based on a job analysis and developed with an eye to clarity of wording, maintenance of difficulty level from year to year, and other technical considerations (Shimberg 1976).

There are some experts, however, who question the adequacy of even professionally developed occupational tests insofar as they measure skills more closely related to academic achievement than to job performance as the indicator of professional competence. Proponents of this point of view argue that the usual description of licensing tests as "job-specific" or "job-related" achievement tests is misleading. A measure of job-related knowledge, they assert, is only a surrogate and, in occupations with a low verbal content, perhaps a poor surrogate for actual performance in situations equivalent to those posed by the job (Pottinger 1979, Pottinger et al. 1980). There is not yet enough evidence to evaluate this assertion.

Formal validation studies of the kind set forth in the *Uniform Guidelines* are not a typical licensing board activity. This is perhaps partly because the Civil Rights Act of 1964 is not believed to extend to most licensing and certification authorities, since they are usually not subsumed under the Title VII categories of "employers, employment agencies, and labor unions," or the Title VI category of government contractors. (See Friedman and Williams in Part II) for a discussion of this point.) When validation studies are done, they are usually done for the boards by the commercial suppliers of the tests. In the District of Columbia, for example, all 22 licensing boards require a written test: 8 of them (36 percent) make up their own tests, while 14 (64 percent) purchase the tests from a professional testing service (see Table 9). Both test validation and, if necessary, compliance with the *Uniform Guidelines* are considered the responsibility of the testing company by those boards that purchase tests. Neither activity is undertaken by the boards that make up their own tests.[4]

---

[4] Telephone interview (April 15, 1980) with the head of the Applications Branch and former head of the Examinations Branch of the District of Columbia License and Inspection Bureau. Incidentally, none of the boards records information on applicants' race, sex, or ethnicity.

THE RATIONALE FOR TEST USE

Ability tests perform a variety of functions in the employment context, from screening and classification to certification and career guidance. Underlying all of these functions is a set of assumptions—historical, economic, and scientific—that create the rationale for using tests. This rationale has been expounded over many years in psychological, business, and personnel management literature.

Why Select?

At the center of the rationale is the economic self-interest of the employer. It is assumed that, under specified conditions, a selected group of workers will do a better job than an unselected one by reducing the employer's costs, increasing productivity, or both. From a broader perspective, a more efficient "selected" work force is believed to be in the national interest because it results in greater overall productivity and optimum utilization of workers.

Selection specialists have long postulated a kind of calculus of increased productivity to be derived from "scientific selection." Its logic was summarized by Haire (1956:115):

Fortunately it has recently become possible to state accurately how much better such a selected population *can* be. The improvement we can hope for depends on three things. All other things being equal, the improvement that comes from a selected population depends on (1) the goodness (validity) of the test battery, (2) the number of people we can afford to reject after testing, and (3) the range of performance in our unselected work group.

In other words, if the information derived from the assessment of applicants has little relationship to differences in performance, collecting that information yields no net economic advantage. Likewise, if it is necessary to hire anyone who applies in order to have the requisite number of workers, as is the case in some manufacturing establishments, there can be no selection. Finally, unless there is considerable variation in performance among workers, little or nothing can be gained from trying to select the better performers. But if the three conditions are met and if the selection procedures cost less than the value of the increased efficiency, then, according to the proponents of scientific selection, measurable increases in productivity will ensue.

Recent theorists, in reaction to the perceived threat to meritocratic selection posed by some federal equal employment opportunity and affirmative action policies, have attempted to calculate the relationship between productivity levels and particular selection procedures in concrete work settings. Some have attempted to express in dollars the loss in productivity to be expected when objective selection procedures are abandoned in favor of less objective practices. Schmidt et al. (1979), for example, estimate that hundreds of millions of dollars in lost productivity are at stake. Others, while feeling that dollar estimates are premature, agree that qualification of objective selection for policy reasons will have a negative effect on productivity.

Why Test for Selection?

Ever since the advent of industrial psychology early in this century, tests have been a favored tool for personnel selection. Although the fate of written tests involved in Title VII litigation has sent industrial psychologists on the search for less vulnerable alternatives in recent years, mental measurement continues to dominate thinking about matching people and jobs as efficiently as possible. The application of psychometrics to problems of employment selection found ready acceptance in this country at least in part because it was grafted onto the somewhat earlier British and American movement for a competitive civil service, chosen by examination and on the basis of talent, rather than on the basis of family or political connection. This wedding of movements served to tone down the authoritarian elements evident in the work of early leaders in psychometrics like Hugo Münsterberg, Harvard professor and founder of industrial psychology (Hale 1980), and clothed scientific testing with the mantle of democratic values.

As we discussed in Chapter 3, the Civil Service Act of 1883 instituted a system of written examinations, open to everyone and designed to be of a practical character. The basic principle of the competitive service was impartial, disinterested selection on the basis of merit, which the 1883 Act defined as "capacity and fitness" for the position (5 USC 3304). Over the years, these have grown to be very popular values. An explanation of the competitive system written in 1940 gives a sense of the feeling with which they have been invested (U.S. Civil Service Commission 1940:85):

There is no more democratic institution in this country than the open competitive examination. Under it rich and poor, society leaders and students, intellectuals and "low-brows" compete for Government employment on the sole basis of character and ability to do the work. American citizens may differ in wealth, in race, or in social station, but they are equal before the law, and they receive equal treatment in the examinations of the United States Civil Service Commission.

To the hopes for a meritocracy, psychometrics added the promise of scientific certainty, or, rather, of a controlled procedure with a known margin of error. Psychologists made the claim—and many have come to accept it—that they could develop tests for employers that would measure applicants' abilities with great accuracy and thereby allow the employer to predict, for a group of applicants, their comparative likelihood of success in a given position. Impartial selection on the basis of fitness for the job thus became a function of the validity of the testing instrument.

The fundamental justification for the use of psychometrics in worker selection lies in the claim that objective measurement is superior to subjective decision making. But not everyone, not even all psychologists, agrees with that claim, even as an abstract proposition. And it is worth noting that employers, whether or not they make use of tests, use the traditional informal interview as an important element in the selection process (Prentice-Hall Inc. 1979:4). Still, objectivity is attractive in the conditions typical of modern mass society, in which all are strangers to one another, and the old signals provided by speech patterns, dress, family connection, or social class are no longer acceptable bases of judgment. Certainly the opinion prevails among industrial psychologists that tests are more valid than alternative procedures such as interviews and letters of recommendation (Reilly and Chao 1980). A fairly sizable research literature in psychology supports the profession's doubts about the reliability of human judgment in comparison with tests (e.g., Dawes 1979, Goldberg 1970, Meehl 1954), but most writers on testing—and the committee agrees—advise that human judgment plays a role even when test scores are the primary source of information about applicants.

Another element in the rationale for test use is the promise of more efficient screening and selection at lower cost. Employment testing came into being as part of a larger movement to rationalize industry. This impulse to streamline operations, to find out more with fewer questions, is still evident in the advertising of commercial test publishers. Moreover, that impulse is the main force behind some of the most important current program development work, in particular the recent attempts by the Office of Personnel Management to develop computer-assisted testing (tailored testing[5]) of basic cognitive skills for entry-level positions. Before abandoning the research due to budget cuts (the Department of Defense is now doing the major work in the area), OPM had forecast that tailored tests with high predictive validity could eventually be developed that

---

[5] So called because the test taker's answer to a question determines the level of difficulty and direction of the next one.

would measure a single ability with as few as five to twenty questions, representing an 80 percent reduction in the number of questions required for comparably reliable measurement on conventional paper-and-pencil tests (Urry 1977).

In addition to impartiality, validity, efficiency, and lowered costs, the rationale for testing includes the belief that tests will uncover talents that would otherwise go undiscovered. Strauss and Sayles (1960:442), for example, find a major advantage of tests to be that

. . . they may uncover qualifications and talent which would not be detected by interviews or listings of education and job experience. Tests seek to eliminate the possibility that the prejudice of the interviewer or supervisor, instead of potential ability, will govern selection decisions.

This argument appears to have genuine merit, which should not be obscured by current controversies about testing.

Finally, the *appearance* of impartiality and objectivity that employment tests impart has been cited as a justification for their use. This reason for the utility of tests is discussed by Yoder (1948:215):

. . . tests are obviously a convenient device for selection because they are relatively inoffensive. The applicant who is turned down tends to blame himself rather than the receptionist or the interviewer. That explains part of their present popularity. Another part is unquestionably due to the fact that test scores seem to represent quantitative, numerical measures of manpower. Administrators are used to such terms; they like and are impressed by numerical statements. Whether the measures thus derived are either reliable or significant for the purpose may make little difference.

Today, of course, one cannot be as optimistic as Yoder was about the reaction to the test of the unsuccessful applicant. Indeed, one of the beneficial side effects of Title VII testing litigation has been to encourage a more critical appraisal of apparently neutral devices for the allocation of opportunity. Under pressure of complaints from test takers, a greater number of test users have learned to ask for information about test validity.

BASIC QUESTIONS OF VALIDITY AND VALUE

With the exception of the point made by Yoder, justification of the use of tests as an important element in employment decisions assumes adherence to the canons of acceptable testing practice. Yet, as V. Jon Bentz, head of the Psychological Research and Services Division of Sears, Roebuck & Co. informed the committee (Bentz 1978:30):

Validity research takes place in an incredibly complicated milieu, where such scientific necessities as control and standardization are extremely difficult to achieve. The attention that needs to be given to criterion and test development, the analysis and interpretation of data, are all arduous in the extreme, calling for very high-level quantitative skills and powers of abstraction.

In view of scientific standards, on one hand, and government policies, on the other, two basic questions arise. The first of these is essentially technical: Can tests measure required skills and abilities? The second is political: Should they be used even when they do? The remainder of this chapter is devoted to providing some answers to the first question and exploring the implications of the second question.

Can Tests Measure Required Skills and Abilities?

We discuss this question of validity, not in terms of what is possible for the research scientist to accomplish in the controlled conditions of the laboratory, but rather in terms of what is most likely to be the case in actual employment settings. The answer depends in part on the complexity of the job for which a test is to be developed. Some test tasks are very close to the content of the job for which they are used. When there is such a close link between test and job, particularly when the relationship is concrete and readily perceived, the chances are good that a test can be developed that is an adequate distillation—sampling—of the job. (It should be emphasized, however, that not all tests that look valid are valid. Face validity, or the apparent reasonableness of a test, can be deceptive; only the validity of a test that has been subjected to careful research can be depended on.)

Clerical positions are the jobs for which there is widest testing because they are among those jobs most amenable to testing. Tests of keyboard skills, written English, reading comprehension, alpha/numeric order, computation, ability to spot errors, and so forth are relatively easy to develop and are not terribly vulnerable to user misinterpretation. This type of test, therefore, is likely to be useful even in organizations that cannot support a highly sophisticated assessment program. And, because the reasonableness (face validity) of a test contributes to its appearance of fairness, this type of test is likely to be accepted by workers and applicants. There has been little litigation involving clerical tests and no successful challenge of a typing test.

Development of tests intended to measure highly abstract job skills like judgment is obviously a far more complicated endeavor, and such tests are more open to question. One difficulty stems from the role of language skills in tests, for example, in the tests for police officers or fire fighters. The conception of intelligence or ability in traditional mental measurement is based on written or formal language. The linguistic demands of the usual paper-and-pencil test may well reduce its predictive power when the job in question does not demand great verbal facility. To the extent that this is so, the tests document lack of facility with English but not necessarily lack of ability to perform well on the job in question. A similar situation exists when training for a job requires more verbal facility than is needed on the job. As we note in Chapter 7, high test scores are significant, while low scores may or may not be meaningful. This is a principle that employers and personnel managers should keep constantly in mind in order to avoid erecting unnecessary barriers to employment.

The most extensive review to date of research on test validation was done by Ghiselli (1966), who searched the published and unpublished literature from 1919 to 1964. He reported validity coefficients averaging just less than .25 for tests of intellectual ability, perceptual accuracy, and personality used in selecting executives and administrators. He reported similar validities for tests of intellectual, spatial, and mechanical abilities used for foreman positions.[6]

In retail sales, Ghiselli reported interesting contrasting data relative to

---

[6] A validity coefficient is a number used to express the relation between performance on a test and performance on a criterion measure; see Chapter 2.

The interpretation of the results of test validation studies rests on the interpretation of the statistic usually used to express the degree of relationship between two variables. That statistic is the Pearson product moment coefficient of correlation, usually denoted by r. In studies of the validity of tests for employment selection, r seems to have been a satisfactory measure of relationship. It is an index number and not to be confused with a proportion. It can take on values from $+1.00$ to -1.00. A value of zero indicates that the two variables of concern display no systematic linear relation. The more closely r approaches either of its two extreme values, the stronger is the linear relationship between the two variables.

Much attention is usually given to the statistical significance of an observed r—can one conclude that it differs from zero? While appropriate attention must be given to the sampling uncertainties of r, especially for small samples, the test of its difference from zero is not as important as the question of whether the magnitude of r allows useful prediction of one variable, given the value of the other variable. Here, a reasonable way to proceed is to calculate a confidence interval (r_a, r_b, with $r_a < r_b$) from the observed r and the sample size, and then ask the question of useful prediction for both r_a and r_b. If r_a is large enough to give useful prediction, useful predictability has been established. If r_b is too small for useful prediction, there is not useful prediction. If neither of these holds, the sample size is inadequate to answer the question.

The question of just what is useful prediction has been a subject of some debate. Early interpretations (e.g., Garrett 1933) equated useful prediction with large values of r^2, the proportion of the variance of one variable (the criterion) that could be accounted for by the other variable (the selection test). However, Brogden (1946) demonstrated that the utility of a test for selection is proportional to r rather than to r^2. This interpretation higher-level and lower-level sales personnel. For sales clerks, tests of intellectual ability have shown no validity for predicting job proficiency; personality tests (not a subject of this study) are more useful, with validities averaging about .35. For higher-level sales positions, the validities are the other way: tests of intellectual ability have average validities of about .31, and personality tests of about .27.

Ghiselli summarized his work as indicating that for all occupations, the average validity of employment tests for predicting success in a training program is .30; for predicting proficiency on the job, the coefficient drops to .19. The difference of about .11 in favor of training criteria holds for nearly all of the major occupational groups. This difference in predictive power is not uniform for all types of tests, however. It appears that intellectual, spatial, and mechanical abilities—as measured by tests—have higher validity coefficients for predicting success in training than for predicting job success, while tests of perceptual accuracy and motor abilities are about equally important in both.

It is probable that Ghiselli's average figures are somewhat lower than the coefficients a survey of current test use would provide, given the pressure of government policy and consequent interest of employers in tightening up their selection procedures. In the petrochemical industry, for example, correlation coefficients of up to .60 between various selection tests and qualification tests at the end of training have been reported to the committee (Carron 1978:231). Ghiselli himself did a second, smaller study of standardized tests used in personnel selection in 1973; for 21 job categories, he reported average validities of .45 for training criteria and .35 for job performance criteria. And it is important to remember that the coefficients underrate the usefulness of tests because the data come from employees and not from the unscreened applicant pool.

In summary, it is clear that the typical coefficients of correlation be-

---

is consistent with most modern treatments of employee selection, e.g., Cronbach and Gleser (1965).

Taylor and Russell (1939) showed that the usefulness of a test with a given validity depends not only on the value of r, but also on the success ratio and the selection ratio. The success ratio is the proportion of successful employees on the job when no selection test was used. The selection ratio is the proportion of the job applicant pool that is hired to fill the job openings available. Taylor and Russell showed that under some conditions, e.g., when most employees are successful without tests or when the applicant pool is small relative to the number of openings, even a test with relatively high validity will not be very useful. Conversely, when few are successful without tests or when the size of the applicant pool is large, a test of relatively low validity can be quite useful. Thus, the usefulness of a test with a given validity coefficient cannot be determined without considering other factors in the selection situation.

tween test score and criterion measure are moderate. Are the tests valid enough to be useful for employee selection? The answer is yes—in some circumstances. Tests that have been carefully matched to jobs can, in particular selection situations, give useful predictions of job performance.

Should Tests Be Used if They Do Measure Required Skills and Abilities?

Government Policy

The salient social fact today about the use of ability tests is that blacks, Hispanics, and native Americans do not, as groups, score as well as do white applicants as a group. When candidates are ranked according to test score and when test results are a determinant in the employment decision, a comparatively large fraction of blacks and Hispanics are screened out. In addition, there has been a substantial amount of misuse of employment tests, whether out of ignorance or from discriminatory motives, that has had the effect of turning away minority applicants.

The goal of the Civil Rights Act of 1964 was to end the economic isolation of blacks and others by prohibiting discrimination in employment practices on the basis of race, color, religion, sex, or ethnic origin. In implementing the statute, the Equal Employment Opportunity Commission and other agencies of the government have applied demanding standards for the development and use of tests and other selection procedures in situations in which an employer's practices have an adverse impact on members of groups covered by the act. The courts have proved willing, by and large, to apply those standards in judging the legality of tests and other selection procedures. The undeniable thrust of the case law has been to strike down the challenged testing procedures when there is evidence of grossly disproportionate rates of selection.

The policies adopted by the Equal Employment Opportunity Commission are those that would be adopted if the desired effect were to force employers to a quota system to achieve a representative work force. The consequences for testing have been complicated, including a decline in test use and a general tightening up of procedures (Peterson 1974, Miner 1976b). The quality of testing is thought by industrial psychologists to have improved (see, e.g., Sparks 1978:222). Nevertheless, the rigidity of the federal standards has created a situation in which adequate or useful tests are being abandoned or struck down along with the bad.

Given these political realities, the committee understands the essential question to be how to achieve the most effective system of employee selection within the context of equal employment opportunity goals.

The compelling practical fact is that employment tests, with all their limitations, are a source of valuable information about prospective employees. Often they provide the only information related to ability and skills that an employer has in making selection decisions. Unlike most school testing, employment testing is used in relatively information-poor situations. In contrast to a teacher, who has daily contact with the pupil and adds a test score to a rich set of impressions, observations, measures of performance, and judgments, an employer seldom has any firsthand knowledge about an applicant. This is particularly true for entry-level hiring for positions that do not require extensive prior training, which is the situation for most employment testing.

In addition, the public interest in protecting the privacy and civil rights of individuals places further constraints on the information available to employers. For example, there are limits on the types of biographical data solicited, including age, medical history, prison record, and responsibility for small children. In addition, there are many self-imposed constraints because the threat of litigation has loomed large in the last decade. As a consequence, it is apparently not unusual for employers to instruct supervisors who have been contacted as references to restrict their remarks to "name, rank, and serial number" so as to avoid the possibility of legal action by a former employee.

Alternatives to Tests

The committee has seen no evidence of alternatives to testing that are equally informative, equally adequate technically, and also economically and politically viable. Assessment center techniques are becoming popular for executive assessment, but they cost anywhere from $300 to $4,000-$5,000 per individual. The only other promising technique at present is the evaluation of biographical information (Reilly and Chao 1980), in which a key is developed empirically on an existing work force that assigns credit for any item of information that is found more frequently among successful workers than among unsuccessful ones. Age and marital status, for example, are usually found to be two of the most consistent predictors of tenure.

Although researchers generally report moderate predictive validities with such biodata evaluations, the technique has important drawbacks. It requires a very large sample (thousands of cases) to validate. In addition, the selection criteria are not likely to find the public acceptance that tests have had because the characteristics measured are often not within the control of the test takers. Many earlier biographical evaluations, for example, were designed to predict on the basis of characteristics like income, social class indicators, age, education, mother's education, or father's occupation. Selection based on biodata of this kind is at the very least injurious to feelings of individual worth; moreover, it could easily become a celebration of the status quo. To avoid this, industrial psychologists have developed within-group predictors. It was found, for example, that items that predict military rank for men were not valid for women. Separate scoring keys for each gender were much more accurate than a key developed on the entire sample (Nevo 1976). While developing separate biodata keys for various subgroups can eliminate bias and enhance the predictive power of the instruments, the procedure does not offer any unique solutions to the problems of balancing adverse impact and fairness concerns when group means on criterion performance are significantly different.

The Need for New Decision Rules

Society has many goals. Productivity is one. Equity is another. As a nation made up of many groups, Americans have long valued pluralism and have considered it a benefit to society to encourage diversity. These fundamental goals exist in a state of tension that can become outright conflict as is illustrated by the controversy about ability testing. The committee cannot take a position on how the goals of productivity, equity, and diversity ought to be balanced in any particular situation. Nor can there exist any psychometric solution to this balancing problem. It is essentially a political problem that must be thrashed out in an open political process in which all interested parties participate.

What is of primary importance is that the integrity of the information being used in the selection process be maintained. At present, the conflict between competing goals is having the effect of eliminating useful tests along with those that make little or no contribution to hiring decisions. Productivity and equity would be far better served by shifting the burden of balancing interests from tests to the decision rule that determines how test scores and other selection criteria will be used.

CONCLUSIONS

In light of the psychometric research findings presented in Chapter 2 and the legal context described in Chapter 3, as well as the evidence presented in this chapter, the committee has reached a number of conclusions about the present state of employment testing.

• Ability tests can provide useful information about the probability of an applicant's performing successfully on the job. Particularly for entry-level positions, tests provide information that is not readily available from other sources. But the benefit of testing is conditional on sensible use, and it also varies with the nature of the job, the size of the employing organization, and the resources devoted by the organization to the testing program. The case law provides ample evidence that tests have at times been so carelessly used as to be irrelevant to the hiring decisions being made.

• We find little convincing evidence that well-constructed and competently administered tests are more valid predictors for one population subgroup than for another: individuals with higher scores tend to perform better on the job, regardless of group identity. However, this generalization does not hold for people who are very different from the norm group, e.g., people who do not have a command of the language in which the test is written or people with handicapping conditions that interfere with test performance. In such cases, test results would be of uncertain or unknown meaning.

• So long as the groups offered protection under the Civil Rights Act of 1964 (particularly blacks and certain ethnic minorities) continue to have a relatively high proportion of less educated and more disadvantaged members that the general population, those social facts are likely to be reflected in test scores. That is, even highly valid tests will have adverse impact. It is important to remember, however, in making the leap from test result to job performance, that predictive decision making is always a matter of probabilities; any individual might, and some would, prove the prediction wrong.

• There is a legitimate governmental interest in promoting the economic integration of blacks, women, Hispanics, and members of other ethnic minorities. In pursuing that interest, the *Uniform Guidelines on Employee Selection Procedures* properly require a close investigation of any selection procedure that has adverse impact. A healthy suspicion of such selection practices is warranted by the discriminatory behavior that has tended to characterize American society. Enforcement of the *Guidelines* has revealed that many employment testing programs did not meet professional standards and were making no verifiable contribution to productivity.

At the same time, there is a genuine societal interest in promoting an efficient and productive work force. The interpretation of the *Guidelines* which EEOC and, by and large, the federal courts press upon employers, has made it exceedingly difficult for test users to defend even state-of-the-art practices. Comparatively few selection systems based on tests have survived legal challenge, particularly when judged under the strict statutory standards of Title VII usually applied by the enforcing authorities.

Some employers have abandoned testing rather than face the prospect of litigation.

• Employment selection is caught up in a destructive tension between employers' interest in promoting work force efficiency and the governmental effort to ensure equal employment opportunity. Although this committee is not in a position to speak to all aspects of the problem, it has concluded that some of the difficulties in achieving a workable balance between the two principles stem from a general failure on the part of those who judge the legal adequacy of selection practices to distinguish between those burdens that can reasonably be placed on tests (i.e., psychometric requirements) and those that should rest elsewhere in the decision process.

For example, a recent consent decree will eliminate the Office of Personnel Management's PACE examination over a period of three years. The test is being phased out because of its adverse impact on minorities. There was, however, no determination made by the court about the validity of the PACE. The ultimate goal of the agreement is the development of alternative examining procedures for each of the more than 100 job classes formerly covered by the PACE. The new procedures will be required to eliminate adverse impact against blacks and Hispanics "as much as feasible," and to "validly and fairly test the relative capacity of applicants to perform the jobs" (p. 3). Adverse impact will be calculated on the basis of comparison of the numbers hired from each group with the numbers who applied. Since it is not clear that alternative cognitive measures of equal validity can be developed that will have sufficiently reduced adverse impact, many knowledgeable observers fear that the psychometric integrity of the selection process, and along with it the goal of efficiency, may be threatened. The goals of efficiency and representativeness are more likely to be brought into a workable balance by altering the decision rule (ranking and the rule of three) that determines how test scores are used. This might be in the form of a weighting formula that recognizes high ability, ethnic diversity, and other socially valued considerations in selecting from the portion of the applicant population that has demonstrated the threshold level of ability or skill necessary to satisfactory job performance.

• While there is clearly a great deal of room for improving the statistical and psychometric qualities of even the more useful tests, there is a danger that, if comparatively valid selection procedures are abandoned as a consequence of administrative pressure, the morale of the work force and the productivity of the economy will suffer.

• In considering validation strategies, the size of a given work force presents an important constraint that is often not sufficiently appreciated.

Since the vast majority of employers in this country have relatively few employees, conducting research and development activities to support testing is difficult and their studies of test effectiveness are necessarily severely limited.

RECOMMENDATIONS

Testing and Selection

1. The validity of the testing process should not be compromised in the effort to shape the distribution of the work force.

2. Federal authorities should concentrate on providing employers with guidelines that set out the range of legally defensible decision rules to guide their use of test scores. Federal and state lawmakers, for example, should seriously consider revising merit system codes. The typical requirements for ranking candidates by test score and selecting according to the "rule of three" should be replaced by a selection system that recognizes the dual interests of equal opportunity and productivity. This would necessitate a rule that avoids either extreme: strict ranking or quotas.

3. It is of utmost importance that judges and compliance authorities distinguish between the technical psychometric standards that can reasonably be imposed on ability tests and the legal and social policy requirements that more properly apply to the rules for using test scores and other information in selecting employees. To that end, we recommend strongly that the Administrative Office of the Courts and other appropriate agencies underwrite a study for the use of judges and compliance officers that analyzes legal doctrines such as job-relatedness in relation to various kinds of ability tests and validation strategies and describes alternative decision formulas that can be applied to a selection situation.

4. Government agencies concerned with fair employment practices should accept the principle of cooperative validation research so that tests validated for a job category such as fire fighter in a number of localities can be accepted for use in other localities on the basis of the cumulated experience. It would remain incumbent on the user of such a test to develop a persuasive showing—based on close examination of the test, the work, and the applicant pool—that it is appropriate for use in the conditions that obtain in the local situation.

5. Employers who use tests, including the federal government, should give greater attention to improving the statistical and psychometric properties of their tests.

Selection and Training

1. The federal government should provide tax incentives and other measures to encourage programs in industry (e.g., focused training programs, relocation) that will enhance the employment opportunities of members of racial, gender, and ethnic groups who have in the past been excluded from full participation in the work force.

Research Agenda

1. The U.S. Department of Labor and the U.S. Office of Personnel Management should support research on the generalizability of validation results and on ways in which jobs can be grouped for purposes of test development and validation.

2. We recommend support of research on the relationship between the employment practices of individual firms and the distribution of human resources among firms.

REFERENCES

Becker, G. (1971) *The Economics of Discrimination*, Rev. 2nd ed. Chicago: University of Chicago Press.

Bentz, J. (1978) An overview of psychological testing in Sears, Roebuck & Company. Statement presented at the hearings of the Committee on Ability Testing, November 17-18, National Research Council, Washington, D.C.

Brogden, H. E. (1946) On the interpretation of the correlation coefficient as a measure of predictive efficiency. *Journal of Educational Psychology* 37:65-76.

Carron, T. (1978) Statement. Presented at the hearings of the Committee on Ability Testing, November 17-18, National Research Council, Washington, D.C.

Campbell, A. K., (1979) Statement on the PACE before the Subcommittee on Civil Service, Committee on Post Office and Civil Service, U. S. House of Representatives, May 15, Washington, D.C.

Cronbach, L. J., and Gleser, G. C. (1965) *Psychological Tests and Personnel Decisions*, 2nd ed. Urbana, Ill.: University of Illinois Press.

Dawes, R. M. (1979) The robust beauty of improper linear models in decision making. *American Psychologist* 34(7):571-582.

Friend v. *Leidinger*, 18 FEP Cases 1052 (4th Cir. 1978)

Garrett, H. E. (1933) *Pschological Tests, Methods, and Results*. New York: Harper & Brothers.

Ghiselli, E. (1966) *The Validity of Occupational Aptitude Tests*. New York: Wiley.

Ghiselli, E. (1973) The validity of aptitude tests in personnel selection. *Personnel Psychology* 26:461-477.

Goldberg, L. R. (1970) Man versus model of man: a rationale, plus some evidence for a method of improving on clinical inferences. *Psychological Bulletin* 73:422-432.

Haire, M. (1956) *Psychology in Management.* New York: McGraw-Hill.

Hale, M. (1980) *Human Science and Social Order: Hugo Münsterberg and the Origins of Applied Psychology.* Philadelphia: Temple University Press.

Hogan, D. B. (n.d.) Unpublished position statement on licensing counselors and psychotherapists.

Hogan, D. B. (1978) *The Regulation of Psychotherapists: A Study in the Philosophy and Practice of Professional Regulation.* Cambridge, Mass.: Ballinger Publishing Co.

Luevano v. Campbell, (1981) (D.C.D.C., 1981) Civil Action No. 79-0271. Consent decree filed January 9, 1981, amended February 26, 1981.

Meehl, P. E. (1954) *Clinical vs. Statistical Prediction.* Minneapolis: University of Minnesota Press.

Miner, M. (1976a) *Selection Procedures and Personnel Records.* Personnel Policies Forum Survey No. 114 Washington, D.C.: Bureau of National Affairs.

Miner, M. (1976b) *Equal Employment Opportunity: Programs and Results.* Personnel Policies Forum Survey No. 112. Washington, D.C.: Bureau of National Affairs.

Nevo, B. (1976) Using biographical information to predict success of men and women in the Army. *Journal of Applied Psychology* 61:106-108.

Peterson, D. (1974) The impact of Duke Power on testing. *Personnel* 51:30-37.

Pottinger, P. (1979) Competence assessment: comment on current practices. *New Directions for Experimental Learning* 3:25-39.

Pottinger, P., Wiesfeld, N., Tochen, D., Cohen, P., and Schaalman, M. (1980) Competence Assessment for Occupational Certification. In *The Assessment of Occupational Competence.* Prepared for the National Institute of Education, Contract NIE 400-78-0028. Available from ERIC Clearinghouse, #(CH): CEO27162.

Prentice-Hall, Inc. (1975) P-H Survey: *Employee Testing and Selection Procedures—Where Are They Headed?* Englewood Cliffs, N.J.: Prentice-Hall, Inc.

Reilly, R. R., and Chao, G. T. (1980) Alternatives to Tests for Employment Selection. Unpublished paper.

Rutstein, J. J. (1971) Survey of current personnel systems in state and local governments. *Good Government* LXXXVII:1-28 (National Civil Service League, Washington, D.C.).

Schmidt, F., Hunter, J., McKenzie, R., and Muldrow, T. (1979) Impact of valid selection procedures on work force productivity. *Journal of Applied Psychology* 64:609-626.

Shimberg, B. (1976) *Improving Occupational Regulation.* Final report to the Employment and Training Administration, U.S. Department of Labor. Grant No. 21-34-75-12. Princeton, N.J.: Educational Testing Service.

Sparks, P. (1978) Statement. Presented at the hearings of the Committee on Ability Testing, November 17-18, National Research Council, Washington, D.C.

Strauss, G., and Sayles, L. R. (1960) *Personnel: The Human Problems of Management,* 3rd ed. Englewood Cliffs, N.J.: Prentice Hall.

Taylor, H. C., and Russell, J. T. (1939) The relationship of validity coefficients to the practical effectiveness of tests in selection: discussion and tables. *Journal of Applied Psychology* 23:565-578.

U.S. Civil Service Commission (1940) *Federal Employment Under the Merit System.* Washinton, D.C.: U.S. Government Printing Office.

U.S. Office of Personnel Management and Council of State Governments (1979) *Analysis of Baseline Data: Survey on Personnel Practices for States, Counties, Cities.* Washington, D.C.: U.S. Government Printing Office.

Urry, V. W. (1977) *Tailored Testing: A Spectacular Success for Latent Trait Theory.* Technical Study 77-2. Washington, D.C.: U.S. Civil Service Commission.

Wright, G. (1978) Statement. The use of ability tests in the merit system employment setting of a large public jurisdiction employer. Statement presented at the hearings of the Committee on Ability Testing, November 17-18, National Research Council, Washington, D.C.

Yoder, D. (1948) *Personnel Management and Industrial Relations*, 3rd ed. New York: Prentice Hall.

5
Ability Testing in Elementary and Secondary Schools

INTRODUCTION

There has been ferment about the public schools and their performance throughout much of the last 30 years. Fears generated by the Cold War brought changes in public education, as did the demands of the civil rights movement, concerns about handicapped children and children whose native language is other than English, and, most recently, the belief of many people that large numbers of students are not acquiring the basic skills necessary to function successfully in contemporary society.

In the course of the 30 years, national and state governments have become increasingly involved in the conduct, policies, and financing of the public schools. A significant consequence of that involvement has been the proliferation of mandated testing. The policy and program responses of federal and state governments to educational issues have typically included the use of tests: tests for selection, placement, diagnosis and remediation, guidance, program evaluation, and certification of competence. Education has come to be treated—perhaps even to be thought of by practitioners—as a measurable, quantifiable product, with tests the favored instrument of measurement of the product.

As a matter of government policy and public expectation, the United States expects education to be a major instrument of social change, placing on schools, administrators, teachers, and pupils the task of reversing the effects of poverty, disadvantage, and discrimination. Since tests provide the measure of the educational product, it is small wonder that educational testing is embroiled in controversy.

In this chapter we discuss the various educational purposes that professionally developed tests are intended to serve and offer guidance for the reasonable use of tests in achieving those purposes. The discussion focuses on questions of test design, administration, scoring, and the interpretation of test results as they affect educational goals. We first outline the overall pattern and extent of test use and then turn to an analysis of three major functions of testing in the schools: classification of students, certification of competence, and policy making and management. To the extent that controversies about testing practices are a reflection of conflicts about broader social issues, far removed from the purposes for which tests are employed, we note here that those conflicts will not be resolved by making changes in tests and testing practices; those broader issues are discussed in the final chapter of this report.

THE PATTERN AND EXTENT OF TEST USE

Schools are the foremost users of standardized tests in the United States. According to figures supplied by the Association of American Publishers (AAP), school purchases accounted for 90 percent or more of standardized test sales by commercial publishers in the years 1972-1978; the remaining 8 to 10 percent of the market was divided among employers, postsecondary educational institutions, and clinical users.[1] Estimated sales for the entire test publishing industry (commercial and nonprofit) grew from $26.5 million in 1972 to $52.0 million in 1978. In 1977, according to AAP estimates, educational sales totaled $44.9 million, or about 1/10 of 1 percent of the total school instructional budget (Association of American Publishers, Test Committee 1978).

The educational testing industry is dominated by a small number of sizable firms. Buros' *Tests in Print: II* (1974) lists 496 publishers of tests. Of these, six commercial publishers produce and market the majority of tests used in the schools: Addison-Wesley Publishing Company, California Test Bureau/McGraw-Hill, Houghton Mifflin Company, Scholastic Testing Service, Inc., Science Research Associates, and the Psychological

---

[1] The AAP figures are based on an annual survey of major test publishers conducted for the association by John P. Dessauer, Inc. Sales reported by participants in the survey for those years were estimated to represent between 45 and 50 percent of total sales for the test publishing industry. The assumption is being made that the breakdown of sales by type of purchaser is not significantly different for the rest of the industry, an assumption encouraged by the statement of the AAP Test Committee (1978) to the Committee.

Corporation/Harcourt Brace Jovanovich, Inc. Typically, the test producers also provide scoring and reporting services: some maintain their own scoring facilities, while others use outside processing organizations. In any event, most scoring is done outside the school and with electronic equipment.

There are several other sources of tests worth noting. Many state departments of education have instituted testing programs in the last two decades, either for the purpose of allowing district comparisons or, more recently, for minimum competency testing. While most state programs have relied on commercially published tests, an increasing number of state departments of education are beginning to develop their own tests or to contract with professional test developers for custom-made tests.

Test development at the local level has also increased significantly in recent years. Spurred by the criterion-referenced testing movement of the early 1970s, some school districts, often with the participation of local teachers, have turned to developing their own tests on the assumption that such tests will be more responsive to community objectives and will reflect more closely the local curriculum (see Anderson in Part II).

Finally, tests are also available to the public schools from the National Assessment of Educational Progress (NAEP), a federally funded survey of academic performance, based on tests, of a sample of students at several age levels. As one of its ancillary activities, NAEP makes test items available at minimum cost to public and private schools or school systems for incorporation into their own tests.

From what we could learn about test use in the public schools, standardized ability tests are used most heavily in the primary and elementary grades, rather less in high schools. The vast majority of tests used are measures of achievement of the basic skills of reading, mathematics, and language. Norm-referenced achievement tests continue to be almost universally used despite the opposition of the National Education Association and the new popularity of domain-referenced tests (see Chapter 2, Anderson in Part II, and Boyd et al. 1975). Group-administered aptitude tests, particularly tests yielding an "intelligence quotient," on the other hand, are far less frequently used today than 10 years ago; some jurisdictions have prohibited group intelligence testing (although individually administered tests of intelligence are widely used in making placement decisions for instruction outside the regular classroom).

How many standardized tests is an American child likely to encounter during her or his progress through the public schools? In the absence of hard data, Houts's (1977) oft-quoted estimate seems reasonable: each child takes from 6 to 12 full batteries of achievement tests during the years from kindergarten through high school. It can also be said that any child who falls outside the norm—in school performance, socioeconomic status, mother tongue, or handicapping condition—is likely to be given additional tests. (See Anderson in Part II for profiles of the testing programs in 10 elementary, junior high, and senior high schools in the Northwest.)

STUDENT CLASSIFICATION AND INSTRUCTIONAL PLANNING

The history and current practice of testing are intimately tied to the pedagogical principle of adapting instruction to the various capabilities of children. The widespread adoption of group intelligence testing in American schools in the 1920s was prompted by the belief that placing children in classes of students with roughly the same intellectual ability would permit more effective instruction for children at all levels of ability.

In recent years, many educators have come to reject this tracking concept in favor of individualized instruction within a heterogeneous classroom. But the link between testing and teaching remains strong. Within the heterogeneous classroom, it is argued, tests could be used "diagnostically" to plan a program of instruction compatible with each pupil's aptitudes and current state of knowledge and skill. The educator's responsibility, as Snow (1976:269) recently put it: ". . . is to adapt instruction to the individual learner—to seek an optimal match between the individual's characteristics and the characteristics of alternative possible educational environments."

In assessing the actual and appropriate role of tests in grouping and other forms of classification, we consider in this section testing both in the educational mainstream and in selection for special education. For each of these situations we discuss: (a) the extent of the practice in the public schools, insofar as data are available; (b) the extent to which standardized tests are an important element in the selection decision; (c) recommended testing practices.

Tracking and Grouping Students in Regular Education

Tracking has been a highly valued practice during much of this century. Elementary schools, if they were large enough, tended to divide their pupils into "fast" and "slow" classes at each grade level. As high school attendance expanded beyond the traditional clientele, most jurisdictions also instituted separate high schools or separate programs within high schools for vocational and academic training.

Current thinking is much less favorable to tracking, and it seems to be reflected in school practice, at least at the elementary school level. Instead of channeling elementary school pupils into fast and slow classes, it is now common to assemble children into small groups within a classroom. In a classroom of 25 or 30 children there might be four or five separate reading groups and perhaps three arithmetic groups. These groups are roughly sorted by level of performance in the particular subject: there is a "high" reading group and a "low" one, and often several in between. While in-class grouping avoids the problem of racial and ethnic separation posed by a system of ability tracking into homogeneous classes—which was one of the arguments against it—there are no sharp distinctions between the two with respect to the appropriate role of tests in assigning students to instructional groups.

There is also a special kind of instructional grouping practiced in most elementary schools, which falls somewhere between formal tracking and in-class grouping with respect to its potential for permanently separating students on the basis of a real or perceived ability differences: selection for compensatory education classes, usually in basic subjects such as reading and mathematics. Approximately 14,000 of the 16,000 school districts in the country receive federal funds under Title I of the Elementary and Secondary Education Act of 1965 to support compensatory education programs. Schools qualify for Title I funding on the basis of the average economic status of the families they serve, but only some of the children within a school normally participate in the compensatory classes and these are usually selected on the basis of low school achievement. A typical pattern is for these students to spend an hour or two per day in enrichment classes and the remainder of the time in the regular course of instruction.

There seems to be more tracking in junior high schools than in elementary schools, and, as in the past, some form of tracking within comprehensive high schools is virtually universal. Students can choose from college preparatory, general academic, or vocational programs. While attendance in a particular course of study is largely a matter of self-selection rather than assignment by authority in most school systems, schools with strong counseling programs try to encourage students whose records and test scores promise good academic work to select the college preparatory course and to steer those with doubtful qualifications into the other programs. Because of both departmentalization (separate teachers for separate subjects) and the greater incidence of homogeneous ability grouping as a consequence of career tracking, there is less in-class grouping in junior and senior high schools than in the primary schools.

The Role of Tests

It is difficult to estimate the actual role of standardized tests in grouping and tracking assignments in regular education. It is possible to have highly tracked school systems that use few or no standardized tests (the French school system is an example), and in most American schools, tracking does not seem to depend in any absolute way on test results. There are highly tracked elementary schools in which standardized tests (generally achievement tests) are used as one indicator of ability, but a teacher's or counselor's judgments, a child's reading level, knowledge of the pupil's family, and the like seem to play a more important role than do test scores. In these schools, test scores generally seem to be used to confirm judgments already made (Salmon-Cox 1980).

The same generalization apparently holds true for junior and senior high schools where tracking is more prevalent, but standardized testing far less so. Test batteries such as the Differential Aptitude Tests are used in guidance and counseling in some schools, and it seems probable that the cumulation of earlier records of achievement, including test scores, is significant in track assignments and in student selection of high school programs. But testing does not seem to dominate the decision process; rather it plays a supplementary role.

Although there are schools and school systems in which test scores are used as the principal determinant of a student's class, program, and even school assignment, these cases do not represent the norm. According to Findlay and Bryan (1975), 82 percent of the schools that practice ability grouping use test scores as a criterion, but only 13 percent of them rely on test scores alone.

As is the case with tracking, the available evidence, though partial, indicates that standardized tests do not usually play a central role in the process of assignment to in-class instructional groups. These assigments are, by and large, made by the classroom teacher on the basis of observation and informal assessment of students' ability early in the year (Salmon-Cox 1980) and without reference to tests (Airasian et al. 1977; but see Yeh 1978:27). The teacher may use such standardized test scores (e.g., reading readiness scores from kindergarten or last year's reading achievement test scores) as are in the files, but according to one study (Rist 1970), the teacher is as likely to use cues such as dress, language, and other class-linked information as test data. Testing seems to influence placement decisions when a score indicates higher ability that the teacher anticipated (Salmon-Cox 1980; Yeh 1978). Thus, when used for grouping, tests occasionally provide an "extra chance" for some children.

Tests play a much different, more prominent, role in the selection for compensatory education classes and for classes for "gifted" children. Standardized achievement tests in mathematics and reading play an important and direct role in determining which pupils in a school will attend compensatory education classes. One large city, for example, uses low scores on the spring Metropolitan Achievement Test as the basis for deciding who will be placed in remedial classes in the fall term; variants of this practice are common throughout the country. It is also common practice to use test scores as the sole or principal basis for deciding who will have the opportunity to attend special enrichment classes for the gifted: in this case, the most common practice is to use an IQ or other aptitude test rather than an achievement test.

Testing Bilingual Students

The testing of children who are not native English speakers presents special problems. Some jurisdictions have attempted to avoid them by using translated tests; indeed, the Education for All Handicapped Children Act (see below) mandates that tests used to classify pupils for special education placement be given in a child's native language. This requirement has caused concern among educators and measurement specialists. Modified tests do exist, particularly in Spanish, but they by no means cover all languages and all types of tests; and even in Spanish, it is doubtful whether a single version would fit equally well all the dialects spoken in the United States in families of different national origins.

The reasons for the native language requirement are understandable. There have, for example, been instances of misclassification of children as mentally retarded (e.g., *Diana* v. *State Board of Education*, Civil No. C-70-37 RFP(N. D. Cal. 1973)) on the basis of classroom performance and test scores, when the reason for the poor performance had more to do with language mastery than mental handicap. However, the test requirement is not a sufficient response, not least because translation does not speak to the problem of assessing the bilingual child. Just as an English-language test is not sufficient to assess a bilingual child's performance, so a test translated into the language of the home falls short because the child's pattern of language development is likely to be mixed, with varying degrees of command of listening, speaking, reading, writing, and thinking in English and in the native language (Martinez 1978, Laosa 1975, Matluck and Mace 1973, De Avila and Havassy 1974). For example, it is often found that at school age the Hispanic child in the United States shows greater formal language competence in English than in Spanish.

To plan a proper education, it would be necessary to test language competence and verbal reasoning in both languages. Beyond that, tests of command of basic number concepts and reasoning skills should be given in whichever appears to be the better of the two languages. But if the child's command of the language is shaky, the interpretation of a poor score is equivocal.

There are technical and practical difficulties in modifying tests for non-native English speakers. There are some difficulties in devising tests in another language that measure the same thing as the test in English, but these are probably not prohibitive. The serious problem arises when an attempt is made to produce a "comparable" test, so that scores obtained from Vietnamese immigrants, for example, can be compared with American norms. This is essentially a nonsensical operation, based on the idea that mental functioning is somehow independent of the language and concepts a person is using. Such testing is sometimes forced on school psychologists by legal requirements that tie the classification of pupils to numerical standards. Given the impossibility of collecting norms for a representative Vietnamese population, the numerical standard cannot logically be applied to children from Vietnam. Tests given in any language are a meaningful description of the child's performance in that language; any inference about probable performance in English instruction in an American school can be justified only on the basis of experience with similar children in similar instruction.

All of these considerations make the use of tests to evaluate bilingual children very difficult, and they should be used with the utmost caution. Reliance on a cutoff score seldom represents good practice: when such a score is used for monolingual and bilingual children, the probability of misinterpreting the bilingual pupil's test performance is heightened. Those states that define "retarded" in terms of a simple IQ score, for example, promote the possibility of serious misunderstanding and misclassification.

Special Education: Assignment to Classes for the Mentally Handicapped

Unlike the practice in most regular tracking, test scores have traditionally played, and continue to play, a central role in the decision to place students in special educational programs outside the regular course of instruction. While specific practices vary from state to state, and even from district to district, individually administered IQ tests, such as the Wechsler Intelligence Scale for Children (WISC), are widely used to identify students of subnormal mental ability; cutoff scores of 75 or 80 are used by many states to define mental retardation (Huberty et al. 1980). Achievement tests and assessments of adaptive behavior often supplement IQ tests in the evaluation of children with special needs.

The provision of separate instruction for pupils who are mildly retarded or suffer other learning disabilities presents the issue of test use in the classification of students for instructional purposes at its most perplexing.[2] The intentions of special education programs are laudable, but the practice has been notable for stirring up controversy because of unanticipated results (e.g., resegregation), inappropriate test use (e.g., using English-language instruments to assess the intellectual skills of pupils with little command of the language), and the apparent inadequacy of instruction in the special classes.

In the last decade, special education has become very much the creature of federal and state policy and financial assistance. Of most importance to the present discussion is the Education For All Handicapped Children Act (P.L. 94-142), enacted in 1975, which requires that children with handicapping conditions, including mental handicaps, be educated at the public expense and in the least restrictive environment. The law further stipulates that the instruction of handicapped children be guided by "individualized education programs," which entered the regulatory parlance as IEPs.

P.L. 94-142 is essentially a civil rights law; it creates entitlement for handicapped children and imposes requirements on state and local education agencies. In response, most states have significantly increased the number and range of their special education programs; state funding of special education increased by 66 percent between 1975 and 1980 (Odden and McGuire 1980). One noticeable consequence of this increased activity has been that the law, intended to bring previously unserved handicapped children into the public school system, has also had the effect of removing many children with substandard academic skills from the regular program, thus increasing the amount of tracking in the schools. In addition to possible fiscal incentives to maximize the number of children in special programs, the very existence of such programs tends to encourage teachers to think of referring a problem learner for assessment and possible placement. In view of the greatly increased availability of special education programs in the schools, therefore, it is crucial that assessment, and particularly tests of aptitude and achievement, be used carefully and with sophistication.

The Role of Tests

P.L. 94-142, as clarified by implementing regulations in August of 1977, established specific requirements for the use of tests in evaluating can-

---

[2] The Panel on Selection and Placement of Students in Programs for the Mentally Retarded of the Committee on Child Development Research and Public Policy, National Research Council, is studying this issue and is expected to issue a report of its findings in 1982.

didates for special placement. Some of these have been widely adopted, while others ask more than the schools or the tests can currently provide. For example, the requirement that tests be used that will reflect the handicapped child's true aptitude or achievement level rather than reflecting the impaired sensory, manual, or speaking skills cannot be complied with in many instances because such tests do not exist.[3]

Perhaps the most important requirement is that no single procedure be used as the sole criterion for placing a child: multiple sources of information are to be used, including aptitude and achievement tests, teacher recommendations, an investigation of social and cultural background, and an assessment of adaptive behavior, which is an attempt to look at a child's ability to manage everyday affairs as distinct from school tasks. Another critical requirement is that the placement decision must be made by more than one person. Typically, the school psychologist, classroom teacher, principal, and parent are involved. It is important that both psychologist and educator take part in the placement decision, for it must involve not only the determination of the special problems and needs of the child, but also provision of an educational program suitable to those needs.

Two further requirements, that tests be validated for the intended use and that they be administered by a trained person, also contribute to sound practice. It is particularly important that individual tests like the WISC be administered by qualified personnel because scoring depends upon the judgment of the test giver.

Problems in Using Tests for Special Education Placement

Tracking or ability grouping of any sort has two important drawbacks: negative labeling of the less able students and separation from peers. In the case of special education the potential for harm is accentuated partly because governmental regulations defining eligibility categories have institutionalized labels—"educable mentally retarded" (EMR), "emotionally disturbed," "learning disabled"—that give them a concrete reality outside of textbooks and clinical practice. Test scores can also add to the labeling problem, particularly in light of the tendency to define retardation by a cutoff point (whether it is 75, 80, or any other number). Given the amount of discussion about testing and test scores in recent years, the public, including teachers, may be coming to understand that

---

[3] See the report of the Panel on Testing of Handicapped People (Sherman and Robinson 1982) for more extensive discussion of this point and a general analysis of issues surrounding the testing of people with handicapping conditions.

psychologists no longer think of intelligence as fixed and innate. But most people do think of retardation as an unchanging state; the effects of misclassification could well persist in future placement decisions concerning a child once given the EMR label. We have already made the point in discussing other, less extreme sorts of ability grouping, that assignments tend to be stable, even in within-class groupings. A similar inertia is likely to be found with special education placements (especially so long as outside funding depends on the number of children so classified).

The question of separation has taken on legal significance because minority children are placed in EMR classes more often than white children. In California schools, for example, Hispanic children constitute 15.22 percent of the general nonhandicapped population, but make up 28.34 percent of the EMR enrollment (California State Department of Education 1970). (Although if similar calculations were made for white children of parents with comparable socioeconomic status, it is likely that a similarly "disproportionate" placement into special education would be found.) The visibly large representation of minority group children in special classes has generated litigation alleging that tests have a discriminatory impact. The legal analysis has been grounded in the standards and precedents developed in employment testing litigation, including the emphasis on statistical proofs.

Labeling and separation would probably not loom so large in special education placement if there were widespread confidence that such placement were to the educational benefit of the children. The two major court challenges (Larry P., PASE v. Hannon),[4] though they came down differently on the validity of the intelligence test used, made it clear that, in many school systems, placement does not result in the intensive and effective instruction called for by P.L. 94-142. Indeed, the educational research community has not yet reached any broad agreement about the teaching methods likely to be most effective with children who are mildly retarded, have specific learning disabilities, or are emotionally disturbed (Kaufman and Alberto 1976), despite the optimism of the federal law on this point. If the evidence presented in Larry P. is representative, special education classes are too often places in which virtually no serious instruction is offered and little is expected of the students.

At least one state (Massachusetts) is presently experimenting with meth-

---

[4] Larry P. v. Riles, No. C-71-2270 RFP(N. D. Cal., Oct. 11, 1979) and Parents In Action on Special Education v. Hannon, 49LW 2087 (N. D. Ill., July 7, 1980); see Chapter 3 for discussion.

ods of assigning special education resources to students without resorting to categorical labeling. However, the more typical practice involves assignment of students to specific handicap categories, and state laws and guidelines frequently mandate the use of test scores in this process. While tests of many kinds are useful to offset stereotyped impressions and to fill the gaps in casual observations, attempts to define disability categories in terms of test scores are not scientifically justifiable. In particular, the use of a single critical score to establish mental handicap is unwarranted.

There is another misuse of test scores that is apparently common: making the decision to assign children to learning disability classes on the basis of discrepancies between intelligence test scores and achievement test scores. This occurs because the regulations define the category "learning disabled" in terms of a discrepancy between school performance and the "ability to learn." It has been demonstrated over and over that the difference between the two kinds of test cannot be directly interpreted in this fashion. Both categories of test measure developed abilities and, therefore, they both give indications of "ability to learn." Moreover, their degree of correlation is so great that a large fraction of observed differences are attributable to measurement error and would be reversed on a retest. Patterning of test scores can be suggestive to the sophisticated interpreter, but it should not be the basis for an automatic decision formula.

THE USE OF TESTS IN CERTIFYING COMPETENCE

Standardized tests have long been used in employment settings to certify competence. Bar examinations, medical boards, and many other tests have served as measures of minimum levels of competence for entry into controlled occupations. But the idea of testing for a set of minimum skills or competencies that a student must have in order to graduate from high school is a new and powerful enthusiasm. Born of evidence of declining test scores and anecdotal accounts of high school graduates who can barely read and write, the minimum competency testing movement is the fastest growing manifestation of concern about public education. Many Americans are uneasy about their schools; they question whether the schools are doing an adequate job of teaching children, and they are seeking some way of ensuring that certain minimum skills will have been mastered by those who receive a high school diploma.

As a consequence, programs are being set up all over the country to define and test for the intellectual skills considered necessary to function successfully in modern society. More than most, this seems to be a grass roots movement: it is the only major educational reform impulse of the last 10 or 15 years not fueled by Washington. An early impetus for the movement came from the minimum graduation requirements proposed by the Oregon State Board of Education in September 1972. Since that time at least 36 states have set up some sort of minimum competency program; in addition, many local school districts have instituted minimum competency testing—some prior to, or as a supplement to, state legislation and some in states that have no mandated minimum competency testing (Pipho 1978, Gorth and Perkins 1979). In some cases, it appears that the programs were initiated in response to public pressure. In others, the state boards of education seem to have been the prime movers.

At the heart of the minimum competency movement is a possible conflict of motives that, unless carefully handled, could threaten significant damage to the one powerless party in the educational process, the student. On one hand, competency testing is offered as an instrument of accountability. It signifies a consumer or taxpayer loss of trust in what the public schools are doing: people want to know if the product justifies the expense. On the other hand, the movement is also the expression of a desire to improve the education of young people, particularly disadvantaged and minority children, so as to prepare them more adequately to be workers and citizens. The first motive has tended to evoke talk of sanctions; the second, extra expense and effort.

In a survey of the characteristics of typical minimum competency testing programs, we found that where sanctions are involved, they are generally imposed, not on those who control the quality of instruction—teachers, principals, school district administrators, state legislators, and education officials—but on students, who are denied a high school diploma. While it seems reasonable to hold students responsible for their learning efforts, it would seem more equitable to divide the burden of accountability among all the parties. States, schools, and teachers should shoulder responsibility for providing effective remedial instruction to bring students willing to expend the effort up to acceptable levels of performance. Otherwise, the end result of the movement could well be to make those who fail the tests less able to make their way in the world than they otherwise would have been.

Basic Characteristics of Competency Testing

Most minimum competency testing programs emphasize the performance of basic academic skills, such as reading and arithmetic; many also test language arts and writing. Usually these academic skills are assessed in life-context situations. The student may be asked to fill in the blank spaces on a check, read a timetable, calculate the amount of paint needed to cover a certain area, figure interest rates, or determine which of several products is the best buy per unit. Some programs have developed "listening and speaking" competencies; others test such subjects as history, citizenship, and economics; one program has a series of tests dealing with science.

Some states and local districts develop their own tests, some hire consultants for test development, and some use commercially available tests; often a combination is used. A multiple-choice format is used for most of the testing, but many programs require a writing sample, and some require students to give an oral presentation. A few programs sample directly such skills as answering a phone and taking messages, writing business letters, completing common forms, participating in a discussion, giving directions, or making various measurements.

About two-thirds of the state and local programs test competencies in both the elementary grades and high school, while the remainder test only at the secondary level. In an attempt to ensure that all students master certain skills, 17 states (and many local districts) have tied the demonstration of competencies to high school graduation or grade-to-grade promotion or both (Gorth and Perkins 1979).

This committee has looked at the minimum competency movement at a time when the programs are too new to have either proved their worth or fulfilled the forebodings of critics. Most of the programs are not yet fully implemented, and many are not yet fully thought out. In a survey conducted in 1978, for example, Smith and Jenkins (1980) found that 40 percent of the state programs did not have established policies regarding the competency testing of students with physical handicaps. More generally, a number of states look to curricular improvements as the main purpose of their minimum competency program, although it is unclear how such improvements are to be effected. Other programs aim to identify students in need of remedial help, but have no plan for dealing with school districts that are unable to provide effective remedial instruction (Ramsbotham 1980, Gorth and Perkins 1979). No doubt many eyes will be trained on the state of New Jersey, which has instituted a system designed to hold individual schools accountable for the outcome of their educational efforts. Beginning in 1980, the state will monitor basic skills test scores. If a school's students fail to meet minimum standards over a specified period of time, various remedial efforts will be prescribed, culminating in review of the school's classification status and, if necessary, direct corrective action by the state commissioner of education (Burke 1980).

Impact on Students

Minimum competency testing may or may not prove to be a useful vehicle for reestablishing educational standards and restoring the value of a high school diploma; it will have an impact, for good or for ill, on certain students. The major impact of minimum competency testing will be on students who risk failing. Those who pass the test after remedial instruction will presumably have gained by the experience. But failure can have serious consequences, not the least of which is the damage to a student's self-esteem that must accompany being classified as "incompetent" or "functionally illiterate." It is likely that minimum competency tests will appear a large enough barrier to marginal students to increase the probability of their dropping out of school. In the 14 states in which receipt of a high school diploma is or eventually will be tied to passing a minimum competency test, failure will diminish a student's educational and employment opportunities. Although the military will accept a certificate of attendance in place of a diploma, federal and state employment agencies will not, nor will most state colleges.

The problem of restricting a student's range of opportunity by tying graduation to competency test scores is complicated by the fact that the consequences of such a policy will fall with greatest weight on those who are most likely to be marginal by circumstance of birth—children of the poor, racial and ethnic minorities, and students with handicaps. For example, when Florida's functional literacy examination was administered for the first time in 1977, 78 percent of the black students failed, as compared with 25 percent of the white students.

Nevertheless, while tests used as a standard of performance can stigmatize poor performers and limit their employment mobility, the personal and social costs of a demanding diploma standard are not nearly so great as the costs of having failed to educate the substandard student during 12 years of schooling. Being illiterate in a society that requires a high degree of literacy in most of its parts is far more destructive to self-esteem and life chances than being labeled as such. If, by imposing standards of competency and using tests to chart each student's progress toward the goal, the number of students who do not master the rudiments of education can be significantly reduced, the impact of minimum competency testing on students will have been, on balance, beneficial.

Impact on Curriculum

If scores on the minimum competency test are important—for promotion, graduation, district-wide comparisons, or school funding—then it would be reasonable to expect teachers to focus their instruction on material that will help their students pass the tests. Indeed, there will be considerable general pressure on teachers for their students to do well (although most programs assume that students' performance will not be used to evaluate an individual teacher's effectiveness). This pressure can have both positive and negative effects. The effects will be positive if teachers focus on skills they have previously taught inadequately. The effects will be negative if other important subjects are neglected because too much time is spent on test-related topics and coaching.

That external tests can influence school curricula has been well documented (e.g., Madaus and Airasian 1977, Spaulding 1938, Gayen et al. 1971, Madaus and MacNamara 1970). If a state or national exam (for example, the British 11 + examinations, the Irish Leaving Certificate Examination, or the New York State Regents Examination) has a marked impact on the future life chances of the students, then the examinations come to influence the teaching and learning process more and more. Faced with a choice between learning objectives in the state or local syllabus and objectives that are implicit in the examinations, students and teachers generally choose the latter (Madaus and Airasian 1977; Spaulding 1938). Indeed, the quickest way to introduce new curricular material may often be to include it in the examinations. For example, the New York State Department of Education had little success in changing the emphasis in language teaching from grammar and translation to conversation and reading skills until the corresponding changes had been incorporated into the regents examination (Tinkleman 1966).

There is some indication that minimum competency tests are beginning to influence school curricula. In Florida, for example, in order to make time for remediation for low-scoring students, the students dropped one or more of their regular subjects or reduced time spent in elective areas such as art and music (Task Force on Educational Assessment Programs 1979). That concentration of effort may well have been entirely to the educational advantage of the low-scoring students. The danger lies in allowing the tests to dominate the curriculum and in letting the minimum become a maximum, so that instruction for all students is geared to the achievement of the least able.

Setting Standards and Constructing Tests

The decision to establish a program of testing for minimum competency requires, at the very least, two judgments: what the significant competencies are and what constitutes a "minimum" level for each. Each of these judgments has social implications; neither is neutral. They contribute to the consequences that will flow from the determination that minimum competency has or has not been demonstrated.

Florida's experience illustrates the difficulty in deciding what constitutes a minimum competency, that is, how difficult the questions should be and what the cutoff passing score should be. The Florida State Board of Education decided—detractors would say arbitrarily—on a cutoff score of 70 percent for their functional literacy test. Much to the public's consternation, that cutoff score resulted in the failure of 25 percent of the white and 78 percent of the black high school juniors. In the opinion of most who read a facsimile of the test in the *Miami Herald* (January 6, 1978), it was much too difficult for one to consider that students who scored below 70 percent were "functionally illiterate."

The decision regarding a cutoff score is particularly crucial when promotion or receiving a high school diploma depends on passing the test. If the cutoff score is set too high, a large number of students will fail. If the cutoff is set too low, the tests will be meaningless in terms of their stated goal. Most importantly, it must be remembered that there is no scientific basis for determining a cutoff point. The decision is a social and political one, and it will affect students, schools, and the community.

The integrity of any test depends upon careful item selection, adequate reliability and validity, and extensive pretesting. Competency testing requires particular attention to the appropriateness of test content. If testing is to be used to hold schools accountable for teaching and to hold students accountable for learning basic arithmetical and language skills, then the test questions should indeed elicit those skills and should represent a reasonable sample of the skill domain.

The purpose of competency testing is to certify that individual students have met predetermined standards of performance and not to compare students. Officials charged with establishing a competency program should keep in mind that the primary thrust of mental measurement—the demonstration of individual differences—is not particularly relevant to the certification function.

The psychometric and statistical techniques used to amplify indications of individual differences tend to compromise content validity. Test items are selected and combined in such a way that they will illustrate performance differences; a question that everyone answers correctly will not aid the differentiation process, nor will obviously wrong answers that do not tempt anyone. An important element in the development of normed tests, therefore, involves balancing the difficulty of items so that the scores of test takers will fall in the desired distribution. These attributes of normed tests are of secondary value when the purpose of testing is to certify competence, although information about score distributions could initially provide guidance in setting passing scores.

The ultimate goal of minimum competency programs must be to bring every student to the level of achievement defined as competent. The use of normed tests and the accompanying scales for the interpretation of scores could defeat the purpose of the programs. The determination of what tests to use, or what principles of test development to emphasize if the tests are being custom-made, is, therefore, of great importance.

Setting standards, choosing appropriate tests, and interpreting competence test results are difficult in any case, but special problems are posed by students with the kind of physical handicaps that make a conventional test an invalid measure (Morrissey 1980, McKinney and Haskins 1980). It has long been known that modifying test formats has significant effects on test results (e.g., Davis and Nolan 1961) and, therefore, destroys the comparability of test scores. Furthermore, there is very little data available about the validity and reliability of modified competency tests; Florida and North Carolina are the only states that have yet done extensive development work on tests with modified formats (Regional Resource Center Program n.d.).

Competency testing of handicapped students is being handled in a variety of ways. Some programs require handicapped students to follow the same procedures and meet the same standards as nonhandicapped students. Other jurisdictions are attempting to prepare tests with special formats (e.g., braille) or to allow modified testing conditions (e.g., supplying a reader or an amanuensis). Because of the difficulties of developing and interpreting tests for students with handicapping conditions, some jurisdictions exempt them; but in some cases, exemption means ineligibility for a regular diploma (McKinney and Haskins 1980:9, National Association of State Directors of Special Education (NASDSE) 1979). Until there is far more evidence available about modified competency tests than is currently the case, special care must be taken not to penalize students for the shortcomings of testing technology.[5]

THE USE OF TESTS IN POLICY MAKING AND MANAGEMENT

Just as in other public services and in business, those with supervisory responsibility in education consider it important to inform themselves

[5] For further discussion of this issue, see Jaeger and Tittle (1980) and the report of the Panel on Testing of Handicapped People (Sherman and Robinson 1982).

about the performance of the system and about the worth of innovative practices whose wider use they could encourage. Tests are frequently called on to play a part in both these evaluative functions because they provide an efficient, accessible indicator of educational achievement.

The most significant development in management (and testing) in recent years has been the increasing demand for central oversight of educational results. This comes partly because of the increased reliance of local schools on state funds since the late 1960s,[6] partly because education has come to be viewed explicitly as a weapon with which to combat poverty and increase equality, and partly because of a suspicion that teachers and local administrators are falling down on the job.

The centralization of educational policy formulation has led to the imposition of external tests—external in the sense that they are created or selected in a central office, not the classroom. It seems safe to say that the purpose of most of the standardized achievement tests taken by students in elementary and secondary schools is to supply the information to administrators at the district, state, or federal levels or to implement their policy decisions in the schools.

The proliferation of externally imposed tests has not been a neutral phenomenon. When responsibilities overlap, tension between central and local administrative bodies is to be expected. Central officials search for rules and standardized procedures that are comparatively easy to manage and try to judge the performance of all units on a common scale. Local officials, on the other hand, are aware of the realities that define the status of education in particular classrooms or schools; teachers are understandably defensive about potentially adverse comparisons and the possibility that tests will give an incomplete, hence unfair, picture of what their work is accomplishing.

The Use of Tests in Surveys

External tests are most useful—and least threatening to local interests—when constructed to provide aggregate data about performance. Surveys, for example, serve an important purpose when they raise questions for educators, legislators, and the public. Data collected periodically from a carefully drawn but modest sample of schools can perform a valuable monitoring function without making great inroads on instructional time. But designing surveys and interpreting their results are complex undertakings.

[6] Odden and McGuire (1980) report that states are now carrying about 50 percent of local school costs.

The survey of equality of educational opportunity, mandated by Congress in the Civil Rights Act of 1964, was a landmark. The investigators surveyed school facilities and the quality of faculties, but they also chose to examine pupil performance, giving various ability tests and breaking down the average scores by region, by characteristics of student bodies, and by individual characteristics such as race and family background (Coleman et al. 1966). Conventional assumptions were challenged by several findings, perhaps the most important being the wide variation in average achievement found among schools with similar resources. The very fact that performance as well as facilities was surveyed contributed to widespread acceptance of the view that educational outputs, rather than inputs, must be the central issue from now on (Mosteller and Moynihan 1972). The original interpretations of the study were later modified, when time permitted a thorough look at the data from many angles (Mayeske et al. 1972, Mosteller and Moynihan 1972), but the attention of policy makers has remained focused on the *effects* of schooling.

From this pioneering study and its successors, much has been learned about schools, and much has also been learned about the hazards of hasty interpretations of surveys. Perhaps the most important lesson, however, has been that survey data, while they can be valuable to the process of policy formation, are frequently ignored. A major conclusion drawn from the Coleman report was that the factors most strongly related to academic success stemmed from the student's home background, variables largely beyond the reach of school policy. Yet policy makers continue to concentrate their efforts to improve the educational achievement of poor and minority children on school-based interventions.

Evaluation is not simply a matter of gathering facts. The decision about what to measure and what not to measure is value laden. And even when it is agreed that a particular performance measure (a reading test, for example) is pertinent, disagreement can still arise about what (how high an average, for example) a certain program should produce if it is to be judged a success. At times, inadequate tests are used and adequate tests are misinterpreted (though even if the tests were impeccable, controversy would arise out of the multiplicity of educational ideals and organizations).

Surveys almost always highlight performance differences between regions, between urban and suburban schools, between schools in the same district, etc. Those differences are easily misread as signs of corresponding differences in the adequacy of instruction. But schools draw their student bodies from different parts of the population, and if it were possible to make allowance for differences in home background, the rankings of schools and of categories of schools would be radically different. Although statistical corrections can be made, these adjustments have often proved to be seriously inadequate. "Adjusting" results must, at best, rely on assumptions (Cook and Campbell 1979, Meehl 1970), and whether defensible conclusions can be drawn must be examined closely in each instance.

It is especially pertinent in the present report to comment on the common but mistaken practice of using a test of general ability (aptitude or intelligence test) to decide whether achievement test scores are better or worse than they should be. A school district, for example, may take an aptitude test as a baseline for judging achievement. When the rank of the local group in reading is higher than its rank on a test of general ability, the school district concludes that it is doing an excellent job of teaching reading. But this kind of difference cannot be so interpreted without looking behind the scores for an explanation. The evidence from the two kinds of test is no more than a report on distinct and useful abilities; the home and school each contribute, directly or indirectly, to *both* kinds of ability.

A more transparent error in interpreting surveys is that of taking the part for the whole. Surveys ordinarily cover those few subjects that are most universally taught and most easily assessed. To give but one example, formal English usage is far more likely to be surveyed than clarity and style of expression. It is important for the interpreter of an assessment to be mindful of the kind of accomplishments that were not assessed.

The Impact of Surveys on Schools

District officials often gather comparative information about schools, classes, or programs in order to guide budgetary or curriculum decisions. State agencies may look to detailed surveys of achievement for purposes of program evaluation. Surveys set up by central authorities, therefore, often apply the same test to everyone and provide scores on pupils, teachers, and schools. Educators disagree about the wisdom of this practice, both because it can feed unsophisticated assumptions about accountability, and because it can exercise an influence of uncertain value on the curriculum. Once teachers and school superintendents know that the "grade" they receive in the survey will depend in part on how well their students can convert English measures to metric measures, for example, they are strongly motivated to allocate classroom time to that topic. Whoever writes the specifications for the test begins to exert influence on instructional decisions. Those who impose the external test, if not mindful of this consequence, may unintentionally shift the balance toward standardization and away from adaption of the curriculum to local circumstance.

External tests are most likely to distort the course of study when heavy sanctions follow in their wake. The threat of sanctions can narrow the curriculum to what the test covers, to the exclusion of topics of special local importance and topics diversified to match individual interests and talents of students.

External tests are sometimes used as deliberate means of control. The minimum competency testing movement is the obvious current example. Legislators or other officials in 37 states, believing that the schools are setting too easy a course and awarding diplomas to students who have not achieved even basic literacy, have mandated testing programs as a means of imposing standards of performance. The fundamental weakness of a system of external testing backed up by sanctions is that while test scores can identify unsatisfactory outcomes, they cannot identify the cause of the outcome. In the absence of discretionary authority, the sanctions can fall arbitrarily.

Control schemes based on tests sometimes envision "payment by results." The most famous example is the plan employed in England during the last third of the nineteenth century. At the end of each year, visitation committees examined the pupils to see how many were up to standard in key subjects, and a school teacher received payment proportional to that count. The imposition of monetary sanctions on the teacher was not then—or now—conducive to excellence of teaching or learning. Students who reached the standard were neglected for the rest of the year while the teacher struggled with the laggards.

Modern formulas are usually less direct about the imposition of rewards and penalties. Funds intended to improve education for the disadvantaged have ordinarily been allocated in proportion to the number of impoverished families districts serve. Some legislators, however, wishing to link funding directly to eductional need, have tried to route funds to districts enrolling many students with low test scores. In such plans, funding in subsequent years may be made contingent on the end-of-year scores the students achieve. At best, plans of this sort require an elaborate system of centrally controlled test administration to produce trustworthy scores. Since there is no way to ensure that a student puts forth maximum effort on an ability test, offering payments contingent on low scores seems to invite cheating. This committee suspects that even the most ingenious arrangement for gearing school funding to test scores would place on tests a weight they cannot sustain. Test information can rightfully influence funding policy, but is not a proper ingredient for an administrative formula.

In contrast to these uses, the National Assessment of Educational Progress (NAEP), initiated in 1968, was designed with great care so as to avoid any direct influence on schools, school districts, or even states. It was conceived of as a white paper on the status of education in America, informative about the educational attainments of students, charting the ups and downs over time, but without in any way making normative judgments about particular schools, programs, or policies. NAEP succeeded in avoiding direct influence on school practices (some would say in having any influence whatsoever).

NAEP surveys, one at a time, a wide range of curriculum areas: career planning, government and citizenship, writing, science, and music, for example, as well as reading and mathematics. National samples are drawn of students aged 9, 13, and 17, and of adults who have been out of school for a decade or more. Repeat surveys at intervals of about 5 years identify the fields and subfields in which students are learning more, or less, than in previous years.

Instead of giving the same test to all 13-year-olds, NAEP prepares dozens of items and assembles them in as many as 15 different booklets. Scores are calculated not for single students or classes but for whole regions (or for such subdivisions as rural schools within a region). Data are compiled on more diverse content than any single test booklet includes. And, as the variation in test forms precludes comparing specific pupils or teachers, teachers and students are unlikely to spend their classroom effort on a topic merely because it will appear in the test.

CONCLUSIONS

Testing for Tracking and Instructional Grouping

Three general principles ought to dominate any plan for classification of students: reversibility of assignments; combination of information; and instructional validity.

• Reversibility of Assignments: What is known about educational development does not warrant allowing a classification or instructional plan to stand without periodic review. The pace of children's development is not regular and foreseeable, but has spurts and lags over time and in particular subject areas. When a pupil spurts ahead or encounters a blockage in some area of learning, that should be a signal for a change in the rate or character of instruction. A shift in instructional pace would be warranted for many children during any one year, and for most children a shift would be appropriate from time to time. No one knows how attentive teachers and counselors are to this possibility in practice, and there have been documented instances of assignments to slow groups or to other nonstandard instruction that, once made, were never changed (Rist 1970). Furthermore, there is rarely a provision for systematic reconsideration of the decision, made early in high school, that a student is or is not "college material." Under these unfortunate circumstances, a student's initial classification has long-lasting effects on her or his educational opportunities.

• Combination of Information: Instructional plans, including classifications, should not rest on any single test score. Tests are at best estimates of performance capabilities in relatively narrow domains of human competence. Instead, an educational decision should take into account many kinds of information and from a number of sources.

• Instructional Validity: Classification of pupils is warranted only when the classification rules—whether based on tests or not—have instructional validity. The educator who recommends one instructional program for a child rather than another is saying that, according to professional experience, the former plan works better for students like this one. Such expectancy statements are difficult to validate explicitly because children, and instructional alternatives, differ in many relevant respects.

The choice of a basis for classification should start with an examination of the differences between the instructional alternatives and the abilities they require; the examination of the child should focus on the abilities that are requisite for the instruction. No child should be assigned to a program that is not expected to enhance her or his achievement. However, research on the ability requirements of specific methods of instruction has not been carried far, and no coherent body of findings is available to guide practice (Snow 1976; Brown and Ferrara 1980). Hence educators should be asked only to exercise a conscientious judgment that any tests they use are relevant to proposed instructional tasks. Research should continue, with the aim of developing instructional alternatives suited to particular patterns of abilities and demonstrating the validity of any proposed methods of assignment.

Tracking and Grouping in Regular Classes

• In most school systems, tests do not seem to dominate tracking decisions; rather, they serve as a cross-check and to raise questions. The generic exception is in classification for placement in federally or state funded programs, such as Title I compensatory education classes. In these programs the documentation and evaluation requirements encourage reliance on test scores.

• There is no necessary correlation between testing and any particular grouping or tracking practice. If it is considered pedagogically desirable to sort students into instructional groups of differing difficulty levels, subject-matter orientation, or pace, then tests can provide one useful sort of information. If it is judged undesirable to sort students that way, tracking should be challenged directly; attempts to reduce tracking by eliminating testing probably will not succeed.

• Used with other information, standardized test scores can be useful in deciding about the level or type of instruction to be given to a student. However, for more detailed instructional planning, other forms of tests more closely keyed to the curriculum need to be developed.

• For the most part, test predictions correlate with academic performance. In testing bilingual children, however, there are important technical problems and interpretive uncertainties.

Special Education

• Test scores play a central, often a determinative, role in special education placement. Used appropriately, they can help to identify pupils who should be studied individually to determine in what educational setting they will prosper.

• An unbiased count of the children who are expected to have severe difficulty with instruction at the regular pace would surely find a greater proportion of poor children, including minority children, in that category. Radical social change would have to take place to alter that prediction significantly.

The Use of Tests in Certifying Competence

• Since it is well established that substantial numbers of students go through 12 years of schooling and are awarded high school diplomas without having achieved elementary skills in reading, writing, and mathematics, there are possible benefits to be derived from mandated minimum competency testing programs. Such testing programs may encourage teachers to try harder and states to make additional resources available to them to sustain the effort; they may stimulate unresponsive students to take basic lessons seriously and could ultimately provide the public with assurance that all graduates have demonstrated a level of achievement judged by the school and community to deserve a diploma. However, there are also possible disadvantages to instituting minimum competency testing programs, particularly the distortion and downgrading of the curriculum in schools or classrooms in which a substantial portion of students are in danger of failing. To be assured that everyone can read at a cost of having no one read well, or to be assured that all can do arithmetic but that none learn the methods of science—these are unhappy possible consequences of a total effort to achieve minimal competence.

• There are troublesome social implications in competency testing programs in which high school graduation is tied to passing the test. Insofar as diplomas are necessary to get jobs, the impact of competency testing will be to reduce the marketability of a group of young people largely characterized by low socioeconomic or minority status. It is true that neither the individual nor society benefits from a pseudo-certificate of accomplishment that allows students to persuade themselves that they have acquired knowledge or skills they in fact have not. However, the practical effect of competency testing programs is likely to be detrimental to the economic opportunity of groups already in a marginal position unless such programs are constructed to emphasize remedial training to combat the weaknesses that competency tests reveal.

• It is imperative that special consideration be given to the assessment of students with physical handicaps. Tests that have been modified so that they can be administered to students with physical handicaps do not produce scores comparable to regularly administered tests. Nor do all individuals with the same handicapping condition find a particular modified format equally amenable. Moreover, suitable modifications are not available for all types of handicap.

• If the only result of minimum competency programs is to deny diplomas to some students who would otherwise be passed through the system, then the test will have fulfilled neither the goal of producing a functionally literate school population nor that of holding schools to account for the product of their efforts.

The Use of Tests in Policy Making and Management

• It is frequently easier to gather than to use information. Throughout our investigation of educational testing we have found that, despite the large amount of testing that goes on in the elementary and secondary schools, test information often plays a minor role in decision making. With regard to school-level use, major exceptions to that general pattern occur when direct sanctions are involved (e.g., minimum competency testing) and when federal or state reporting requirements necessitate the documentation of a decision (e.g., Title I placements).

• An extensive ongoing investigation of the use of testing information at the school district level (the sample included urban, suburban, and small town school districts) indicates that the information from district testing programs is not particularly salient to district-level decision making (Sproull and Zubrow 1981). Central office personnel perceived the main benefits of the testing programs to accrue to school officials—teachers and principals—a perception the local people did not share. District administrators did report occasional use of test results in planning curriculum, but reported no use of the information for making decisions about personnel or budgetary matters. Nevertheless, surveys of school performance based on testing can be, and have been, extremely important sources of information. We would by no means conclude that such testing ought to be abandoned entirely, merely more carefully considered.

• Those who use or publish test survey results must guard against the common fallacy that score differences between schools necessarily indicate corresponding differences in the adequacy of instruction. Media stories could also be better informed in this regard.

• Test users should also guard against the practice of using one test score as establishing an "expectancy" for a school's performance on another test, a practice that is encouraged by the form in which some standardized test scores are reported to schools. There is no reason to give special status to aptitude tests or to some items in a test battery that are thought to define general ability and therefore "expectancy" or "anticipated achievement." All of the tests used in schools are measures of currently developed competence and should be considered as providing estimates of students' present level of functioning in some domain.

• When externally mandated tests are used as instruments of control, backed by sanctions, administrators must be especially sensitive to the possibility of curricular distortion.

• An administrative formula that gears school funding to test scores would place on tests a weight they cannot sustain; test information can reasonably influence funding policy, but should not define it.

RECOMMENDATIONS

Testing for Tracking and Instructional Grouping

Tracking and Grouping in Regular Classes

1. No important decision about an individual's educational future should be based on a single test score considered in isolation. This should hold for tests that purport to measure educational achievement as well as for tests that purport to measure aptitudes or disabilities. Scores ought to be interpreted within the framework of a student's total record, including classroom teachers' observations and behavior outside the school situation, taking into account the options available for the child's instruction.

2. If a school or school district institutes testing to guide placement decisions, it is imperative that the faculty, parents, and all others playing a role in placement decisions be instructed in interpreting test data and understanding their limitations.

3. Careful attention should be given to the question of the instructional validity of ability grouping decisions. Schools should make a continuing effort to check on the educational soundness of any plan they use for grouping or classifying students or for individualizing instruction. Regular monitoring should be instituted to ensure that instruction is contributing to the child's growth over a broad spectrum of abilities. Beyond that, special attention should be paid to determining which kinds of children thrive best in alternative programs. Assignment policies should be revised if there is any evidence that pupils being assigned to a narrower or less stimulating program are progressing more slowly than they would in regular instruction.

4. Because the concept of instructional validity is only now in the process of articulation, we strongly urge that the National Institute of Education and other agencies with interests in this matter encourage research and demonstration projects in:

(a) The development and use of tests as diagnostic instruments for choosing among alternative teaching programs the one most appropriate to a given student's mental traits or abilities (that is, matching aptitudes and instructional treatments);

(b) The development and use of tests to assess current learning status as it relates to a child's ability to move on to more complex learning tasks.

Special Education

1. There is little justification for making distinctions and isolating children from their cohort if there is not a reasonable expectation that special placement will provide them with more effective instruction than the normal instruction offers. The fundamental challenge in dealing with children who seem ill-adapted to most regular instruction is to devise alternative modes of instruction that really work.

2. Skepticism about the value of tests in identifying children in need of special education has probably been carried too far; people making those decisions should, wherever practicable, have before them a report on a number of professionally administered tests, in part to counteract the stereotypes and misperceptions that contaminate judgmental information.

3. We recommend against the use of rigid numerical cutoff scores

(applying to a test, a set of tests, or any other formula) as the basis for decisions about mental retardation and special education.

The Use of Tests in Certifying Competence

1. Fair and accurate assessment of competencies includes: Clear specification of the kinds of academic and other skills that are to be mastered; methods of evaluation that are tied closely to these skills, e.g., tests with high content validity and construct validity; a reasonable justification of the pass/fail cutoff point that takes cognizance of community expectations; many opportunities to retake the test; gradual phasing in of the program so that teachers, students, and the community can be prepared for it; and stability of requirements, both as to content and difficulty level, so that standards are known and dependable.

2. Since the desired result of minimum competency testing is to encourage intensive efforts on the part of students and teachers to increase the general level of accomplishment in the schools, the tests should be introduced well in advance of the last year of high school in order to provide ample opportunity for schools to offer and students to take extra training geared to the problems revealed by the tests.

3. Above all, minimum competency programs must involve instruction as well as assessment. We can see little point in devoting considerable amounts of educational resources to assessing students' competencies if the information so gained is not used to improve substandard performance. Furthermore, schools should carry the burden of demonstrating that the instruction offered has a positive effect on test performance. Diagnosis without treatment does no good and, quite literally, adds insult to injury.

The Use of Tests in Policy Making and Management

1. Testing for survey and policy research purposes should be restricted to investigations that have a good chance of being used; testing should not degenerate into routine compilation of data that are filed and forgotten. Moreover, any testing should be designed to collect adequately precise data with a minimum investment of effort (for example, when the purpose is system monitoring, sampling rather than administration of the same long test to every pupil every year).

2. Tests introduced for the purpose of guiding policy should be examined both before and after introduction for undesirable side effects, such as unintended standardization of curriculum or making a few subjects unduly important.

3. Surveys of performance of groups should emphasize performance descriptions and avoid comparisons between schools or school districts.

REFERENCES

Airasian, P. W., Madaus, G. F., Kellaghan, T., and Pedulla, J. J. (1977) Proportion and direction of teacher rating changes of pupils' progress attributable to standardized test information. *Journal of Educational Psychology* 69:702-709.

Association of American Publishers, Test Committee (1978) Unpublished letter to the Committee on Ability Testing, National Research Council, December.

Boyd, J., Jacobsen, K., McKenna, B. H., Stake, R. E., and Yashinsky, J. (1975) *A Study of Testing Practices in the Royal Oak Public Schools.* Royal Oak, Mich.: Royal Oak Michigan School District.

Brown, A. L., and Ferrara, R. A. (1980) Diagnosing Zones of Proximal Development: An Alternative to Standardized Testing? Unpublished paper, Center for the Study of Reading, University of Illinois.

Burke, F. G. (1980) *Guidelines for the Evaluation and Classification of Schools and Districts in New Jersey.* Trenton, N.J. Department of Education.

Buros, O. K. (1974) *Tests in Print II.* Highland Park, N.J.: Gryphon Press.

California State Department of Education (1970) *Placement of Underachieving Minority Group Children in Special Classes for the Educable Mentally Retarded.* Sacramento: California State Department of Education.

Coleman, J. S., Campbell, E. Q., Hobson, C. F., McPartland, J., Mood, A. M. et al. (1966) *Equality of Educational Opportunity.* Washington, D.C.: U.S. Government Printing Office.

Cook, T. D., and Campbell, D. T. (1979) *Quasi-Experimentation: Design and Analysis of Field Experiments.* Chicago: Rand McNally.

Davis, C. J., and Nolan, C. Y. (1961) A comparison of the oral and written methods of administering achievement tests. *The International Journal for the Education of the Blind* 10:80-82.

De Avila, E. A., and Havassy, B. (1974) The testing of minority children: a neo-Piagetian approach. *Today's Education* (November-December):72-75.

Findlay, W. G., and Bryan, M. M. (1975) *The Pros and Cons of Ability Grouping.* Bloomington, Ind.: Phi Delta Kappa, Inc.

Gayen, A. K., Nanda, P. D., Mathur, R. K., Duarti, P., Dubey, S. D., and Bhattacharyya, N. (1961) *Measurement of Achievement in Mathematics: A Statistical Study of Effectiveness of Board and University Examinations in India,* Report I. New Delhi: Ministry of Education.

Gorth, W. P., and Perkins, N. R. (1979) *A Study of Minimum Competency Testing Programs: Final Summary and Analysis Report.* A report by National Evaluation Systems, Inc. Washington, D.C.: National Institute of Education.

Houts, P. L., ed. (1977) *The Myth of Measurability.* New York: Hart Publishing Co.

Huberty, T. J., Koller, J. R., and TenBrink, T. (1980) Adaptive behavior in the definition of mental retardation. *Exceptional Children* 46:256-261.

Jaeger, R. M., and Tittle, C. K., eds. (1980) *Minimum Competency Achievement Testing: Motives, Models, Measures, and Consequences.* Berkeley, Calif.: McCutchen.

Kaufman, M. E., and Alberto, P. A. (1976) Research on the efficacy of special education for the mentally retarded. *International Review of Research in Mental Retardation* 8:225-255.

Laosa, L. M. (1975) Bilingualism in three United States Hispanic groups' contextual use of language by children and adults in their families. *Journal of Educational Psychology* 67:617-627.

Madaus, G., and Airasian, P. W. (1977) Issues in evaluating student outcomes in competency based graduation requirements. *Journal of Research and Development in Education* 10:79-91.

Madaus, G., and MacNamara, J. (1970) *Public Examinations: A Study of the Irish Leaving Certificate.* Dublin: Educational Research Centers.

Martinez, O. (1978) Problems associated with assessment of minority children: the Chicano child. Written testimony submitted for the public hearings of the Committee on Ability Testing, National Research Council, November.

Matluck, J. H., and Mace, B. J. (1973) Language characteristics of Mexican-American children: implications for assessment. *Journal of School Psychology* 11:365-386.

Mayeske, G. W., et al. (1972) *A Study of Our Nation's Schools.* DHEW-OE-72-142. Washington, D.C.: U.S. Department of Health, Education, and Welfare.

McKinney, J. D., and Haskins, K. G. (1980) *Final Report: Performance of Exceptional Students on the North Carolina Minimum Competency Tests, 1978-1979.* Submitted to North Carolina Board of Education.

Meehl, P. (1970) Nuisance variables and the ex post facto design. In M. Radner and S. Winokur, eds., *Minnesota Studies in the Philosophy of Science,* Vol. IV. Minneapolis: University of Minnesota Press.

Morrissey, P. A. (1980) Adaptive testing: How and when should handicapped students be accommodated in competency testing programs? In R. M. Jaeger and C. K. Tittle, eds., *Minimum Competency Achievement Testing: Motives, Models, Measures, and Consequences.* Berkeley, Calif.: McCutchen.

Mosteller, F., and Moynihan, D. P. (1972) A pathbreaking report. Pp. 3-66 in F. Mosteller and D. P. Moynihan, eds., *On Equality of Educational Opportunity.* New York: Vintage.

National Association of State Directors of Special Education (1979) *Competency Testing, Special Education and the Awarding of Diplomas.* Washington, D.C.: National Association of State Directors of Special Education.

National Research Council (1982) *Report.* Panel on Selection and Placement of Students in Programs for the Mentally Retarded, Committee on Child Development Research and Public Policy, National Research Council. Washington, D.C.: National Academy Press.

Odden, A., and McGuire, C. K. (1980) Financing educational services for special populations: the state and federal roles. Working Paper No. 28, Education Finance Center, Education Commission of the States, Denver, Colorado.

Pipho, C. (1978) Minimum competency testing in 1978: a look at state standards. *Phi Delta Kappan* 59:585.

Ramsbotham, A. (1980) *The Status of Minimum Competency Programs in Twelve Southern States.* A Report of the Southeastern Public Education Program (SEPEP). Columbia, South Carolina.

Regional Resource Center Program (n.d.) Handicapped students and minimum competency testing programs: An analysis of the state-of-art of service delivery and technical assistance activities provided to SEAs and LEAs under P.L. 94-142. Draft report, submitted to U.S. Office of Education, Bureau for Education of the Handicapped.

Rist, R. C. (1970) Student social class and teacher expectations: the self-fulfilling prophecy in ghetto education. *Harvard Educational Review* 40:411-451.

Salmon-Cox, L. (1980) Teachers and Tests: What's Really Happening? Paper presented at the American Educational Research Association annual meeting.

Sherman, S. W., and Robinson, N., eds. (1982) *Ability Testing of Handicapped People:*

Dilemma for Government, Science, and the Public. Panel on Testing of Handicapped People, Committee on Ability Testing, National Research Council. Washington, D.C.: National Academy Press.

Smith, J. D., and Jenkins, D. S. (1980) Minimum competency testing and handicapped students. *Exceptional Children* (March):440-443.

Snow, R. E. (1976) Aptitude-treatment interactions and individualized alternatives in higher education. In S. Messick and Associates, *Individuality in Learning.* San Francisco, Calif.: Jossey-Bass, Inc.

Spaulding, F. T. (1938) *High School and Life: The Regents Inquiry into the Character and Costs of Public Education in the State of New York.* New York: McGraw-Hill.

Sproull, L., and Zubrow, D. (1981) Standardized testing from the administrative prospective. *Phi Delta Kappan* (May).

Task Force on Educational Assessment Programs (1979) *Competency Testing in Florida: Report to the Florida Cabinet,* Part I. Tallahassee, Florida.

Tinkleman, S. N. (1966) Regents examination in New York State after 100 years. In *Proceedings of the 1965 Invitational Conference on Testing Problems.* New York: Educational Testing Service.

Yeh, J. (1978) Test Use in the Schools. Center for the Study of Evaluation, University of California, Los Angeles.

6
Admissions Testing in Higher Education

In the last 30 years, more and more postsecondary educational institutions have required entrance examinations for admission. The model established by a small group of Eastern colleges with the founding of the College Entrance Examination Board in 1900 has come to characterize the process nationwide; that is, an external examining agency provides the measure that each educational institution uses in a way suited to its character and needs.

CURRENT PRACTICE IN UNDERGRADUATE INSTITUTIONS

Applicants to undergraduate colleges and universities are generally required to submit scores on a professionally developed ability test for the use of the admissions office. There are some exceptions: many junior and community colleges and a few 4-year institutions have an "open admissions" policy and so do not require admissions tests. Tests may also be waived for certain individuals, most notably those with visual or motor disabilities that interfere with test performance.

Data from the American College Testing Program indicate that about 90 percent of the approximately 1,700 4-year undergraduate schools in the United States currently require that applicants take one of two entrance examinations (see Table 10): their own American College Testing Program Assessment (ACT) or the Scholastic Aptitude Test (SAT) administered by Educational Testing Service for the College Entrance Examination Board. Of the colleges and universities requiring submission of test scores, some specify which of the two tests they require while others

TABLE 10 Admissions Tests in Higher Education, 1978-79

Test[a]	Type of School	Number of Test Takers 1978-79	Schools Requiring Test
ACT/SAT	Undergraduate	1,000,000 each	About 1,530 of 1,700 4-year colleges
MCAT	Medical	48,000	124 of 126 schools
LSAT	Law	115,284	All 168 schools
GRE	Graduate	270,700	Data not available
GMAT	Management	190,000	More than 550, including all 55 in graduate admissions council

[a]Full names of tests:
ACT   American College Testing Program Assessment
SAT   Scholastic Aptitude Test
MCAT   Medical College Admissions Test
LSAT   Law School Admissions Test
GRE   Graduate Record Examination
GMAT   Graduate Management Admissions Test

SOURCE: Based on data in Skager (in Part II).

will accept either. In 1978-79, almost 2 million ACT and SAT tests were given. Since an unknown number of students took both tests, however, the total number of students who took college admissions tests that year is less than 2 million.

The SAT yields two scores: verbal (V, based on vocabulary, verbal reasoning and relationships, and reading comprehension) and mathematical (M, based on competency in computation and application of principles in arithmetic, algebra, and geometry). The ACT tests assess competencies in the subject matter fields of English, mathematics, social studies, and natural science and are designed to provide work samples of content-related activities that are relevant to college work. Although the ACT subtests are more closely tied to the high school academic curriculum than the SAT, scores on the two examinations are highly related; on the average, individuals who do well on one do as well on the other.

Schools vary in the specific procedures they follow to make admissions decisions and in the attention paid to test scores. Most, however, appear to rely on a general model in which applicants are initially sorted into three categories: (1) presumptive-admit, those with strong academic credentials; (2) hold, those whose records are less outstanding but may have special qualifications as indicated in letters of recommendation, information contained in the students' application materials, and the like; and (3) presumptive-deny, those whose credentials appear weak (see Skager in Part II). Quantitative data—scores on the ACT or SAT and high school grade-point average (GPA)—are used in this rough sorting. Qualitative data may be used at any stage in the admissions process but are more frequently used after the initial sorting.

Although the practice of using cutoff scores on either test scores or GPA to deny admission is frowned upon by testing organizations, 60 percent of the institutions reported doing so in a study cited by Skager. The minimum grade-point average required by most of those schools was "C." On the SAT, for which the total score possible for the verbal and mathematical sections (V + M) is 1600, the average cutoff was found to be about 750 for both public and private institutions, well below the national average of about 900 for those who take the SAT.

Precise information on the use of test scores in the sorting process is not available, and there is undoubtedly some variability among institutions. Ford and Campos (1977) cite data suggesting that in general test scores are currently being given slightly greater weight than earlier because of grade inflation. Even today, however, GPA appears to be given somewhat greater weight than test scores in the admissions process. (See study by the College Board and the Association of Collegiate Registrars and Admissions Officers, cited by Skager in Part II.) This weighting is supported by research evidence indicating that high school GPA is a somewhat better predictor of academic performance during the first 2 years of college than SAT or ACT scores. However, a combination of the two measures typically increases the accuracy of prediction for either, in part because the contribution of test scores to prediction is to some extent independent of other predictors like prior grades (Friedman and Bakewell 1980).

Qualitative information, such as letters of recommendation, special awards or accomplishments, and other personal data, are most likely to be used to determine which applicants in the "hold" category to admit. There may also be attempts to identify for special consideration applicants who are physically handicapped, come from socioeconomically or educationally disadvantaged backgrounds, are offspring of alumni, come from parts of the country that are underrepresented in the student population, or are eligible for sports scholarships.

Despite the complaints of critics that tests emphasize certain cognitive abilities to the exclusion of other abilities and traits that contribute to successful college performance (e.g., creativity, motivation), there is little use of formal measures of attitudinal and personality variables in the admissions process. Such measures have not been demonstrated to improve appreciably the prediction of academic performance. And even if personality characteristics had an established relevance, the fact that applicants can slant questionnaire responses to paint favorable pictures of themselves would argue against their use in selection.

The importance of test scores, high school grades, and similar indicators of performance in the college admissions process depends on two highly interactive variables: the prestige or reputation for academic excellence of the institution and the composition of the applicant pool. The pool of applicants understandably varies with the reputation of the school, the most prestigious institutions attracting a disproportionately large number of applicants with outstanding test scores and scholastic records. Students with undistinguished records will tend to select themselves out of that pool, which can be considered damaging (a student's judgment of her or his chances might be wrong), but only mildly so, given the number of institutions from which to choose.

To the extent that the number of academically outstanding applicants exceeds the number of openings in the entering class at a given institution, test scores and high school grades are likely to be important. But only a very small proportion of undergraduate schools could be called highly selective. With declining enrollments, an increasing number of colleges are in fact having difficulties filling their entering classes. Realistically, test scores (and GPAs) are likely to be a barrier only to that small group of applicants who want to attend the most selective colleges and universities; few students with a high school diploma fail to find an institution to accept them. In that sense, the public perception of the importance of high scores on the SAT or ACT is misleading: most applicants are admitted to the college or university of their choice (Skager in Part II, Hartnett and Feldmesser 1980).

CURRENT PRACTICE IN GRADUATE SCHOOLS

The general model of sorting applicants into presumptive-admit, hold, and presumptive-deny categories also applies to professional schools and graduate academic departments. Unlike undergraduate institutions, however, most professional schools and many Ph.D.-granting graduate departments currently have far more well-qualified applicants than they are prepared to admit. Except under unusual circumstances or in the case of students with special qualifications, applicants put in the presumptive-admit and hold categories are likely to have undergraduate grades or scores on required admissions tests (or both) that are far above average. In order to narrow down further this select group to the number to be admitted, graduate schools and departments, more than undergraduate colleges, depend on qualitative sources of information to assess applicants' motivation and personal suitability for pursuing postgraduate study and, ultimately, entry into the profession. Depending on the particular school or department, those sources may include letters of recommendation from undergraduate professors in related disciplines or other individuals active in the profession, personal interviews with the applicant, and special indications of the applicants' talents and interests, such as research papers, relevant job experience, and other kinds of extracurricular activities and background.

Data from four types of graduate programs—medical schools, law schools, graduate schools (which encompass a number of academic disciplines), and graduate schools of management—indicate that scores on professionally developed tests are typically required of applicants.

Medical School Admissions

All but two of the 126 medical schools in the United States require applicants to take the Medical College Admissions Test (MCAT), an instrument composed of six subtests. Scores on the MCAT are reported for each of six subtests and there is no composite score. The admissions process at medical schools is different from that of most other professional schools in that about 95 percent of the medical colleges interview applicants during the second of a two-stage selection process. While objective data, such as test scores and college grades in science courses, receive heavy weight in the initial selection of candidates to be interviewed, qualitative information is also used. Skager found no evidence that admissions decisions are based on a cutoff on any or all of the MCAT subtests, but there is a sharp decline below a GPA of 3.3 (B+) in the percentage of students admitted. Thus, while test scores are important in the admission of students to medical schools, the single most important factor appears to be undergraduate grade point average.

The striking fact about medical school admissions is the great disproportion between the number of applicants and the places available. To begin with, applicants to medical school are highly self-selected; 58 percent of the applicants in 1978-79 had undergraduate grade point averages of B+ or better. Of the applicants, 45 percent received at least one offer of admission, but the more prestigious schools exercised a high degree of selectivity. According to Gordon (1979), 43 of the 48 private medical schools admitted less than 10 percent of applicants in 1977-78.

Law School Admissions

Almost all law schools require that applicants submit scores on the Law School Admissions Test (LSAT). In addition, almost all of them also require that applications be submitted through the Law School Data Assembly

Service (LSDAS), which provides an index predicting first-year law grades for each applicant based on undergraduate grades and LSAT score. This index is reportedly used by admissions offices to sort applicants into the presumptive-admit, hold, and presumptive-deny categories. Qualitative information is most likely used to select from the hold category those applicants to be admitted.

Skager reports that LSAT scores receive more weight in decisions on law school admissions than do scores on tests for other programs. LSAT scores are also reported to be a better predictor of first-year law grades than undergraduate grade point averages (Schrader 1977), perhaps because there is no common prelaw curriculum that undergraduates are required to take. LSAT scores have even been used by some law schools to adjust an applicant's GPA so that grades can be compared across different undergraduate schools, although this practice is now being revised.

Graduate Management School Admissions

More than 550 schools of management require the Graduate Management Admissions Test (GMAT). This number includes the 55 schools that constitute the Graduate Admissions Council. Schools of mananagement are unlike other graduate and professional schools in that they stress the importance of prior work experience and sometimes award deferred admission status to promising undergraduates.

Other Graduate Admissions

Requirements of other graduate programs are difficult to summarize because applicants are most often screened by individual professional schools or departments within the university rather than by a central admissions office. A summary of a few selected programs from the Association of Graduate Schools (48 schools including the largest and most prestigious) indicates that scores on the Graduate Record Examination (GRE) are required of some or all applicants by most schools offering degree programs in biology, chemistry, the humanities, and by about half in education (Skager in Part II). Many graduate school applicants are required to take the Miller Analogies Test (MAT), either in addition to or in the place of part of the GRE.

Problems of Test Misuse

As is the case with other kinds of tests, entrance tests can be useful only if admissions officers respect their limits. One of the most common misconceptions about the tests used for admission to graduate and professional schools is that they predict who will be a good lawyer or doctor. In fact, there has been very little research on the correlation between test scores and later performance in a profession. The tests are designed to predict a much more limited outcome: which applicants are likely to perform well in the academic segments of professional training. The criterion measure is usually first-year grades.

Another common misconception concerns the importance of small score differences. As was explained in Chapter 2, the 200-800 scale used in scoring most of these tests was originally chosen arbitrarily as a convenient scale on which to display performance differences. Time has invested the numbers with more meaning than they should be expected to carry. The Law School Admissions Council has recognized that the 200-800 scale can create a false impression of precision. The Council has decided that the new LSAT, which is now under development, will be scored on a 10 to 50 scale. This change to a scale with fewer digits and fewer score intervals will, it is hoped, discourage admissions officers from exaggerating the importance of small differences.

The most important element in proper test use is, of course, demonstration of the validity of the test for the intended use. There are a number of pitfalls in the context of graduate admissions:

• An admissions office might use test scores as a determinant of admission, even though the validity of the test for that particular program had not been examined.
   (a) Tests sometimes are used inappropriately for admission to programs in disciplines for which validity has been established neither locally nor nationally.
   (b) In other cases, for a given discipline, national studies may show a test to be valid for admission to programs generally. Still, it may not be appropriate to the local situation.
• An admissions office might adopt an absolute minimum cutoff score below which applicants are uniformly rejected. Unless the cutoff score is validated, it might exclude applicants who could succeed in the program or include some who have little chance of success.
• An admissions office might use composite test scores for admissions decisions when only one or more component scores have been demonstrated to be valid in the program. For example, total GRE (V + Q) may be used despite the fact that only one has predictive validity.

In all of these situations, the admissions officers would be relying on unclear and possibly irrelevant information.

THE CONTROVERSY ABOUT ADMISSIONS TESTING

Given the clear evidence that most undergraduate institutions are not very selective, and that test scores play a significant role only for a very small portion of students—those applying to highly selective undergraduate institutions or to graduate and professional schools and those who rank low among high school graduates—one might not expect the furor that has in fact surrounded admissions testing in the last 5 years. The SAT has been the subject of numerous articles in the popular press. Educational Testing Service (ETS) was the subject of a lengthy investigation by a team connected with consumer advocate Ralph Nader (Nairn 1980), and test disclosure laws have been passed in two states and introduced in several others, as well as in the U.S. House of Representatives.

Truth in Testing

There is a vocal, deeply felt, and fairly widespread sentiment that the tests used for admission to higher education and the admissions process to which they contribute are unfair. While an earlier generation saw tests as an opening to equal opportunity for all because they select on the basis of ability and without regard for social class or national origin, standardized admissions tests are now branded by critics as barriers to equal opportunity and supports for the status quo in part because test scores correlate positively with indicators of socioeconomic status.

Two arguments have been advanced concerning the unfairness of using tests of cognitive ability as a criterion for admission to higher education. One involves the question of "test bias" and its possible effects on the competitive position of blacks, Hispanics, other minorities, and females; this is discussed below. The other argument, which has been marshalled in support of disclosure legislation, has to do with the alleged secrecy of the testing industry and the right of students to compare their test results with the correct answers and to examine evidence of validity for the particular decisions that may be made on the basis of their test scores.[1]

It is not necessary to hark back to Star Chamber to point out that openness in the exercise of power is important to the American concept of equity. Because the allocation of educational opportunities has come to be recognized as an exercise of power, many are no longer willing to let the admissions process go on entirely behind closed doors. Tests, the most tangible if not necessarily the most important element in postsec-

---

[1] See Brown (1980) and Strenio (1979) for two recent useful summaries of the debate over test disclosure.

ondary admissions decisions, have been the target of the greatest popular dissatisfaction. Given this climate, the central question concerns control of the test instruments and of the decision rules that govern the admissions process. Federal affirmative action policy is shaping college and university admissions practices by changing the decision rules (e.g., *Bakke*[2]); supporters of open testing seek to influence the process by bringing testing under greater public scrutiny.

It must be remembered that it was as recently as 1958 that the College Board decided to tell students their scores. The truth-in-testing movement is the culmination of those modest beginnings. It represents an important assertion of the interest of students, and of society in general, in the allocation of educational opportunity. As a general principle, it is desirable that tests—indeed the entire selection process—be open and known. How openness can best be achieved is a difficult question.

There are those who claim that only government regulation of the testing companies can ensure openness. Proponents of governmental oversight of the industry have drawn analogies to various regulatory precedents: some argue that testing companies have a monopoly on the instruments of human resource allocation that would justify their treatment as a public utility; some draw on the example of sunshine laws to justify opening up the process of test development and validation to public scrutiny; others believe that "truth in lending" and "truth in advertising" provide models for the protection of consumer interests.

We have not, however, seen evidence of systematic abuse by the testing companies serious enough to make government intervention imperative. Nor do we consider it obvious that federal regulation of the testing industry will serve the interests of test takers, although the testing companies might well find federal regulation less burdensome than a patchwork of state laws. It will not affect how tests are used. Thus, while we support the general principle of openness, we question both the need for federal legislation and the efficacy of the laws currently in operation or under discussion for significantly improving tests or the way they are used.

This is not to deny that the disclosure law passed in New York State in 1980 has had positive effects. The publication of test forms has resulted in the detection of a number of errors or ambiguities in the test questions, which has resulted in extra points for some test takers and, presumably, improved tests for future applicants. But the larger hopes expressed by supporters of the test disclosure laws, that governmental regulation will result in better test research or a fairer admissions system, seem mis-

---

[2] *Regents of the University of California* v. *Bakke*, 57 L.Ed. 2nd 750(1978).

placed. Kenneth B. Clark's remarks about the New York law (*The New York Times*, Aug. 18, 1979) point up some of the problems of the legislative approach:

. . . this law cannot deal with the complex issues of test validity and the role of cultural factors in influencing test results. The construction, evaluation and interpretation of tests are highly technical matters which must be dealt with by ongoing research by those who are trained in this specialty. The important problem of the use and abuse of standardized tests cannot be resolved by a simplistic law which confuses this issue with consumer protection problems.

Many test developers have expressed concern that test disclosure will have negative effects on the quality of the tests. Some feel that the pool of possible items is so limited and item development so difficult a process that disclosure after each administration of a test will soon give test takers what amounts to prior knowledge of the test questions. They have also expressed the concern that the reliability of the tests, which relates to the consistency of test scores, will be reduced because full disclosure rules out the traditional equating techniques (see Chapter 2). But there are other test developers who feel that the industry will be able to respond to these challenges, that they will be able to develop new item pools and new equating techniques rapidly enough to maintain test quality.

Instead of speculating about the technical costs and consumer benefits of disclosure, we suggest that states, Congress, and the research community take advantage of the current situation. Largely because of the pressure brought by supporters of open testing, the conditions now exist for an empirical investigation of the effects of various kinds of test disclosure. California and New York have passed state "truth-in-testing" laws. The California law, while stopping short of full disclosure, requires that facsimiles of postsecondary admissions tests, along with validity data and scoring information, be filed with the Postsecondary Education Commission. Test takers are to be given information about the purposes of the tests, the nature of the subject matter, scoring procedures, and sample questions, thus placing a legal obligation on test publishers where formerly voluntary action sufficed. The New York law goes further, requiring full disclosure. Under the terms of the Lavalle Act, test producers must file with the Commissioner of Education and supply to the test taker upon request the actual test questions and answers within 30 days of administration.

In addition to these state disclosure plans, some of the testing companies and client boards, despite continued concern about the effects of full disclosure on test quality, have begun to respond positively to the challenge. The Educational Testing Service has developed "public interest principles" to guide its staff and its relations with the client boards and colleges and universities that use its admissions tests (see Novick in Part II). Of more immediate consequence, three client boards, the Law School Admissions Council, the Graduate Management Admissions Council, and the Graduate Record Examination Board, have decided to disclose their examinations nationwide. The experience with these efforts over the next few years will indicate whether full disclosure is technically feasible and what the financial costs will be.

The decision to disclose these tests nationwide, together with the two existing state open-testing programs, provides all parties to the truth-in-testing debate with the opportunity to establish the effects of disclosure empirically. It would be useful for the Department of Education, through the National Institute of Education, to underwrite research projects on the experience with various disclosure plans and to ensure that a wide variety of psychometricians and other experts are involved in the collection and evaluation of data needed to provide the basis of future policy.

A policy of empirical study will also allow assessment of the accuracy of the assumptions that students are interested in, and will benefit from, knowing more about their performance on the tests. Early evidence from New York is mixed, with the lowest interest in disclosure indicated for the GRE (about 1 percent at each of the two administrations in spring 1980) and the highest for the LSAT (requests in 1980 were 17 percent in February and 25 percent in June). Disclosure requests for the SAT were in the lower range: 7 percent in March 1980 and 5.3 in May. There is reason to believe, however, that disclosure-request rates are significantly influenced by the method of request adopted. To get a copy of the SAT, for example, a student must send in a disclosure-request form (and $4.65) within a given period after the test administration. The Law School Admissions Council experimented with a simple check-off on the exam registration form for the June 1980 administration; 60 percent of the students offered that option elected for disclosure, as compared with 25 percent of the control group who had to initiate a request (Educational Testing Service 1980). Easier access would no doubt increase disclosure requests for the other examinations as well.

As to the question of which students benefit from test disclosure, an Educational Testing Service staff analysis of the first two SAT administrations since the New York law took effect indicates that the students who requested a copy of the test booklet and answer sheet had significantly higher mean scores and (self-reported) family incomes than those who did not (Educational Testing Service 1980). The hope of many supporters of the Lavalle Act that disclosure would improve the competitive position of disadvantaged and minority students is not borne out by this early evidence.

Admissions Tests and Minority Students

Among the social issues of recent years, none has proven more vexing than those related to providing minority and disadvantaged citizens with access to equal educational opportunities. Although the general issue of equal opportunity is discussed in Chapter 7, this specific aspect of the problem is deserving of special note.[3]

The basic problem in connection with admission to programs of higher education arises because test score distributions for identifiable subpopulations differ systematically. There is, for example, an average score difference of about 1 standard deviation between white and black applicants. To the extent that admissions decisions are influenced by those test scores, and to the extent that the number of applicants exceeds the number of available places, those subgroups displaying high average test scores will be relatively heavily represented among the students, and lower scoring subgroups will be underrepresented, in comparison with their representation among the applicants.

The observed differences in score distributions between various subpopulations raises questions of validity and questions of fairness. Whether test data are appropriately used in admissions decisions regarding minority applicants is first of all a factual question: Are predictions made from test scores as accurate for minority as for majority applicants? On the basis of the evidence currently available, the answer is yes (see Linn in Part II). That evidence dispels two contentions regarding within-group and between-group comparisons.

One contention, which pertains to within-group validities, is that tests do not predict which of the black students will achieve the best college records. In fact, however, predictions for blacks as a group are as accurate as predictions for whites as a group. Hence, insofar as admissions officials want predictive information to improve the comparison of competing applicants from the same ethnic group, tests provide useful data.

The second contention, which pertains to between-group comparisons, is that experience tables based on the general student population un-

---

[3] Because the technical and popular uses of the term "test bias" are so different, we hope to avoid confusion by omitting the term here and speaking instead of validity and fairness issues; see Chapter 2 for a discussion of the meanings of test bias.

derstate the probable success of black students. However, the bulk of the evidence concerning commonly used admissions tests suggests that their predictive validity differs at most only very slightly for blacks and whites (Breland 1978, Linn in Part II). With the important qualification that only scanty evidence is available for minorities other than blacks, subgroup differences in average ability test scores seem to predict similar differences in academic performance as measured by course grades.

Reasonable people differ over the definition of equal opportunity as well as over the means by which equal opportunity can be assured. And scientific evidence concerning test validity does not provide answers to questions of social justice. The evidence does indicate, however, that a policy decision to base an admissions program strictly on ranking applicants in order of their expected success will tend to screen out minority candidates (see, for example, Evans 1977, Brown and Marenco 1980). Lest this statement appear to establish polar options—decisions must be based either on ability or group quotas—we hasten to add that it is meant to preface a counsel of flexibility.

There is nothing in psychometric theory to encourage a strict and mechanical application of any ranking principle. Test scores are admittedly statements of probability, not of fact. They seek to measure a relatively narrow (if also very important) range of cognitive skills. And they predict against a limited, if also very useful, criterion (usually first-year grades). Hence, while they can provide important information about an applicant's probability of success, there is no reason, when there are many applicants capable of succeeding, for test scores to dominate a decision process. As the Carnegie Council on Policy Studies in Higher Education (1977) commented a few years ago, using numerical predictions to make fine distinctions can look attractive to admissions officers, but it is a misuse of tests. Even recognizing the inherent difficulties, we believe that admissions officers have to exercise judgment, case by case, as, in fact, many now do. The goal should be to effect a delicate balance among the principles of selecting applicants who are likely to succeed in the program, of recognizing excellence and of increasing the presence of identifiable underrepresented subpopulations.

Coaching and Test Scores

A final part of the controversy surrounding admissions tests concerns the effects of coaching on test results. The Educational Testing Service and its client, the College Board, have long stated that special preparation has no beneficial effects on SAT scores. In the 1977-78 College Board booklet for students and their advisors, it was noted, for example, that "the abilities measured by the SAT develop over a student's entire academic life, so coaching—vocabulary drill, memorizing facts, or the like—can do little or nothing to raise the student's scores" (Educational Testing Service 1977:24). Yet numerous coaching programs have sprung up, many of them commercially sponsored, and both researchers and popular critics of admissions tests have disputed the validity of the College Board position (Pike 1978, Slack and Porter 1980, Nairn 1980; but see Messick 1980).

Evaluation of the influence of coaching on test performance is not a simple matter. Coaching programs vary in their duration and intensity, some lasting only a few hours and others for weeks. They also vary in purpose, effectiveness, and in the background of the students they serve. No matter what its accuracy regarding coaching for the SAT, for example, the College Board position presented above does not speak to the courses offered to law school graduates preparing for the bar exam or to medical students facing their first board exams.

Partly because it is difficult to design evaluation studies of coaching, the evidence on coaching effects is not clear. Few controlled experiments have been conducted in which the performance of students who have been coached can be compared with comparable uncoached students. The much-discussed Federal Trade Commission study (1979) of the coaching industry provides some hints that, in certain circumstances and for certain limited kinds of students, coaching efforts may improve scores on college admissions tests, but problems with the data analysis qualify the importance of the findings. Messick's (1980) review and reanalysis of research from the 1950s to the present concludes that a 30-point average gain on the SAT-V comes at 300 hours of coaching-tutoring, and 10 points at about 15 hours; gains below 10 hours were too irregular to be predictable. Messick emphasized that the longer programs were more like regular instruction or curriculum than what is usually thought of as coaching.

Messick's finding about long-term tutoring seems to carry over to medical school boards. A recent study of coached and uncoached students who took the National Board of Medical Examiners, Part I, showed sizable positive coaching effects from an extremely intensive review course consisting of up to 134 90-minute tapes. Unfortunately, however, the results are muddied by the fact that 72 percent of the coached students reported that the examination included a number of questions (averaging 10) identical to questions they had encountered during the review sessions (Scott et al. 1980).

Studies of short-term coaching programs, which tend to concentrate on test-taking skills, indicate that such coaching produces, *on the average*, very little improvement in test scores. Nevertheless, because conclusions on the subject are tentative, it is reasonable to encourage schools or school districts to make sure that students are familiar with test-taking techniques. ETS currently supplies students and their advisers with explanations of test item formats and full-length sample tests. For students who are both test wise and well-schooled, informal study of the information provided by test publishers is probably sufficient preparation for college admissions tests. But students who lack experience with standardized tests and have not been drilled in test-taking techniques—such as knowing when to guess, when to pass over questions, how to allot time, etc.—may benefit from some drill in the techniques of taking tests.

The issue of public responsibility for providing intensive coaching is difficult. Long-term coaching programs tend to have greater, although not necessarily dramatic, effects on the test score of the average individual. In some of these programs, students are given training in both general and specific academic skills that are useful in mastering college courses as well as in test performance. In effect, such programs provide remedial training for students who, for some reason, did not acquire these skills in their high school courses.

Provision of longer term, intensive test preparation courses in public schools would make access to such courses less dependent than now on the financial means of students or their families, since most intensive courses are now run on a private fee-paying basis. The prospect of establishing high school courses for test preparation immediately raises the question of whether schools and students ought to spend valuable time in preparing for a selection test when that time could be devoted to the study of some appropriate subject matter. The answer depends on the value placed on the subject matter and reasoning skills measured by the test. There is no necessary disadvantage, and there may be considerable advantage, to explicitly preparing students for an examination if the examination tests abilities and knowledge that are educationally worthwhile.

CONCLUSIONS

Admission to Undergraduate Institutions

• Despite the lack of selectivity in many colleges, the vast majority of them continue to require applicants to submit SAT or ACT scores. To the extent that test scores are not used, students who are not planning to apply to selective schools are incurring unnecessary expense and inconvenience. There is also danger that students with poor or mediocre test scores may be discouraged from applying even to nonselective institutions in the mistaken belief that their chances of being admitted are small.

Admission to Graduate and Professional Schools

• Tests can predict which applicants are likely to perform well in the academic portion of professioinal training. But there has been little effort to demonstrate a correlation between test scores and performance in the profession to which applicants wish to enter. Admissions tests cannot be said to predict which applicant will be a good doctor or a good lawyer. This means that tests should not be allowed to completely determine the admissions process, since some people who do somewhat less well in the academic program may be outstanding in the profession.

• Validity studies of the GRE, the LSAT, the MCAT, and the GMAT (postgraduate) support the thesis that, for many programs, not only are test scores correlated with student's grades in the program, but also the tests' contribution to the prediction is to some extent independent of the contributions of other predictors, e.g., prior grades.

• Admissions tests can be useful selection aids if admissions officers respect their limits. An important such limitation is that the use of test scores as one of the criteria for admission to graduate programs—and to highly selective undergraduate programs—is justified only to the extent that validity of the tests for that purpose has been demonstrated or shown to be reasonable. (The same restriction should be imposed on other predictors, i.e., earlier grades and recommendations.) Therefore, it is incumbent upon each institution to justify the use of test scores as a criterion for admission to a program of study. Ideally, that justification would take the form of a local validity study demonstrating that the test has a relation to some meaningful criterion, e.g., GPA or retention in the program. When that is not feasible, it may be possible and reasonable to justify the use of the test by noting close similarity of the local program to those programs to which the national validity studies pertain. Unless close similarity is established, it is unwarranted to generalize from results of national studies that a test is valid for the local program. The population of applicants may differ, the selection ratio may differ, or the requirements for success in the program may differ.

• It is unwise to adopt a rigid minimum cutoff score. Candidates barely below that score probably are not appreciably less likely to succeed than candidates barely above that score. For applicants whose predictor scores are in a marginal range, it is especially desirable to consider other evidence, e.g., commitment to study, past experience relevant to the field of study, contribution to desirable diversity in the enrolled student group, and other nonquantified factors. This conclusion also applies to selective undergraduate institutions.

• When only certain subtests of an admissions test have demonstrated validity, e.g., an advanced (achievement) test on the GRE or the verbal section on the SAT, it is not appropriate to use other subtest scores for admissions decisions.

Test Disclosure

• As a general proposition, openness in test development and use is to be encouraged. It contributes to better understanding of a complex technology, helps to protect the interests of students and the public in the allocation of educational opportunity, and encourages necessary research.

• Full test disclosure will have definite but unknown effects on test development, test quality, and test use. For example, new methods will have to be found for ensuring comparability from test to test. These effects may or may not be negative, but will certainly take time to work out.

• It is not clear that there exists a systematic abuse or a clear public interest requiring governmental regulation of the testing industry.

Admissions Tests and Minority Candidates

• The evidence indicates that predictions made from test scores are as accurate for black applicants as for majority applicants; there is only scanty evidence available for other minority groups. Subgroup differences in average ability test scores appear to mirror like differences in academic performance as measured by course grades. In this sense, the tests are not biased.

• The basic selection problem for professional schools and selective undergraduate institutions is an overabundance of qualified applicants. When there are many applicants capable of succeeding, admissions decisions should be based on social and educational values broader than a comparison of predicted grade averages.

Coaching and Test Scores

• It does not appear that short-term coaching produces significant improvement in test scores for most students, although it may reduce test anxiety, and it may be of value to students who have little experience with standardized tests. Research indicates that long-term coaching does have some effect, which appears to differ with the type of test, coaching program, and test taker (e.g., high school senior, medical student, lawyer, disadvantaged student, bilingual student).

RECOMMENDATIONS

Admission to Undergraduate Institutions

1. College admissions officers ought to examine closely their policies and gauge the usefulness of requiring applicants to take admissions tests. They should inform potential applicants how test scores and other sources of information are used in making decisions. This information should be provided, even if the tests are optional, so that students can decide whether or not to take them.

Admission to Graduate and Professional Schools

2. For deciding about admission of applicants to graduate or professional programs, the criteria for admission should include test scores only when such test scores are valid for that program. Even then, since small differences in test scores are unlikely to be associated with appreciable differences in academic performance, relevant factors other than test scores should be given considerable weight in admissions decisions. This recommendation also applies to selective undergraduate institutions.

3. In order to establish the validity of an admissions test, when the local situation does not seem to warrant reliance on the national validation studies, graduate and professional school admissions officers should explore the possibility of participating in a cooperative validity study of the kind offered by the Graduate Record Examination Board. Such cooperative ventures can bring essential technical assistance to schools that do not have the expertise to conduct an independent study.

Test Disclosure

4. A number of experiments with test disclosure now exist: New York and California have passed disclosure laws and the Law School Admissions Council, the Graduate Management Admissions Council, and the Graduate Record Examination Board have decided to disclose their tests nationwide after each administration. We recommend a policy of watchful waiting to allow the developments of the next few years to inform judgment about a workable balance between openness in testing and the integrity of the tests and the selection process to which they contribute and about the effects of government involvement in admissions practices.

5. The Department of Education should support research on the effects of test disclosure on test quality and on the response of test takers to supplement industry-sponsored studies.

Admissions Tests and Minority Candidates

6. We recommend *against* admissions decisions based solely upon ranking of applicants' test scores or high school record or a combination of the two. We also recommend *against* fixed quotas or other mechanical systems (such as adding points to test scores) for increasing the minority student population as being unsound policy.

7. We recommend flexible decision rules that balance likelihood of success in the program (as measured by tests, GPA, and other predictors), recognition of academic excellence, and support of demographic diversity in the student population.

Coaching and Test Scores

8. We recommend that schools or school districts routinely take such steps as are necessary to ensure that students are familiar with test-taking techniques.

9. If schools decide to institute long-term, intensive coaching courses, it is important that the time devoted to preparing students for an examination be spent on content that is educationally worthwhile in its own right and that excessive concern for what is most testable does not lead to serious sacrifice of other educational content.

REFERENCES

Breland, H. M. (1978) Population validity and college entrance measures. College Board Research and Development Report. RDR 78-79, No. 2. Princeton, N.J.: Educational Testing Service.

Brown, R. (1980) *Searching for the Truth About "Truth in Testing" Legislation*. Report No. 132. Denver, Colo.: Education Commission of the States.

Brown, S. E., and Marenco, E., Jr. (1980) *Law School Admissions Study*. San Francisco, Calif.: Mexican-American Legal Defense and Educational Fund.

Carnegie Council on Policy Studies in Higher Education (1977) *Public Policy and Academic Policy, Selective Admissions in Higher Education*. San Francisco, Calif.: Jossey-Bass, Inc.

Educational Testing Service (1977) *Guide to the Admissions Testing Program*. New York: College Entrance Examination Board.

Educational Testing Service (1980) Testing Programs Affected by Lavalle Act, Compliance Policies and Disclosure Experience. Internal memorandum to the Executive, Finance, and Audit Committees' Meeting October 22-23.

Evans, F. R. (1977) Applications and admissions to ABA accredited law schools: an analysis of data for the class entering in the Fall of 1976. *Reports of LSAC Sponsored Research,* 3 vols. Princeton, N.J.: Law School Admission Council.

Federal Trade Commission, Boston Regional Office (1978) *Staff Memorandum of the Boston Regional Office of the Federal Trade Commission: The Effects of Coaching on Standardized Admission Examinations.* Boston, Mass.: Federal Trade Commission, Boston Regional Office.

Federal Trade Commission, Bureau of Consumer Protection (1979) *Effects of Coaching on Standardized Admission Examinations: Revised Statistical Analysis of Data Gathered by Boston Regional Office of the Federal Trade Commission.* Washington, D.C.: Federal Trade Commission.

Ford, S. F., and Campos, S. (1977) *Summary of Validity Data from the Admissions Testing Program Validity Study Service.* New York: College Entrance Examination Board.

Friedman, C. P., and Bakewell, W. E. (1980) Incremental validity of the new MCAT. *Journal of Medical Education* 55:399-404.

Gordon, T. L. (1979) Study of U.S. medical school applicants, 1977-78. *Journal of Medical Education,* 54:677-702.

Hartnett, R. T., and Feldmesser, R. A. (1980) College admissions testing and the myth of selectivity: unresolved questions and needed research. *American Association of Higher Education Bulletin* 32(March):3-6.

Kingston, N. M., and Livingston, S. A. (1981) *Effectiveness of the Graduate Record Examinations for Predicting First-Year Grades: 1979-80 Summary Report of the Graduate Record Examinations Validity Study Service.* Princeton, N.J.: Educational Testing Service.

Messick, S. (1980) *The Effectiveness of Coaching for the SAT: Review and Reanalysis of Research From the Fifties to the FTC.* Princeton, N.J.: Educational Testing Service.

Nairn, A., and associates (1980) The Reign of ETS, The Corporation That Makes Up Minds. The Ralph Nader Report on the Educational Testing Service.

Pike, L. W. (1978) *Short-Term Instruction, Testwiseness, and the Scholastic Aptitude Test: A Literature Review with Research Recommendations.* College Entrance Examination Board Research and Development Report 78-2. Princeton, N.J.: Educational Testing Service.

Schrader, W. B. (1977) Summary of law school validity studies, 1948-1975. Pp. 519-549 in *Reports of LSAC Sponsored Research,* Vol. III. Princeton, N.J.: Law School Admission Council.

Scott, L. K., Scott, C. W., Palmisano, P. A., Cunningham, R. D., Cannon, N. J., and Brown, S. (1980) The effects of commercial coaching for the MBME Part I Examination. *Journal of Medical Education,* 55(September):733-742.

Slack, W. V., and Porter, D. (1980) The scholastic aptitude test: a critical appraisal. *Harvard Educational Review* 50:154-175.

Strenio, A. (1979) The Debate Over Open Versus Secure Testing: A Critical Review. National Consortium on Testing, Staff Circular No. 6, October.

Wilson, K. (1979) *The Validation of GRE Scores as Predictors of First-Year Performance in Graduate Study: Report of the GRE Cooperative Validity Studies Report.* GRE Board Research Report GREB No. 75-8R. Princeton, N.J.: Educational Testing Service

7
Ability Testing
in Perspective

INTRODUCTION

As previous chapters have shown, ability testing emerged in this century in response to a need for a uniform, rational system for evaluating a person's attainment—relative to some standard, relative to someone else's attainment, or relative to a previous level of attainment. In a rapidly expanding economy and a mobile society, testing had great appeal. It held out the promise of rewarding a person's merit independent of class or family connection, ethnic origin, or race. That goal continues to have widespread appeal, but long experience with testing and changing social conditions have generated conflict about the impact of the technology of testing on the realization of the goal of rewarding merit.

THE CONTROVERSY ABOUT TESTING

At its core, the current controversy about testing is a product of greatly expanded aspirations and contracting opportunities. During the 1960s, scarcity seemed obsolete, a relic of war and depression. Abundance— automobiles and washing machines, housing subdivisions and credit cards— seemed the natural condition of American society, poverty an anomaly. As noted by Harrington (1980:12), social thinkers described the central problem of the age as the management of abundance and predicted "that a fine-tuned affluence under conditions of price stability would create fiscal dividends sufficient to make justice not only possible, but profitable." Buoyed by faith in the possibility of legislating social change, the federal government launched preschool and educational enrichment programs, job-training programs, health care programs, legal aid programs, and housing programs. Cities, counties, and states devoted sizable resources to establishing community colleges, and universities admitted a much broader range of students than ever before.

Allocating greater resources to the poor, the aged, and the powerless appeared a matter of social justice, and there was a sense of moral uplift in these years. But the distributive impulses of the 1960s spawned frustration along with increased expectations. The revolution of rising expectations, as Daniel Bell (1972) remarked, is also the revolution of rising *ressentiment*. Hence this period of optimism witnessed an increase in social unrest and in political activity aimed at forcing the system to live up to its promise.

Today, the philosophical legacy of the 1960s is being played out in a world in which the perception of abundance no longer prevails: the belief in equality as an economic promise has taken firm root even as the economic conditions that nurtured it have changed. It is easy to favor amelioration of the condition of the poor in an expanding economy, but in a stagnant or declining one the inclination is to protect one's own share. The concordance of interests that supported the social policies of the 1960s is being replaced by the conflicts of interests of various groups in the society. As organized interest groups—community organizations, labor unions, business associations, ethnic and racial associations—apply political pressure to influence policy, the sense of a larger social good is bowing before the concerns of particular groups. Indicative of the disintegration of the generous impulses of the 1960s is the so-called tax revolt: resentment of the cost of social programs extends in some cases even to public education and public libraries, two of the most traditional kinds of publicly supported institutions designed to promote the general welfare.

The diminished prospects of the average American give the debate about testing an especially sharp edge. Because they are visible instruments of the process of allocating economic opportunity, tests are seen as creating winners and losers. What is not as readily appreciated, perhaps, is the inevitability of making choices: whether by tests or some other mechanism, selection must take place.

Criticism of testing by professional, public, and advocacy groups reached a peak in the early 1970s, and the level has remained high. And testing is vulnerable to criticism in at least two respects. First, there have been enough instances of poor testing practice, which have been headlined in the press, to make all testing suspect. Second, testing organizations have been so convinced of the superiority of their methods that they have not been sufficiently sensitive to legitimate criticisms about testing. In particular, they have been slow to extend their accountability beyond the institutional client to encompass the interests of the test taker.

It is likely, however, that even if only the most rigorously developed and psychometrically advanced tests were used to fill jobs or choose among applicants for graduate and professional education and even if they were used only under the most stringent standards of public accountability, the outcome would not satisfy current demands for social justice. And this fact reveals a confusing, indeed, a destructive element of the testing debate. Americans have, on the whole, expected too much of tests and, conversely, have blamed too much on tests. People have wanted tests to produce social justice, to be "fair" in some absolute sense. And, when disappointed in the results of the testing process, people have charged them with being "unfair," with producing inequality.

Are Tests Fair?

In all of the controversy about testing, selection by test results has been the object of the most intense criticism. On the surface, selection on the basis of standardized test scores seems to satisfy the concept of fairness in that all test takers are treated alike, without regard to race, sex, religion, or any other irrelevant consideration. But, as the following very simple example illustrates, the automatic application of such a selection process does not necessarily serve the ends of fairness or of rational decision making. It assumes that individual promise can be compared by considering only the relative level of accomplishment and skill attainment at the decision-making point, without regard to the environment in which this accomplishment and attainment were achieved.

Suppose that for admission to a university (all other specified qualifications being equal), the selection rule is that any candidate with a score of 700 on a highly valid test is to be selected over any candidate with a test score of 650. Certainly, such a rule would preclude overt discrimination. But suppose that the test in question were the advanced mathematics test of the Graduate Record Examination; that the student who scored 700 was the son of a mathematics professor, who had attended an exclusive and prestigious private school, received special instruction in mathematics, and studied in the mathematics department of one of the best universities in the country; and that the student with the score of 650 was a woman of working-class background, who grew up and attended school in modest circumstances and worked her way through an urban open college. If a single opening remained in the graduate class, which candidate would deserve to be selected?

Though a rigid interpretation of the concept of equal opportunity might dictate impersonal selection of the higher scorer, fairness and rationality could also lead to choosing the other candidate. She started at a lower base of accomplishment than the professor's son and nearly caught up with him. Apparently, she learned faster than he did. A projection of this performance into the future, even without other considerations, might support the belief that in time she would match and surpass his level of attainment. And she exhibited a higher learning rate despite being exposed to a lower quality of educational opportunity than the young man. It is at least arguable that if she were given equal or superior education, she would excel. She also has clearly demonstrated an ability to overcome adversity and therefore would be likely to prove successful in career opportunities in which motivational factors are as important as cognitive factors. Finally, it might well be in society's best interest to reinforce behavior that produces results beyond the expectations of a given educational and cultural background.

While this simple example demonstrates that mechanical use of test scores may not lead to fairness, it also demonstrates one critical value of tests: without the test score, the young woman might have had no way of demonstrating that her absolute level of achievement was nearly that of her competitor, whose background was so much more auspicious. The moral of the story is that the use of ability tests may be a necessary element, but it will seldom be a sufficient basis for selection decisions. Objective assessment can inform, but it cannot supplant, judgment.

An important goal of this report is to provide a balanced picture of tests and the effects of testing. Previous chapters have discussed the appropriate uses of tests and their potential value in educational settings and in the workplace. Because one must understand the character of a tool to use it well, the following section focuses on the limitations of ability tests—limitations that arise from the inherent nature of the testing effort, from the way in which testers have gone about their work, and from the shortcomings of present knowledge about abilities. Then, in order to place the whole question of testing in perspective, the concluding section of the chapter looks at a number of aspects of American society today—ranging from the concrete (the structure of the labor market) to the philosophical (changing conceptions of accountability)—that have fueled the testing debate, but that transcend and are essentially independent of testing. From that perspective, testing is less a source of various social problems than the occasion for their manifestation; to the extent that this is true, complaints about testing are functioning like a distractor item on a multiple choice test and drawing public attention away from more fundamental issues. When people stop thinking of tests as panaceas or using them as scapegoats, when they understand that testing is a useful, but limited, means of estimating one of the characteristics of interest in selecting or assessing people, i.e., ability or talent, then a good part of the conflict about testing will be alleviated.

LIMITATIONS OF TESTING

The task that testers took on early in this century was shaped by the ideal of a scientific approach to human behavior and social order. Above all, they drew from the new field of applied psychology an interest in human variation and its implications for social efficiency. They tended to view society in organic terms and assumed a natural harmony between the variety of human capacities and the requirements of the social order. They were excited by the vision of the psychological expert, who could measure individual mental and physical capacities, guiding everyone into his or her proper place in the social hierarchy. Professional norms and techniques evolved from this base, and a consensus emerged about how to test. But the methodology necessarily exacted a certain price, which is evident in the following discussion of four aspects of testers' work: the measurement of difference; the attempt to produce comparable information on large numbers of people at low cost; the concentraton of effort on one segment of the spectrum of abilities; and the limited role that the theory of abilities plays in test development. And since improper or misguided use of test results probably causes as many problems as any shortcoming of tests themselves, this section on limitations includes a discussion of some common types of misuse.

Measurement of Individual Differences

The major goal in much test construction has been to reveal individual differences. Sometimes the goal is to separate people who are exceptionally good or poor. Sometimes the goal is to rank the test takers along a scale: the developer tries a large number of test items and forms a combination that will produce the desired spread. This technique is especially important when the test is to be used with people who are much the same in ability—for example, to choose executive trainees from a group of people with MBA degrees. If all examinees answer a particular item correctly, it is of no value in sorting the group. An item on which all examinees choose an incorrect answer likewise does not differentiate. It is items in the intermediate range that efficiently identify differences.

As was explained in Chapters 2 and 5, item selection based on the need to spread examinees' scores over a wide range of correct/incorrect ratios compromises the integrity of test content to some degree: the developer may pay more attention to the statistical properties of an item than to the importance of its content, and in any case there is an unavoidable tendency toward the homogenization of content.

Compromises Required by Large-Scale Testing

The development of standard conditions of testing and particularly of group-administered testing programs represents an attempt to provide a reasonable accommodation of the need for information about individuals to the conditions of mass society. If comparisons are to be made among people or institutions, it is essential that they be observed under comparable conditions. Standard conditions are also important if one wishes to interpret a performance in the light of past experience with examinees who performed similarly or if measurement is to detect change from one occasion to another. But constraints are introduced by the very fact that testers are attempting to obtain comparable information on many people in many places.

Standardizing leads to a preference for questions that can be easily administered and scored. This in turn tends to set limits on the content of tests and on the conditions of testing (time, space, number of test takers, type of response, manner in which instructions are given, etc.). The need to test large numbers of people with minimum expense and minimum investment of time has given a near monopoly to pencil-and-paper tests, multiple-choice items, and group administration.

Test developers try to keep time pressures moderate. One general rule of thumb in developing tests (although we recognize this is an oversimplification) is to try for a limit that will allow 75 percent of the test takers to complete the test. Still, time constraints are a significant aspect of standardization. Arguably, time pressure rewards the mentally quick and penalizes the ruminative. And, since older people tend to fall behind young adults when working under time limitations, they may score lower on a test with time liitations than they would on a different test. And if the time pressure during a test is appreciably greater than the time pressure in the educational program or the job, the older test taker is at an unfair disadvantage.

Conventional group-administered written tests are intended to be uniform, not flexible. But even on a strictly uniform test, performance depends on personal working styles and inquiry strategies, specific learning history, stamina, tolerance of stress, and individual confusions and idiosyncracies. A tester giving a test to one person can detect and adapt to these variations; a tester of a group cannot. In a group test, for example, a person's failure to respond to a large fraction of the items produces a low score of uncertain meaning. An individual tester observing nonresponse can usually discriminate lack of knowledge from lack of motivation or lack of confidence. As a result, a test that is individually administered offers far more suggestions regarding causes of difficulties in performance and learning. Individual testing on a large scale, however, is expensive, often prohibitively so.

Yet another effect of the kinds of tests currently used is to reward certain personal or cultural styles. For example, people who are accustomed to competing for recognition as individuals are comfortable with the requirements of the usual testing procedure; those who lack this confidence and independence can feel threatened. Performance in cooperative tasks is rarely tested, although cooperative work is obviously to be valued in many work situations. Indeed, in some American subcultures it is the most valued style of work, and children in those cultures are encouraged to become effective in collaborative work. It can be argued, then, that conventional tests require a style that does not show some people and some groups to their best advantage.

It is possible to devise rule-governed, hence reproducible, testing procedures that break the traditional mold. In practice, however, testers have exploited those possibilities only for decisions for which there are large risks that are thought to warrant large expenditures. For example, airlines and the military test the pilot trainee in the cockpit of a computerized flight simulator. Instruments like those on airplanes display a sequence of readings that closely resemble flight situations, including the rare emergencies that demand extraordinary responses. In this kind of computerized test, the domain of possible tasks is infinitely diversified, and it is easy to adjust items so as to challenge the examinee neither too much nor too little. Testing is "standardized," but not at the same level for everyone. The test can be tailored to the examinee in a way pencil-and-paper tests do not allow. This kind of test can function as a diagnostic instrument and, by repeating types of questions or problem situations in which the examinee performs inadequately, can promote learning.

What Tests Do Not Measure

There is much that tests do not cover. The concentration on "objective" tests in large-scale programs does not allow one to get information on tasks such as writing or oral presentations. The standard tests also place the examinee in a reactive role. The usual test item makes a strong demand on the processes of critical verification and very little demand on more imaginative processes. But independent productive work requires a subtle combination of intuition, invention, and synthesis with the processes of self-regulation.

Throughout the history of ability testing interest has concentrated on a limited number of cognitive skills. Three of them—verbal abilities, quantitative abilities, and analytic reasoning ability—appear over and over in the most-used tests, the tasks changing little from decade to decade. Typically, the verbal items require reading comprehension, vocabulary, analogic reasoning, sentence completion, and command of grammar. The quantitative items call for computations (with or without numbers), quantitative comparisons, and higher mathematical manipulations (e.g., algebra, geometry). The analytic reasoning items generally include logical reasoning, analysis of explanations, interpretation of graphs and charts, and data sufficiency problems. In most tests, the analytic reasoning component is incorporated in the verbal and quantitative sections of the test, though the GRE has recently provided a separate analytic reasoning component.

The traditional triumvirate of abilities, extensive as it is, leaves out many abilities important in practical activities. Few of the most widely used group tests touch upon synthesizing abilities, spatial reasoning, problem solving for which alternative solution strategies are necessary, and problems of sequential linkage. (The Differential Aptitude Tests and other batteries for vocational guidance or classification do cover some of these abilities.) Far more important than the possible neglect of specific reasoning skills, however, is the fact that most ability tests do not address creativity, intuition, perseverance, insight, and the like. The few attempts to assess them have not been conspicuously successful. Walter Lippmann (1922) said of test developers in the early 1920s: "What their foot rule does not measure soon ceases to exist for them. . . ." The years have not stilled that complaint.

The subordinate abilities measured by subgroups of items in most testing programs are not reported separately nor usually validated separately. Reading comprehension, for example, calls on resources different from those required in vocabulary subtests. Analogic reasoning is the product of yet other mental skills. Some of these could be more important to one course of study or type of job and some to another. Up to now, psychologists have developed only a limited body of research relating the component abilities to particular and varied performance criteria. Because these efforts have not met with great success, validation research has concentrated on composite verbal and composite quantitative scores and on gross outcome measures such as grade averages. It therefore gives users little specific information about how to match instruction or training or job tasks to each individual's strengths.

For the most part, the current procedures serve adequately the needs of institutional decision makers such as colleges, universities, and, somewhat less adequately, those of employers. The additional benefit in having more refined procedures is often not considered by test users to be worth the additional cost. However, many critics of testing point out—and many psychometric researchers going back as far as Thurstone agree—that abilities are not one, two, or even three dimensional and that a sizable minority of test takers is generally not well served by research procedures that group all facets or types of ability into two or three categories. They argue for greater symmetry in the service extended to test takers and test users (Coleman 1970). Despite the fact that both critics and many prominent members of the testing community have argued for reform for several decades, there has been only modest change in this area.

We noted above that test developers had not been particularly innovative. Innovation did thrive in the early days of testing, but the tests that sell well today can, with few exceptions, be described as finely tooled versions of the tests of the 1920s. Invention wilts in the absence of a market. The market has not encouraged automobile manufacturers to venture beyond the internal combustion engine, and it has not encouraged test developers to turn in new directions.

One example of the effect of market forces on test innovation occurred with regard to testing of cooperation. Social psychologists have long had ways to study cooperation, and at least one tester (Damrin 1959) built on that experience to produce a standard test. In her Russell Sage Test of Social Relations, the examiner (a stranger) takes charge of a classroom while the teacher watches from the sidelines. The children are to build a picture from pieces they have been given—one piece to each child. Classes differ markedly in their ability to coordinate their efforts. This test obviously could be as suggestive for educators as most tests that are scored for individuals, given that almost all schools profess the objective of developing the child's effectiveness in social relations. In fact, however, the test faded into obscurity. The test was made available to schools by a prominent publisher, but so few educators showed interest that it was allowed to lapse. Had the educational users of tests been eager to branch out in this new direction, it would not have been difficult to provide continuing research and development like that provided for tests of arithmetic computation. A science can perhaps forget about the market, but a technology cannot.

The Role of Theory in Test Development

The Explanation of Abilities

The social sciences have been characterized in this century by a methods-oriented approach to inquiry. The sociologist Robert Nisbet (1976) draws attention to the risk that methodology will be elevated from handmaiden to master of the process of inquiry. That risk exists in the field of testing because mental measurement has been deliberately quantitative, empirical, and pragmatic. Modern psychology is characterized by a determination to go beyond philosophy and to displace theories that described the mind in terms of unobservable powers and instincts. As a result there have been great advances in the mathematical aspects of measurement theory. Tremendous energy and talent have gone into elaborating statistical methods, refining measures to bring out individual differences, investigating the interrelations among measured abilities, and correlating test performance with other indicators of ability. But there has not been similar progress in the understanding of what is being measured.

There are two basic approaches to the study of abilities: one focuses on internal processes and their ontogenesis; the other concentrates on external correlates of test scores. The first style of inquiry tries to find out exactly what growth in the command of logic, the techniques of deploying attention, and the skill in using knowledge enables the developing human mind to solve increasingly difficult problems with each passing year. Psychologists working in this internal vein—Binet, Piaget, Wertheimer, and Simon, for example—have used exceedingly varied techniques: simple observation of sources of confusion, clinical interviewing, timing steps in the performance to a fraction of a second, and writing computer programs that "act like" a child in a certain stage of development (mistakes and all). The second style tries to link up test performance with external variables: with scores on tests that are better understood, with antecedent conditions in the person's upbringing, and with outcomes in later activities. Most of the pioneers of testing—Cattell, Galton, Thorndike, and Terman, for example—worked in this external vein. This research has found much that is important; indeed, it supplied much of the documentation for Chapters 2 through 6 of this report. Nevertheless, it has limits as a means of explaining abilities.

Almost 60 years ago Walter Lippmann took proponents of testing to task in the pages of *The New Republic* (Vol. 33, 1922-23) for suggesting that their instruments were capable of measuring intelligence when, in fact, there existed neither an accepted definition of what constitutes intelligence nor reliable evidence of the nature of the abilities that tests measure. Understanding of the factors that influence scores remains seriously incomplete. While there has been some interplay between the internal and external lines of psychological research, the external line has continued to dominate the development of group testing. Research on test scores has been parallel to but not integral with research on internal processes. Specialists in test development have not devoted as much effort to or have not had as much success in interpreting tests substantively as they have had in relating test performance to other measures of ability. Theories of cognition (including theories of "intelligence," "creativity," and the like) do not currently play a central part in test development. As a result, the task of explaining even so long-recognized an ability as reading comprehension in terms of a theory of information processing or other advanced psychological concepts has barely begun. If more psychologists who worked on theories of cognition had also worked on test development, testing today might be further advanced. This kind of research is difficult, but the effort is needed. There is some evidence of a heightened interest in the profession in addressing the question of what tests measure and room for some optimism about new directions in research (Messick 1980, Snow et al. 1980, *Construct Validity in Psychological Measurement* 1980).

Ability Tests, Abilities, and Performance: Uncertain Connections

Test development and the interpretation of test results have benefited from advanced psychometric methodology, but this methodology has not been a powerful source of explanations. The best efforts of students of human abilities have not created a generally accepted theory linking success in reasoning tasks to the descriptions of mental processes coming from the laboratory. We can summarize the comments of J. B. Carroll (1976:29), a senior figure in the field of measurement, on the research program of J. P. Guilford in a slightly earlier generation. Guilford's research, says Carroll, was thorough, brilliant, and informed regarding the findings of laboratory experiments; even so, it could not resolve the problem of classifying abilities. Creditable in its own terms, the research was "certainly not adequate for the extrapolations that have been made from it by . . . [followers who] propose applications of it to school learning problems." As Carroll goes on to say, nearly all the abilities of concern outside the laboratory, including most test tasks, involve a complex mixture of the elementary processes. Theory now emerging from the laboratory may make it possible to say how an individual operates with multiple processes in an efficient sequence, but no one any longer looks forward to sorting abilities into the kind of "periodic table" that was the principal aim of psychological research on tests between 1930 and 1960.

Testers necessarily set up artificial, insulated, schematized situations to assess problem-solving behavior. The work of Cole et al. (1978) on the distinction between solving problems in a closed system and in an open-ended situation suggests that the link between test and nontest behavior may be more tenuous than has been generally assumed (Sarason 1980). People acting in their usual circumstances rely heavily on familiar cues, many of them social; they differentiate their behavior according to their own wants and the expectations held by others; they choose responses on the basis of impression and hunch more than by formal analysis, and they consider the concrete setting of the problem as well as its logical, abstract core. A test item, however, ordinarily strips a problem of its concrete and social context and demands the most purely analytic response the respondent can give. Cole et al. believe that laboratory controls prevent subjects from displaying the kinds of behavior organization they use outside the laboratory. If so, theories and data derived from stripped-down tasks are a poor basis for predicting what people will do after they leave the laboratory or the testing room.

In a similar vein, instructional psychologists (Neisser 1976, Brown and French 1979) lament the aridity of test tasks for which examinees are to attend only to the information given by the examiner. The formal intelligence that ignores context and preconceptions so that a problem can be treated in words and equations is worth measuring and worth developing, they say, but they concur with Cole and his colleagues that abstraction is not the whole of intelligence and perhaps not the part most important for most people most of the time. This line of thought leads instructional psychologists to try to tease apart the tasks presented in the usual ability test (e.g., Glaser 1978, Sternberg 1977). Identifying the underlying processes tapped by particular tasks may serve to improve the diagnostic potential of tests. This is clearly an agenda for coming decades; it will not be accomplished in a few years (Brown and French 1979).

In the meantime, the relationship between problem solving on tests and everyday performance has taken on new relevance to public policy, as attention has come to focus (largely as a result of governmental concerns about equal employment opportunity) not on those selected, as was the case when tests were perceived primarily as identifying excellence, but on those not selected. This shift in focus has brought new prominence to the question of what is being measured by a given test or item type and has pointed up insufficiencies from a public policy perspective in validation strategies based solely on the demonstration of external statistical relationships. This brings us back to the theme of internal and external approaches to ability. Both the empirical route and the theoretical route have contributions to make; it is unfortunate that the progress in testing has come almost exclusively from the former. Scientists have now developed a remarkable amount of theory of cognition out of studies of language and culture, of human development, of memory and retrieval, of perception, and so on. There is no one theory, and on some central issues there are conflicting views. Even so, many valuable ideas are available that were not available when the basic structure of present ability tests was established. The time surely has come for the testing profession to see what use it can make of these ideas.

Test Misuse

While tests themselves have important shortcomings, problems arising from technical limitations are probably not as significant as the problems stemming from improper or misguided test use. The distance between laboratory conditions and everyday use may sometimes be so great that test users are buying peace of mind rather than scientific selection.

The Dominance of Quantifiable Information in Judgments

Any tendency of test developers to leave unmentioned what they cannot measure or to overstate the importance of what can be measured feeds a more general tendency to place unwarranted faith in numbers. The national penchant for numerical and statistical information both predates and extends beyond psychometrics. There is an apparently insatiable demand for numbers—census data, educational summaries of pupil performance, fertility rates, death rates, GNPs, batting averages, and Dow-Jones averages—that taxes those involved in data collection. At the same time, some scholars suspect the expression of information in quantitative form of eroding critical inquiry and thus debasing the decision process.

The attempt to quantify carries with it the seeds of a dangerous illusion: that what has not been reduced to numbers can safely be left in the background. Researchers have found that statistics tend to drive out what is called soft data (Tversky and Kahneman 1974). In the realm of policy analysis, for example, critics claim that when administrators make decisions they tend to give too little weight to what is not expressed quantitatively (Center for Policy Alternatives 1980). But the dilemma for decision makers is that there is no easy or sure way to weight qualitative, supplementary, and especially idiosyncratic information. Says historian Lynn White (1974): "Some of the most perceptive systems analysts are pondering today how to incorporate into their procedures for decision the so-called fragile or nonquantifiable values to supplement and rectify their traditional quantifications. Unhappy clashes with aroused groups of ecologists have proved that when a dam is being proposed, kingfishers may have as much political clout as kilowatts. How do you apply cost-benefit analysis to kingfishers?" Making decisions about people is at least as difficult.

Although the Committee favors giving attention to a college applicant's history and the circumstances under which he or she will study, as well as to test scores, we cannot suggest a strict rule of procedure. For example, if a law school applicant dropped out of two colleges before earning a BA degree at a third, how heavily should that fact count? One admissions officer might see it as a bad sign and prefer another applicant with the same test score and grade record who went to only one college; another officer may be favorably impressed by the student's "determination." Personal and perhaps prejudiced opinions tip the scales. Because experience tables can rarely be compiled for qualitative and situational information, the interpretations of such data cannot be validated. Worse, there is evidence that human readers, making predictions on the basis of rich case files, often miss the mark by more, on the average, than do predictions by formula about the same cases made from quantitative data (Meehl 1954, Dawes 1980). Yet it remains true that quantitative scores are often interpreted with greater emphasis and finality than they deserve.

Overreliance on Test Data

Ability test results—like other data—have limited dependability and significance, yet those who use test results do not always keep the limitations in mind. The content and form of a test limit the inferences that can justifiably be drawn from it, but the reporting of test performance as a numerical score tends to veil the limitations. Critical observers from within and without the field of psychometrics have noted that the public (and professionals) discuss scores out of context as if they were the reality, and neglect to think about the many processes generating the behavior that the scores, at best, only summarize.

The issue of test score decline illustrates the problem of reading more into test results than they can reveal. A steady if small annual decline in average performance on the two major college admission tests over the last 10 years has been widely reported and discussed in the press and popular literature. Among the explanations advanced for the decline were the inferior quality of teacher education, increased disciplinary problems in the classroom, an increase in the percentage of minority students in the college-bound population, the negative effects of television on the young, and the deleterious psychological effects of a contracting economy. In the absence of supporting evidence, the test producers had very little confidence in any of the explanations of score declines. They considered the scores to be programmatic data (as distinguished from data collected under rigorous experimental conditions or critical survey and poll sampling constraints) and therefore not appropriate, sufficient, or reliable indices of educational quality. However vigorously these caveats may have been voiced, however, few press accounts questioned the adequacy of the test data to support any or all of the hypotheses. And while the testing organizations undertook extensive studies to check the calibration and technical adequacy of the instruments in question, they did not undertake a program of public education on the limits of reasonable inference from SAT and ACT scores. The hypotheses lingered in the media that the test scores were adequate measures of a general deterioration in education, when in fact they could only suggest provocative possibilities (for a recent discussion of the research on some of those possibilities, see Jones 1981).

Scores as Labels

People who rely on test data as sufficient in themselves often oversimplify even more drastically by reducing test information to a label. Members of the academic community refer to their "700 students," meaning those who had scores in the upper ranges of the SAT. IQ scores are used to designate "genius" and "retardation."

Recent controversy over the all-volunteer army provides a telling example of incautious test interpretation. Since World War II, the armed forces have used a succession of tests for purposes of selection. The successive tests provide scores that cannot be directly compared from year to year, so some of the technical calibration procedures mentioned in Chapter 2 have been used to put them on a comparable basis. It was decided a long time back to mark four division points on this common score scale, creating five categories. Category V ("Cat V" in the jargon) spans the score range of the lowest-scoring 10 percent of the people in service in 1944; in postwar use of the tests, examinees scoring in this range were considered unsuitable for military service.

A recent controversy has focused on Category IV. Rightly or wrongly, military officials and legislators looked on scores in Category IV as only minimally acceptable; they assumed that if "Cat IVs" made up a sizable proportion of an army, it would be unable to do its job properly. The Department of Defense had thought—and had told Congress—that in recent years the percentage of enlisted personnel in Category IV remained steady at about 5 percent. Troublesome questions about the calibration of the measure in current use cropped up, however, which led the Department of Defense to commission technical studies. A review of the studies by a committee of three psychometricians resulted in a report (Jaeger et al. 1980) that indicated that 30 percent—not 5 percent—of recruits were in Category IV. The press relayed this information under such headlines as "Recruits' Mental Ability Far Lower Than Reported" (*Washington Post*, August 1, 1980), but the press generally neglected the report's challenge to the way the question itself had been framed. The committee pointed out that the long-used categories are arbitrary and that the relationship of Category IV status to on-the-job performance had been assumed, not established. It recommended phasing out the categories and the labels "mental category" or "mental group." A major recommendation of the report was an ambitious research program to learn how the measured skills of recruits relate to their performance in the armed services and to define standards for particular levels of responsibility accordingly.

An early College Board report (Brigham 1926:55) proposed a rule of thumb about the meaning of SAT scores that seems worthy of resurrecting and extending: "[T]he test scores are more certain indices of ability than of disability. A high score in the test is significant. A low score may or may not be significant. . . ." Test users should more often corroborate low scores with other evidence and should consider the relevance of *all* scores—high and low—to the selection decision being made. Then labels like "Cat IV" would less often be used to short-circuit the process of assessment that testing is intended to facilitate.

Matching a Test to Its Function

All too often a test is badly matched to the function it is intended to perform. Group-administered written tests can be useful as mass screening devices. They can fulfill a broad institutional objective of quality assurance. But they are not designed to provide a full portrait of the abilities of any individual test taker. Test users have a great responsibility to find the kind of test that serves their objectives *and* to understand the limits of the information the test offers.

Costs are inevitably a consideration. Large business firms can afford to seek extensive information about candidates for executive positions. Many have set up assessment centers at which candidates spend one to three days undergoing all kinds of assessments: written tests, oral tests, interviews, in-basket routines and other work samples, observed small-group interactions, and so on. Such assessment programs cost anywhere from

$350 to $5,000 per participant. No small employer could afford such a system.

While one can hope for further progress, there is little prospect that test misuse will be eliminated. For example, a recent survey of several hundred school teachers indicated that many of them did not understand percentiles or grade equivalent scores (Yeh 1978). Many of the problems discussed above do not lend themselves to short-term or easy solutions, but some obvious steps can be taken to improve the way tests are used. Given the prevalence of testing in the schools, for example, school officials ought to ensure that teachers, parents, and students understand something about the tests and how they should be used. The test makers, for their part, can provide test users with much more information about their products and specific advice about interpreting scores.

The limitations of testing technology and the problems caused by its misuse lead us to a cautionary conclusion. Tests are tools. They provide an efficient way to gather certain kinds of information systematically and they extend to a decision maker one means of making judgments about people. But when a test score is taken out of context and treated as if it tells all that matters about a person, scientific assessment is degraded to dogma.

TESTING IN THE CONTEXT OF BROADER ISSUES

We now turn to an examination of a number of social developments that have focused public attention on ability testing and have helped shape current attitudes toward tests, but that far transcend any possible effects of testing. The five subjects treated here are attempts to ensure fair process; the expansion of the concept of a public function; the expansion of the concept of accountability; changes in the population and the structure of the labor market; and equal opportunity. Our purpose is to place testing in perspective, not to pass judgment on the developments and intellectual currents described.

Fair Process

Part of this society's heritage is the belief that individuals are entitled to fair treatment, with decisions about them made on the basis of openly stated rules and according to procedures carried out publicly. Like any such belief, it has been adhered to in varying degrees at various times. Certain institutions have developed formalized procedures to ensure fair treatment, e.g., the record-keeping and due process rules of the courts. The norms for others, particularly private institutions, are less clear. Until recently, the hiring and firing of workers was subject to considerably less demand for known and open process. But the past few decades have seen an increased insistence on fair process in all aspects of people's lives, and this increased insistence has been manifest in a variety of ways that involve tests and testing.

Access to Information

Recent laws have established the right of individuals, with certain exceptions, to have timely access to information concerning them personally or about the general workings of government. For example, people now have the right to see any files a federal agency has gathered about them, including information obtained for security clearances, unless there is evidence that releasing such information would be contrary to the national interest. Further, the burden of proof in such instances is not on the person to demonstrate that he or she requires the information; the agency must establish that such information may be withheld.

Rights of access have also been extended to certain types of records held by academic institutions. Students now may see letters of recommendation teachers write about them when they apply for admission to schools or for jobs, unless they specifically waive this right.[1]

Although people today have more formal access to the personal information that influences decisions about them than they did a few years ago, it must be noted that inevitably the system has adjusted to dilute the impact of the change. For example, unless students waive the right to see teachers' letters of recommendation, they may have difficulty obtaining such letters in the first place. In some cases, the information that is made available to individuals may not be the same information as that on which decisions are based; for example, information obtained by telephone, which is not subject to disclosure, may have more influence than letters.

The trend toward increased access to information quite naturally has included the right to see test scores.[2] In fact, the disclosure of test scores to test takers preceded the right to information in other areas, such as access to letters of recommendation.

---

[1] Subject to the outcome of current litigation, applicants for faculty positions in the University of California system may be allowed to see all letters of recommendation written in their behalf.

[2] Some years ago, test scores were not considered the property of the test takers, so they had no right to see their scores. For more than two decades, however, test takers have generally had direct access to their own scores.

Privacy

Related to the right of access to information is the right of privacy. It is increasingly being accepted that information about a person may be made available to others only with the specific authorization of that person. For instance, a letter of recommendation written by a teacher in support of a job application may not be shown to another potential employer, except as specified by the applicant. Without the applicant's permission, the letter is to be displayed only to those clearly assumed by the nature of the application to be authorized to receive the information.

Past and current census questionnaires are also subject to privacy restrictions. By law, information obtained in census questionnaires may not be divulged to any person or agency outside the Census Bureau, and census workers are sworn to secrecy in this matter. Similar protection exists for people who are subjects in medical or psychological experiments. Such information may be used in statistical analyses, but only in the rarest circumstances could it be divulged in any way in which the data about any one person were identifiable.

The application of this principle to educational testing has raised a number of questions about school record keeping, which were the subject of a conference sponsored by the Russell Sage Foundation at the beginning of the decade: Should schools be required to obtain parental or pupil permission before collecting certain kinds of test information? Should schools be required to obtain parental or pupil permission before releasing test data to parties outside the school? What rights should parents or pupils have regarding access to test information? Under what circumstances may such information be responsibly withheld? Should the pupil have the right to restrict parents' access to test information? (Russell Sage Foundation 1970).

The testing companies have developed procedures designed to protect the privacy of individual test takers. Nevertheless, they must be able to make aggregate test data available for research as a part of the validation process, and it is very difficult to guarantee absolutely that individuals cannot be identified. This is a problem common to all computerized record systems.[3]

---

[3] It should be noted that the protection of test takers' privacy goes beyond the question of validation research. The Educational Testing Service and the American College Testing Service, in addition to their testing programs, have provided data-assembly services. These files include such information as the detailed statements of family finances needed for a student to qualify for financial aid. The testing companies have been faced with requests from government agencies for access to these financial files; indeed, one of the companies has gone to court repeatedly to avoid subpoenas by the Internal Revenue Service (Privacy Protection Study Commission 1977:411).

Privacy concerns are much more immediate, however, in the case of tests whose primary purpose is diagnosis of personality or capability problems. Not all specialists agree even that the results of an individual test given to determine whether a young student is mentally retarded should be made available to the parents or guardians of the child, even for the purpose of deciding whether the child could benefit from some form of special education. The arguments against disclosure include misunderstanding of the test score and the danger of labeling as well as lack of awareness of the limits of tests. Yet the general trend toward full access to information suggests that full disclosure of such information will become regular practice; indeed, the Education for All Handicapped Children Act requires that parents have access to such information and be brought into the decision process if a child is to be placed in a special education program.

Open Decision Making

The concept of fair process includes the idea that decisions made about peple should be based on open criteria and ground rules known in advance by all interested parties. Most large industries, especially those with strong labor unions, now openly state their rules for hiring and firing. Employers are no longer completely free to make idiosyncratic decisions to hire, fire, or promote employees: they must follow a set of rules, which has been established in a collective bargaining contract between the union and management.

It is not yet clear how open decision-making rules will affect testing practices. Currently, for example, most test results are not evaluated on the basis of rigid cutoff scores, with people whose scores are above the cutoff score being accepted and those whose scores are below being rejected. The application of open decision-making rules to the interpretation of tests for admissions, hiring, or promotion might require that cutoff scores be established and made known in advance. Even if the test scores were only one basis for the decision, along with such considerations as grade point averages, letters of recommendation, and supervisors' ratings, it might be argued that the weight to be given to each type of evidence would have to be stated in advance. But rigid, established rules might not serve the purpose of providing a given number of suitable, successful applicants. If many applicants were competing for only a few places, the scoring rules might need to be more stringent; if the converse were true, the rules might need to be relaxed.

Open decision making is also pertinent to another aspect of standardized testing: people's right to know the basis on which their test score is determined. A test taker's access to his or her own score has been established for some time, but only recently has legislation been introduced or passed that assures the test taker of the right to know how the score was determined. The LaValle law in New York, for example, requires that copies of tests used for admission to colleges and to graduate or professional schools be made available to test takers at their request, within 30 days of administration. This allows a test taker to see what the right answer was considered to be and even to challenge the derived score. While this practice is a matter of considerable controversy at the present time, it is a development that is consistent with open decision making, which permits individuals to verify the legitimacy of all aspects of decision processes that affect them. (See Chapter 6 for a discussion and recommendations on the issue of test disclosure.)

Impartial Evaluation

The right of an individual to impartial evaluation means that the decision maker should not have a personal interest in the outcome of whatever decision is being made. This is not a new concept of fair process, of course. The society generally has frowned on nepotism, for example, because a decision can hardly be impartial if an important personal relationship exists between the decision maker and the person about whom the decision is being made. For many purposes, however, the idea of impartial evaluation has its natural limits. The owner of a small business would hardly be criticized for giving preferential treatment to family members. In practice then, the principle of impartial evaluation refers to the use or potential use of power in decision making that goes beyond the legitimate concerns and interests of the decision maker.

Impartial evaluation is especially important in grievance procedures. This familiar application of fair process allows a person who feels an injustice has been done to file a grievance that will be evaluated by neutral examiners according to an established, open process. A supervisor who fires an employee or a school principal who disciplines a student should not be a member of the body that will arbitrate the complaint brought by the employee or student in response to the action. Most labor union contracts specify grievance procedures in which decisions rest with people not involved with the incident in question.

A special need for impartial evaluation exists in the realm of testing when a test taker is charged with cheating. Most standardized testing programs have some basis, usually statistical, for establishing the likelihood of cheating. For example, the answers of the test taker under suspicion can be compared with those of the people seated nearby. If the correlation in answers is beyond statistical reason, there is a presumption of cheating. Most testing organizations pursue such cases in some form of a hearing in which the verdict is reached by people, within or outside the organization, who are not involved in the testing program or with the individual.

The Costs of Fair Process

The gains society realizes by putting fair process principles into practice are not without costs. Some sacrifice in institutional efficiency is inevitable, and in many, if not most, cases the monetary costs of institutional performance are increased. In some contexts, the costs of fair process practices may outweigh the benefits. For example, the benefits of making the SAT, ACT, and similar tests available shortly after use are clear, but such disclosure will entail monetary costs and possibly will also reduce the technical quality of the tests. Furthermore, the benefits gained may not be equitably distributed, so that "fair process" in this instance may have unfair results. For example, full disclosure of test material could benefit advantaged test takers more than disadvantaged ones because of differences in the ability to use the information disclosed. This, too, is a cost in terms of social values.

Determining whether the trade-off of costs for benefits is acceptable will require careful evaluation of the nature of the costs and benefits of each element of fair process and considerably more empirical evidence than now exists.

The Concept of Public Function

In recent decades there has been a general social trend toward a broadened concept of what government should do for its citizens. Government now plays a greater role than ever before in determining how various functions that affect the public, as individuals or as a whole, are carried out. This tendency has manifested itself primarily in two ways: in the protection of individuals and in the monitoring of institutional practices.

Government Protection of Individuals

The old principle of caveat emptor has been considerably weakened in recent years. Government has established safety standards, consumer protection agencies, and even ombudsmen who protect the right of individuals against government itself.

Increasing governmental regulation of the private sector has been accompanied by an extension of the concept of public function to private institutions. This development has clearly influenced society's attitude toward standardized tests, particularly with regard to protecting the rights of test takers. Not too many years ago, test producers and such test users as industrial or educational institutions were the sole determiners of how a test was constructed and how it was used. Individual test takers had little, if any, right to decide whether to take the test or what decisions would be made on the basis of the test result. That situation is changing, both as a result of general social change and as a result of specific legislative action. In addition, access by third parties to individual test scores is severely limited, while access by test takers has expanded.

Government Regulation of Private Industry

The idea that some functions, such as delivering the mail, are best performed by public agencies is quite old, and it has also been long accepted that some functions of private industry—communication, transportation, and utilities—are so essential, affect such a large segment of society, and require such large capital investment that they are at least quasi-public in nature. Though in the United States these functions are carried out by private industry, government franchises and regulates their performance. In some cases, the distinction between a publicly owned and operated industry and a privately owned but publicly regulated industry is very narrow, and in a few industries—local transit, for example—the function has moved from the private to the public domain.

The definition of what affects the public now goes beyond the traditional concept of public utility. Monitoring and regulation by government also applies to industries whose processes or products may adversely affect the public. Federal regulation is more likely to be aimed at large industries than small ones, of course, but regulation, in general, is not limited to large industry. The housing industry, for example, traditionally is composed of small local businesses, but it is regulated through local building codes to protect both home buyers and the interests of the community at large.

Education has been considered a public function for a long time. Primary, secondary, and much of postsecondary education is conducted directly by state or local governments. Arguably, then, educational testing, because it exists as a contracted support activity of state and local schools and colleges, constitutes a public function and, as such, should be subject to the same fair process restrictions as the schools and colleges themselves. To date, only professional societies have served to regulate and monitor the testing industry, and clearly professional expertise is necessary in establishing any professional guidelines—legal, medical, testing, or whatever. But the effectiveness of regulation by professional societies has been questioned because they are put in the position of recommending guidelines for their own activities. Recently, some legislatures have become convinced of a need for public regulation of the testing industry, with or without the guidance of testing professionals. Intensified regulation in some form is likely in the future.

Accountability

The concept of accountability goes hand in hand with that of public function because performance of a public function carries with it the obligation of public accountability. And increasingly, society is demanding accountability from the private, as well as the public, sector. Accountability has two related aspects: one is that products or services should not be harmful to users; the other is that the products or services should possess the quality or attributes claimed for them. An important example of accountability is that industry is held liable for the failure of a product to meet quality or safety expectations.

Quality Assurance

One aspect of accountability is the idea that if a product or service is offered for sale and the purchaser expects some value from it, the purchaser should be reasonably assured of the quality and safety of the product or service. When a manufacturer makes and sells toys, it is held accountable for ensuring that the toy is safe for children. Meat sold for consumption is inspected and labeled by government to assure the customer of its quality and safety. The cost of producing an unsafe product can be very high; witness, for example, the costs of recalling the Firestone tire.

In the realm of testing, the obligation of quality assurance falls upon producers both directly and indirectly: the test must do all it purports to do, and applicants selected on the basis of the test must have demonstrated the competencies the test is designed to measure. Like any other manufacturer, a test producer tries to assure test users and test takers that the test is of the quality the purchaser (or taker) is led to expect. This is the purpose of test validation.

The LaValle law in New York is not concerned just with the rights of test takers to information about the test; it is also intended to provide an external spur to quality assurance by allowing a test taker to judge the quality of the test used to make decisions about his or her life. What is required is that a test be as it is advertised and sold. If a test taker believes that a test does not perform as advertised, he or she can file a complaint.

The Committee has some skepticism about these assumptions and expectations of the LaValle law. We are not sure that it will do much good (and we are equally unconvinced that it will cause serious problems). Expertise far beyond the capacity of most test takers is required for any serious analysis of the adequacy of a test and its research base, although disclosure may be valuable in turning up ambiguities in specific items. We believe that wider access of the research community to test data is far more germane to improving the quality of tests than disclosure to test takers.

Tests are a special class of product in that they are themselves used to measure quality—the quality of an individual's training or skill. For example, the testing industry increasingly is called upon to develop competency tests that can be used to establish the credentials of people graduating from high school or entering various professions. The quality of the test is reflected indirectly in its ability to measure test taker competencies. But there may be an inherent contradiction between the direct and indirect requirements for quality assurance in tests: public access to test forms may increase the difficulty of assuring test quality and thus reduce the accuracy of the test in measuring the quality of test takers.

Liability

A corollary condition of quality assurance is that, if the expected quality is not realized, the person or organization offering the product or service is liable for the deficiency. A doctor who makes a surgical error may be sued for damages stemming from the failure to provide service of the quality expected of a licensed physician; a toy manufacturer may be sued if a toy injures a child.

Many court actions with regard to testing thus far have been brought against test users for alleged misuse. The Bakke case is one illustration of this type of action. Bakke did not claim the test itself was at fault; he challenged the decision made on the basis of the test. However, the line between liability for misuse of tests and quality deficiency in the tests themselves can be very thin. Several suits have been brought against employers whose use of tests has resulted in hiring a disproportionate number of white males in comparison to women and minority group members, and in such cases the burden is on the test user to prove that the tests used were valid. But in these cases, too, the liability for the quality of the test lies with the test user rather than the test producer, for it depends on the particular use to which a test is put. A test may be valid in one circumstance but not in another.

Assuring a structure of user responsibility is the knottiest problem in testing. Professional regulation has severe limitations since most test users are not members of professional organizations of psychologists. There are no obvious self-regulating mechanisms to suggest, and the Committee doubts that an elaborate system of federal controls monitoring thousands of users is practical. It seems, however, that many kinds of intermediate bodies could be useful in promoting proper use. Testing companies and organizations like the College Board could set up ombudsman boards to look into cases of misuse. Trade associations whose members use tests might take an active role in promoting responsible procedures.

The Role of Accountability in Education

Public institutions dominate education in this country. Their clear mandate to provide a public service is accompanied by the assumption that they should be held accountable for what they purport to do—educate. Public schools have always been held accountable, but today a new determination has developed to measure the quality of educational processes and to hold schools liable for providing an acceptable standard of education. This concept of public accountability has been given only limited judicial support in educational malpractice suits, however.

Increasingly, the public has come to view all aspects of education as a public, rather than a private, function. To some extent in recent years, the distinction between public and private educational institutions has become blurred because of the large amounts of federal money going to all educational institutions. With this public support, the accountability requirement has extended to almost every facet of college and university as well as to private schools. The rationale is much the same as for noneducational organizations that are largely funded by government: if government money is being spent, then government has a right, even a duty, to hold the spenders of the money accountable.

Tests have a role in educational accountability because they are used to evaluate an educational process or institution. A competency test administered to a student yields a direct assessment of the performance of that student. It may also indicate the effectiveness of the education that that student has received, thereby serving to evaluate the school as it has affected that student. Competency test results for a group of students, then, may serve the purposes of accountability of the educational process.

In sum, the trend toward greater accountability in education is influencing testing in two almost contradictory ways. First, tests are a product whose quality can be questioned and whose use can be challenged. Thus, demand will increase for quality assurance in tests, and test producers and users will increasingly be liable for meeting this demand. Second, competency tests are increasingly called on to provide assurance that individual students and educational institutions are performing adequately. In order to provide this assurance, the individual or school must accept the quality of the tests they use. Inevitably, the quality of the tests individuals or schools use to assure quality is itself being challenged.

Labor Market and Population Changes

Changes in the age structure of the population and in the occupational structure of work have significant effects on society in general and the labor market in particular, and these in turn affect education and training and, hence, the use of tests.

Population Changes

Changes in the population profile have already had profound effects on the labor market and more are projected in the next 20 years. The birthrate has been decreasing for the last two decades, so that fewer children have been entering the educational system. The number of young people entering the labor market is smaller than in previous years, but because of the increase in the overall number of people remaining in, or reentering, the labor market, its size has increased. Often, women who reenter the labor market must undertake additional training or retraining, which has obvious implications for the testing industry.

The "aging" of the population also has significance for educational testing. With fewer students in the educational system, fewer tests will be given. Colleges and universities no longer enjoy an oversupply of applicants from which to choose their students. Thus, they place less emphasis on selective devices like aptitude tests. With some schools near closing for lack of students, only the more prestigious institutions may continue to use tests for selection purposes.

Changing Skill Requirements

With technological advance, the occupational mix of the labor force has come to include a greater proportion of technically trained workers. Today even farming, with its use of large, expensive, and complicated equipment, requires specific technical skills. And ditches are rarely dug with shovels these days; instead, various types of earth-moving equipment are used. Each differs substantially from the others, and each requires special skills to operate. In recent years, the computer has been responsible for increasing the demand for specially trained employees throughout the business world.

These changes in skill requirements have an obvious implication for education: more and more specialized training is required. These training requirements also put greater demands on testing: more tests and more sophisticated tests are needed to determine training eligibility, to establish competence, and to evaluate the training organization. Increasing specialization, particularly, puts an additional burden on the testing industry because it must develop many different specific competency tests to assure quality workers for specialized occupations.

Job Mobility

Geographic mobility has always been a characteristic of American society, starting with the first immigrants to this country and continuing with the settlers who migrated westward. Even without a change in geography, Americans tend to exhibit a large degree of job mobility. Young people today do not necessarily follow the trades and occupations of their parents, and people often change jobs horizontally, simply moving from one job to another at the same level. Vertical mobility also has increased, and people do not expect, and are not expected, to remain in entry-level jobs.

Occupational mobility, whether vertical or horizontal, requires that people, during the course of their working lives, acquire many skills. Acquiring these skills has increased the demand for training and retraining and for specific tests for ability or competence. New jobs often will require a new set of skills that cannot be inferred from test results established for entry into previous jobs. Particularly with vertical mobility, the new, higher skill level calls for training and accreditation.

Even for those who stay in the same occupation or profession throughout their lives, some professions require continued certification or continued training and recertification, of which the health and teaching professions are notable examples. And because of technological change, even some "same" occupations may change significantly in the course of a person's working life. Retraining and recertification put increased demands on test producers to provide the testing tools to measure skills.

Equal Opportunity

Equal opportunity is a longstanding and highly publicized American goal. Strong commitment to the goal for *all* Americans, however, has been slow in developing. Slaves were never considered to have equal rights, nor historically were women, native American Indians, and many immigrant groups. In recent years, commitment to the goal has grown, and few or no exceptions are now admitted. As the goal of equal opportunity has been extended to virtually everyone in the society, new demands are being placed on many institutions and processes; testing is one of them.

The Handicapped

Until recently, a very large segment of our population, the handicapped, did not have equal opportunity or, indeed, much opportunity at all. It was assumed that physical or mental handicaps made equal opportunity impractical or too expensive. Deaf or blind children did not have the same educational opportunities as their normal peers because society was unwilling to bear the costs of special education facilities or because such children were considered not worth educating. Little attempt was made to provide handicapped adults with equal employment opportunities because employers believed that modifying the work environment to accommodate their handicaps would be economically unreasonable.

Now, increasingly the handicapped are given greater opportunities in education, employment, and many other areas. Blind children are educated in Braille or provided with readers; deaf children are taught to read lips or given other special education; accessibility to public transportation and public buildings is required for people with motor handicaps. And people now believe that retarded children should be educated up to the limit of their abilities. Accommodation to the special needs of the handicapped has been made a legal obligation. Schools, employers, and public agencies have a burden to provide equal opportunity up to the limit allowed by the specific handicap.

In testing, it is difficult in some cases to provide equal opportunity for the handicapped because of physical obstacles coincident to the testing process. A person with motor handicaps, for example, may not be able to record test answers; a blind person cannot read a pencil-and-paper test. However, test producers and users are expected or required to provide special facilities so the handicapped can take tests.[4]

The Disadvantaged

Another category of people who have faced limited opportunities is comprised of those in circumstances that may impede educational or skill

[4] The larger problem of modifying tests to accommodate various kinds of handicap is the subject of a study and report by the Panel on Testing of Handicapped People (Sherman and Robinson 1982).

development. This category includes recent immigrants, who have not become fluent in English or have not received the kind of education that would make them employable in modern American society, and children from poorly educated families who live in low-income neighborhoods and attend poor-quality schools.

Historically, many immigrants or their children could not fully develop their potential skills until they became assimilated into American culture. Although Americans take pride in how quickly immigrant groups have been assimilated, some groups have not been able, have not been allowed, or have not chosen, to assimilate, and members of those groups remain disadvantaged. Today, society expects such disadvantaged people to be offered greater opportunity in education and employment. For example, people with language deficiencies are expected to be employed to the limit of their capabilities, and the burden of proof has shifted to employers to demonstrate that a particular function demands greater language skills. And the government has undertaken massive, if only partially successful, efforts to provide compensatory education to the disadvantaged.

Testing the disadvantaged sometimes requires special arrangements. Increasingly, courts and legislatures have ordered that educational tests be given by a person who speaks the same language as the test taker or be written in that language. As is the case for handicapped people, the desire to reduce disadvantage often conflicts with institutional efficiency. Furthermore, the interpretation of test scores, particularly of aptitude tests, is a significant matter for the disadvantaged. Test users cannot rely on test scores alone to indicate potential ability because a particular disadvantage may mask this potential. Instead, they need to consider the test score within the context of the circumstances that have shaped the test taker's experience prior to the test (see below).

Whether right or wrong, it is a common perception among members of disadvantaged groups that tests have been used to justify procedures that exclude minority group members and therefore impede their advancement. Intentions are difficult to judge, but even the appearance of intentional discrimination calls for significant changes in decision-making processes. It is very important that all members of society perceive decisions about them to be fair.

Educational decision making for women poses special problems. While direct, overt discrimination against women has been substantially reduced (although certainly not eliminated), expectations of what women ought to do and are capable of doing are changing only slowly. Women do not receive the same amount of encouragement as men to enter the most rewarding careers, and so they are less inclined than men to take the courses necessary for admission to many academic and professional education programs. Girls are seldom urged, for example, to take four years of high school mathematics, but if they do not, their college choices are severely limited, as are program choices within a college. Such factors should be recognized when test scores are used as admissions criteria.

The appropriateness of standardized tests for black and Hispanic students has been seriously questioned. Comparatively high percentages of students from black and Spanish-speaking families are classified as educable mentally retarded and are placed in classes that provide them few opportunities for educational development. Typically, intelligence tests form an important source of data for the placement decision.

It is frequently—and mistakenly—presumed that these intelligence tests measure innate, and perhaps genetically derived, intelligence and not attained skills. But the reality is that these tests reflect to a significant degree a student's educational advantage or disadvantage. In particular, such tests are highly language dependent. Consequently, the possibility exists that because of these tests, language-deficient students are wrongfully classified and assigned to special education classes.

The language issue is particularly controversial with regard to the Hispanic community. In contrast to earlier immigrant groups, who generally accepted the idea that first-generation children should adopt English as their primary language, some Hispanic immigrants insist on retaining Spanish as the primary language for their children. Because using English is not valued highly in this immigrant culture, the children have little motivation to acquire English skills. But without such skills, these children score low on educational tests, and the naive interpretation of these scores results in many being classified far below their real abilities.

The question of the extent, if any, that this nation ought to become bilingual and the extent to which local, state, and federal governments ought to accept or promote bilingualism is an issue beyond the scope of this report. It is clear, however, that the conflict between the traditional unilingual policy and those who demand that their children be taught in Spanish, with English as a second language, is a source of contention about education and a source of the controversy about testing.

Interpreting and Using Test Results

The relevant factors in the educational decision-making process are not race or ethnicity, but those that derive from disadvantage. It would be difficult to identify all the variables that contribute to educational advantage or disadvantage for particular students. Certain variables have obvious relevance. The language spoken in the family and the peer group is particularly important, as are the educational and income levels of the parents and the neighborhood. The quality of the preschool and primary school is significant, as is involvement in other educational activities before school years. The quality of the college attended is important in judgments about entrance to graduate school.

If these variables were considered in the decision-making process and the performance of students were related to differences and similarities in background, it is unlikely that many inappropriate decisions would be made. The major testing organizations have been gathering background data on students for many years and reporting this information to those responsible for making important educational decisions. Nevertheless, many decisions are still made without taking into account relevant information about a student's background. Testing organizations have no power to force proper use of such information. They, and other professionals, have long condemned the practice of basing decisions solely on test scores.

Because test developers cannot guarantee that tests will be used properly and because many test users continue to make simplistic inferences from test scores, criticism has mounted, and now there are public demands for a moratorium on testing and for federal and state legislation to monitor the testing process. Test developers encourage test users to interpret test scores properly, but the test user is the ultimate decision maker. At present, neither the test developer nor the test taker can easily hold a school district accountable for misuse of an intelligence test, and the courts have come to be perceived by many people as the only avenue of redress.

The Concept of Group Parity

Equal opportunity was originally understood to require an end to discrimination against individuals on the basis of race or ethnic origin and this goal became the law in 1964. The problem of disadvantage was at that time widely believed to result primarily from present and previous racial, ethnic, and other discrimination. Eliminating such overt discrimination was seen as a way to solve the problem of disadvantage in some proximate future.

When this passive approach did not produce the desired results, or at least did not produce them fast enough, the concept of affirmative action was introduced. Institutions were required to actively solicit applications from qualified members of specified groups. Selection, however, was still to be made of the most qualified individuals. However, affirmative action programs did not result in a substantially broadened opportunity for minority persons, at least in the short run. As a result, the concept of equal outcome, or group parity, evolved, aimed at those groups especially identified as protected under civil rights legislation. Many people came to see "equal opportunity" as requiring that minorities be selected from the pool of all qualified applicants in proportion to their representation in the population. Although group parity has significant support from advocacy organizations and some federal agencies, its historical roots in America are limited primarily to some big cities and the governmental jobs controlled by their political machines. The change from equal opportunity to affirmative action and then to group parity has produced conflict because group parity does not easily coexist with traditional conceptions of the rights of individuals. Many people perceive group parity as reverse discrimination. The policy of group parity has been interpreted most broadly by the Equal Employment Opportunity Commission. The federal courts have recognized it to the extent of imposing hiring quotas in specific instances and for a limited amount of time to overcome the effects of past discrimination. The Supreme Court has carefully avoided endorsing a legal mandate for equal outcome, although stringent applications of the *Uniform Guidelines* by the courts at times come very close to requiring equal outcome. The equal opportunity-equal outcome antimony is, as much as anything, the fuel of testing controversy.

SUMMARY AND CONCLUSIONS

In earlier chapters of this report we have discussed the uses of tests and pointed out their potential value as sources of information in educational settings and in the workplace. In this chapter we have emphasized the limitations of tests, which include issues involving the nature of standardized ability tests as well as issues of test misuse. In the concluding section of the report we discussed testing as it has been caught up in and affected by important intellectual and social developments, such as expanded public expectations about the right to privacy or equal opportunity. This chapter—indeed, the report as a whole—is a call for balance. By emphasizing the limitations of tests we mean to counteract the widespread tendency to look to ability tests as a panacea for deep-seated social ills; and by discussing testing in the context of social developments that far transcend it in importance or effect, we hope to counter the equally prevalent tendency to use tests as a scapegoat for society's ills.

Limitations of Tests

• Standardized group testing is a product of mass society. It was developed because there was a need to assess the talents of large groups of people efficiently and at low cost. The techniques that allow assessment in these conditions, however, necessarily impose constraints on the quality of assessment that is possible. Large-scale testing does not allow the flexibility of clinical testing. It cannot equal the advantages of long association in judging a person's abilities. Although a well-developed test can be a reasonably good predictor of the performance of people in the aggregate, it may be a poor predictor of the performance of any particular individual.

• Ability tests do not measure many things that are important to performance in school and at work. First, they focus on a limited number of cognitive skills. Within that domain of interest, the research has been directed largely at composite abilities (verbal ability, quantitative ability) rather than the many distinct component skills. Second, ability tests do not for the most part attempt to assess things like motivation or creativity. These limitations qualify the relationship between test performance and everyday behavior.

• The strength of modern mental measurement has been its mathematical and statistical underpinnings. There has not been similar progress in understanding what is being measured. The relative immaturity of theories of cognition places significant limits on the explanation of abilities that can be derived from test results.

Test Misuse

• An important problem involving all quantified information, including test scores, is that it tends to dominate decision making. Quantification encourages the dangerous illusion that what cannot be reduced to numbers can be left on the periphery of the decision process. A related problem is that test scores, like all data, have limited dependability and significance but are often used as if they were meaningful everywhere and forever. People who rely on test data as sufficient in themselves often oversimplify even more drastically by using a test score as a label rather than as a summary of the information the test was constructed to provide. In the course of its investigation, the Committee has seen enough instances of these kinds of misuse of test scores—from the practice of business firms' requiring scores on admissions tests to professional schools on job applications to the use of unvalidated tests—to conclude that overreliance on test scores is a widespread problem.

• Many users apparently do not understand enough abut the technology of testing—for example, the techniques of scaling scores in order to invest them with meaning or the statistical methods of correlating test scores an criterion performance—to avoid the pitfalls mentioned above.

Testing in the Context of Broader Issues

• The concept of fair process has taken on new meaning for Americans in recent years. Once seen primarily in the light of procedural due process in the court room, fair process has now come to involve making many sorts of governing institutions accountable by giving people access to information about themselves and about the workings of government in general. This right of access to personal information gathered by government has been accompanied by guarantees in the name of privacy that third parties may not have access to personal files. Inevitably, standardized testing has been and will be influenced by this trend. Changes in many practices have demonstrated that industry, schools, and other private and public institutions can adapt to rules that significantly increase people's access to information that affects them. In some circumstances there are convincing arguments against disclosure, but the burden of proof has been shifting to those who wish not to disclose.

• The idea that some private organizations and businesses perform functions so important to society that they are in the nature of a public function has begun to be extended to the production and use of standardized tests because of their role in allocating positions, opportunities, and, ultimately, the fruits of society. Many have argued the need to regard testing companies as performing a public function as the only means of protecting the rights of the test taker; indeed, some of the major companies have developed rules and procedures that recognize a public interest in their activities. Whether by a process of self-regulation, monitoring by professional organizations, or oversight by government, the industry is likely to be held to closer account than in the past. To the extent that government gets involved in regulating the industry, we urge that attention be given to the costs as well as the benefits of regulation.

• The trend toward greater accountability in education is influencing testing in two almost contradictory ways. First, tests are a product whose quality can be questioned and whose use can be challenged. It is likely that demand will increase for assurance of a test's quality, and that test producers and users will increasingly be liable for meeting this demand. Second, competency tests are increasingly called on to provide assurance that students and educational institutions are performing adequately. As might be expected, the quality of the tests used to ensure quality is itself being challenged. This situation emphasizes the ambivalence with which Americans have come to regard testing.

• Changes in the structure of the labor market and the population will have many varied effects on testing. Some will lead to more testing, some to less. The situation surrounding employment testing is complex, and the impact of the changing nature of the labor force and changing technology difficult to assess. Changes in skill requirements in some employment areas will lead to more specialized testing. The decrease in the percentage of young people in the population, however, will tend to reduce the number of ability tests given. In addition, this decrease will result in fewer students entering college, perhaps diminishing the importance attached to such tests in selecting students for higher education.

• The traditional American ethic of equal opportunity was given new vigor with the passage of the Civil Rights Act of 1964. Few acts of government have had greater impact on social assumptions in recent times, yet the continued reality of unequal access to education and jobs and goods has placed an earlier understanding of equal opportunity in contest with the newer demand for equal outcome. The quest for a more equitable society has placed ability testing at the center of controversy and has given it an exaggerated reputation for good and for harm.

REFERENCES

Bell, D. (1972) On meritocracy and equality. *The Public Interest* 29:29-68.

Brigham, C. C., et al. (1926) The Scholastic Aptitude Test of the College Entrance Examination Board. In T. S. Fiske, ed., *The Work of the College Entrance Examination Board, 1901-1925.* New York: Ginn and Co.

Brown, A. L., and French, L. A. (1979) The zone of potential development: implications for intelligence testing in the year 2000. *Intelligence* 3:255-273.

Carroll, J. B. (1976) Psychometric tests as cognitive tasks: A new "structure of intellect." Pp. 27-56 in L. B. Resnick, ed., *The Nature of Intelligence.* Hillsdale, N.J.: Laurence Erlbaum and Associates.

Center for Policy Alternatives, Massachusetts Institute of Technology (1980) *Benefits of Environmental, Health, and Safety Regulation.* Prepared for the Committee on Governmental Affairs, United States Senate. Washington, D.C.: U.S. Government Printing Office.

Cole, M., Hood, L., and McDermott, R. (1978) Ecological Niche Picking: Ecological Invalidity as an Axiom of Experimental Cognitive Psychology. Laboratory of Comparative Human Cognition, Rockefeller University, New York.

Coleman, J. S. (1970) The principle of symmetry in college choice. Pp. 19-32 in *Report of the Commission on Tests, II. Briefs.* New York: College Entrance Examination Board.

Construct Validity in Psychological Measurement: Proceedings of a Colloquium on Theory and Application in Education and Employment. (1980) Sponsored by U.S. Office of Personnel Management and Educational Testing Service. Princeton, N.J.: Educational Testing Service.

Damrin, D. E. (1959) The Russell Sage Special Relations Test: A technique for measuring group problem solving skills in elementary school children. *Journal of Experimental Education* 28:85-99.

Dawes, R. M. (1979) The robust beauty of improper linear models in decision making. *America Psychologist* 34(7):571-582.

Glaser, R., ed. (1978) *Advances in Instructional Psychology.* Hillsdale, N.J.: Laurence Erlbaum and Associates.

Harrington, M. (1980) *Decade of Decision*. New York: Simon & Schuster.

Jaeger, R. M., Linn, R. L., and Novick, M. R. (1980) A review and analysis of score calibration for the armed services vocational aptitude battery. Prepared by a committee commissioned by the Office of the Secretary of Defense.

Jones, L. (1981) Achievement test scores in mathematics and science. *Science* 213:412-416.

Lippmann, W. (1922) A future for tests. *The New Republic* 33(November 29):9.

Meehl, P. E. (1954) *Clinical vs. Statistical Prediction*. Minneapolis, Minn.: University of Minnesota Press.

Messick, S. (1980) Constructs and their vicissitudes in educational and psychological measurement. In *Construct Validity in Psychological Measurement*. Princeton, N.J.: Educational Testing Service.

Neisser, U. (1976) General academic and artificial intelligence. In L. Resnick, ed., *The Nature of Intelligence*. Hillsdale, N.J.: Laurence Erlbaum and Associates.

Nisbet, R. (1976) *Sociology As an Art Form*. New York: Oxford University Press.

Russell Sage Foundation (1970) *Guidelines for the Collection, Maintenance, and Dissemination of Pupil Records*. New York: Russell Sage Foundation.

Salmon-Cox, L. (1980) Teachers and Tests: What's Really Happening? Prepared for the American Educational Research Association annual meeting, April 1980. Learning Research and Development Center, University of Pittsburgh.

Sarason, S. (1980) Book review of A. R. Jensen, "Bias in Mental Testing." *Society* (November/December):86-88.

Sherman S. W., and Robinson N., eds. (1982) *Ability Testing of Handicapped People: Dilemma for Government, Science, and the Public*. Committee on Ability Testing, Assembly of Behavioral and Social Sciences, National Research Council. Washington, D.C.: National Academy Press.

Snow, R. E., Federico, P.-A., and Montague, W. E. (1980) *Aptitude, Learning, and Instruction*. Hillsdale, N.J.: Laurence Erlbaum and Associates.

Sternberg, R. J. (1977) *Intelligence, Information Processing, and Analogical Reasoning: The Componential Analyses of Human Ability*. Hillsdale, N.J.: Laurence Erlbaum and Associates.

Tversky, A., and Kahneman, D. (1974) Judgements under uncertainty: heuristics and biases. *Science* 185:1124-1131.

White, L. (1974) Technology assessment from the standpoint of a medieval historian. *American Historical Review* 79:1-13.

Yeh, J. (1978) Test Use in Schools. Center for the Study of Evaluation, Graduate School of Education, University of California at Los Angeles.

Appendix:
Participants, Public Hearing on Ability Testing, November 18-19, 1978

JOSEPH AWKARD, Association of Black Psychologists
V. JON BENTZ, Sears, Roebuck & Company
RONALD BOESE, (Unscheduled)
THEODORE J. CARRON, American Petroleum Institute
VIRGIL DAY, Ad Hoc Industry Group on the Uniform Guidelines for Employee Selection Procedures
EDWARD A. DEAVILA*
ROBERT C. DROEGE, Department of Labor*
JAMES B. ERDMANN, Association of American Medical Colleges
NANCY GAETA, The American Federation of Teachers
MARTIN GERRY
CAROL GIBSON, Urban League
DONALD ROSS GREEN, CTB/McGraw-Hill
ROBERT HILL, Urban League
ASA HILLIARD, San Francisco State University*
SYLVIA JOHNSON, Howard University
ROBERT KINGSTON, The College Board
ROGER T. LENNON, The Psychological Corporation, Harcourt Brace Jovanovich, Inc.

*Did not attend hearing but submitted written testimony.

RICHARD H. MCKILLIP, U.S. Civil Service Commission
OLIVIA MARTINEZ, San Jose Bilingual Consortium*
JOEL PACKER, United States Student Association
VITO PERRONE, North Dakota Study Group on Evaluation*
MARILYN QUAINTANCE, International Personnel Management
    Association
FRANCES QUINTO, National Education Association
PHILIP R. REVER, The American College Testing Program
DAVID ROSE, Department of Justice
WILLIAM M. ROSS, Recruitment and Training Program*
JAMES C. SHARF, (Unscheduled), Richardson, Bellows, Henry &
    Company
THOMAS SOWELL, University of California at Los Angeles
PAUL SPARKS, Exxon Corporation
GERDA STEEL, National Association for the Advancement of Colored
    People*
JAMES J. VANECKO, ABT Associates, Inc.*
DOUGLAS R. WHITNEY, American Council on Education*
WARREN WILLINGHAM, Educational Testing Service
GRACE WRIGHT, New York State Department of Civil Service
JERROLD R. ZACHARIAS, Educational Development Center*
*Did not attend hearing but submitted written testimony.

Date Due

N